A CULTURAL HISTORY OF PEACE

VOLUME 3

A Cultural History of Peace
General Editor: Ronald Edsforth

Volume 1
A Cultural History of Peace in Antiquity
Edited by Sheila L. Ager

Volume 2
A Cultural History of Peace in the Medieval Age
Edited by Walter Simons

Volume 3
A Cultural History of Peace in the Renaissance
Edited by Isabella Lazzarini

Volume 4
A Cultural History of Peace in the Age of Enlightenment
Edited by Stella Ghervas and David Armitage

Volume 5
A Cultural History of Peace in the Age of Empire
Edited by Ingrid Sharp

Volume 6
A Cultural History of Peace in the Modern Age
Edited by Ronald Edsforth

A CULTURAL HISTORY OF PEACE

IN THE RENAISSANCE

Edited by Isabella Lazzarini

BLOOMSBURY ACADEMIC
LONDON • NEW YORK • OXFORD • NEW DELHI • SYDNEY

BLOOMSBURY ACADEMIC
Bloomsbury Publishing Plc
50 Bedford Square, London, WC1B 3DP, UK
1385 Broadway, New York, NY 10018, USA
29 Earlsfort Terrace, Dublin 2, Ireland

BLOOMSBURY, BLOOMSBURY ACADEMIC and the Diana logo are trademarks of
Bloomsbury Publishing Plc

First published in Great Britain 2020
This edition published in Great Britain, 2024

Copyright © Bloomsbury Publishing, 2020

Isabella Lazzarini has asserted her right under the Copyright, Designs and Patents Act, 1988,
to be identified as Editor of this work.

Cover image © UniversalImagesGroup / Getty images

All rights reserved. No part of this publication may be reproduced or transmitted
in any form or by any means, electronic or mechanical, including photocopying,
recording, or any information storage or retrieval system, without prior permission
in writing from the publishers.

Bloomsbury Publishing Plc does not have any control over, or responsibility for, any
third-party websites referred to or in this book. All internet addresses given in this
book were correct at the time of going to press. The author and publisher regret
any inconvenience caused if addresses have changed or sites have ceased to
exist, but can accept no responsibility for any such changes.

A catalogue record for this book is available from the British Library.

A catalog record for this book is available from the Library of Congress.

ISBN: HB: 978-1-4742-3852-6
PB: 978-1-3503-8588-7
Set: 978-1-3503-8603-7

Series: The Cultural Histories Series

Typeset by RefineCatch Limited, Bungay, Suffolk
Printed and bound in Great Britain

To find out more about our authors and books visit www.bloomsbury.com
and sign up for our newsletters.

CONTENTS

List of Illustrations		vi
General Editor's Preface		x
	Introduction *Isabella Lazzarini*	1
1	Definitions of Peace *Filippo Del Lucchese and Alastair Mordaunt*	15
2	Human Nature, Peace, and War *Andrea Guidi*	31
3	Peace, War, and Gender *Brian Sandberg*	49
4	Peace and Religion *Elena Bonora*	67
5	Representations of Peace *Sean Roberts*	85
6	Peace Movements *Diego Pirillo*	101
7	Peace, Security, and Deterrence *Rebecca Boone*	117
8	Peace as Integration *Kazuhisa Takeda*	133
Notes		149
Bibliography		151
Contributors		177
Index		181

ILLUSTRATIONS

INTRODUCTION

0.1 Formerly Piero della Francesca, *Ideal City*, Galleria Nazionale delle Marche, Urbino (*c.* 1480–4).   2

0.2 Raffaello Sanzio, *The School of Athens*, Palazzi Vaticani, Stanza della Segnatura, Rome (1509–11).   4

0.3 El Greco, *The Adoration of the Name of Jesus* (*Allegory of the Holy League*), Real Monasterio de San Lorenzo de El Escorial (late 1570s).   6

0.4 Diego Velazquez, *The Surrender of Breda*, Museo del Prado, Madrid (*c.* 1635).   8

0.5 Sebastian Dadler, *Medal of Emperor Ferdinand III with the Allegory of the Peace of Westphalia*, National Museum, Warsaw (1649).   9

CHAPTER 1

1.1 Benozzo Gozzoli, *Triumph of Saint Thomas of Aquin over Averroes*, Musée du Louvre, Paris (1468–84).   17

1.2 Anthon von Werner, *Luther at the Diet of Worms*, Staatsgalerie Stuttgart (1877).   18

1.3 Ford Madox Ford, *The Trial of Wycliffe*, Manchester Town Hall (1886).   21

1.4 Thomas Fairland, *George Fox*, Library of Congress (1915).   22

1.5 Lorenzo Bartolini, *Statue of Niccolò Machiavelli*, Loggiato degli Uffizi, Florence (1845).   27

CHAPTER 2

2.1 Ambrogio Lorenzetti, *Effects of Good Government in the City*, Palazzo Pubblico, Siena (1338–9).   34

2.2 Hieronymus Bosch, *The Mocking of Christ*, also known as *The Crowning with Thorns*, National Gallery, London (*c.* 1510).   35

2.3 Hieronymus Bosch or follower, *Christ Carrying the Cross*, Museum of Fine Arts, Ghent (1500–35).   36

2.4 Peter Paul Rubens, *The Consequences of War*, also known as *Horror of War*, Palazzo Pitti, Florence (1638–9).   46

ILLUSTRATIONS vii

2.5 Peter Paul Rubens, *Minerva Protects Pax from Mars* ('*Peace and War*'), National Gallery, London (1629–30). 46

CHAPTER 3

3.1 *Zenobia*, an illustration from Pierre Le Moine's *La galerie des femmes fortes*, by Abraham Bosse, Gilles Rousselet, and after Claude Vignon, Paris (*c.* 1647). 51

3.2 Anonymous, *Elisabeth I of England*, Österreichische Nationalbibliothek, Wien. 53

3.3 Anonymous, *Idealized Portrait of the Mughal Empress Nur Jahan*, India (*c.* 1725–50), LACMA. 56

3.4 Anonymous, *Head of a Queen Mother (Iyoba)*, Benin (*c.* 1750–1800), Metropolitan Museum of Arts, New York. 57

3.5 Bartholomeus Sprangler and Jan Muller, *Minerva* (*c.* 1632), Metropolitan Museum of Arts, New York. 59

CHAPTER 4

4.1 Sebastian Münster, *Map of Europe as a Queen*, in *Cosmographia Universalis*, Basel (1570). 68

4.2 Heinrich Bünting, *Map of Europe Shaped as a Virgin* (Hannover? 1582?). 69

4.3 Peter Paul Rubens, *The Consequences of War*, Palazzo Pitti, Florence (1637–8). 71

4.4 Frans Hogenberg, *The Calvinist Iconoclastic Riot of August 20, 1566* (1588), Kunsthalle, Hamburg. 78

4.5 The Simultankirche of St. Petri in Bautzen, from Johann Leisentrit's *Geistliche Lieder und Psalmen* (*Spiritual Hymns and Psalms*, 1567). The picture shows the Catholic mass in the foreground, the Lutheran Lord's sermon in the back. 80

4.6 Ground plan sketch (1741) of St. Laurentius church in Dirmstein (Rhineland-Palatinate): Protestant part (left third) and Catholic part (right, including the tower). 82

CHAPTER 5

5.1 Gerard ter Borch, *The Ratification of the Treaty of Münster*, oil on copper (1648), Amsterdam, Rijksmuseum. 87

5.2 Andrea del Verrocchio, Candelabrum, bronze (1468–9), Amsterdam, Rijksmuseum. 88

5.3 Fra Angelico (Giovanni da Fiesole), *Last Judgement*, tempera on panel (1431), Florence, Museo di San Marco. 89

5.4 Unknown Florentine smith, *Pax with the Dormition and Assumption of the Virgin,* silver, niello, gilded copper, and enamel (*c.* 1440–1500), Baltimore, Walters Art Museum. 91

5.5 Jan Baptist Weenix, *The Dutch Ambassador on his Way to Isfahan,* oil on canvas (1653–9), Amsterdam, Rijksmuseum. 96

5.6 Peter Paul Rubens and Jan Brueghel the Elder, *The Return from War: Mars Disarmed by Venus,* oil on panel (*c.* 1610–12), Los Angeles, Getty Museum. 98

5.7 Agnolo Bronzino, *Portrait of Cosimo I as Orpheus,* oil on panel (1537–9), Philadelphia, Philadelphia Museum of Art. 99

CHAPTER 6

6.1 Edwin Sandys, *A Relation of the State of Religion*, London: Simon Waterson (1605): title page. 102

6.2 Daniel Mytens, *King James I of England and VI of Scotland* (1621), oil on canvas, London, National Portrait Gallery. 103

6.3 Paolo Sarpi, *Historiae Concili Tridentini*, Dordrecht: Paulus Vink (1658): frontispiece. 105

6.4 Francesco Pucci, *Informatione della religione christiana*. London: John Wolfe, 1580 (Florence, 1579): title page. 108

6.5 Francesco Pucci, *Informatione della religione christiana*. London: John Wolfe, 1580 (Florence, 1579): p. 2. 109

6.6 Alberico Gentili, *De papatu Romano Antichristo Assertiones (ex verbo Dei et SS. Patribus)*, ms. D'Orville 607, title page, Bodleian Library, Oxford. 113

CHAPTER 7

7.1 *Henry IV as Mars*, attributed to Jacob Brunel (*c.* 1605), Musée National du chateau de Pau. 119

7.2 *Toyotomi Hideyoshi.* 121

7.3 *Charles V Enthroned Among his Enemies*, British Library Add. 33733, f. 5, London. 123

7.4 *Suleiman the Magnificent After the Capture of Buda* (1529), sixteenth century, Topkapı Palace Museum, Istanbul. 124

7.5 Hendrik Cornelizs Vroom, *Battle Between Dutch and Spanish Ships on the Harleem Mermeer (The Dutch Revolt)* (1626), Rijksmuseum, Amsterdam. 130

CHAPTER 8

8.1 *The Death of Harold*, La tapisserie de Bayeux, Musée de Bayeux (France).   137

8.2 College of Santa Cruz of Santiago Tlatelolco (Mexico).   144

8.3 *Reducciones*.   145

8.4 Typical plan of a Jesuit Mission, San Ignacio Miní (Argentina).   146

8.5 Jesuit-Guaraní Mission of La Santisima Trinidad, (Paraguay).   146

GENERAL EDITOR'S PREFACE

RONALD EDSFORTH

When people learn that I study and teach peace history, they often look puzzled and ask me, "Does peace have a history?" *A Cultural History of Peace* is an emphatically positive response to that question. Yes, peace has a history. The original scholarly essays collected in these six volumes clearly show that peace always has been an important human concern. More precisely, these essays demonstrate that what we recognize today as peace thinking and peace imagining, peace seeking and peace making, peace keeping and peace building have long recorded histories that stretch from antiquity to the twenty-first century. All of us who have contributed to *A Cultural History of Peace* believe that present and future generations should have the opportunity to recognize and understand the importance of this peace history.

Very few universities and colleges had faculty who taught and researched peace history before the end of the Cold War. Even today, most professors who do peace history moved into it from other specializations in History or other academic disciplines. Most contributors to *A Cultural History of Peace* are professional historians, but Anthropology, Sociology, Political Science, Journalism, Art History, Religion, and Classical Studies are also represented. These fifty-six contributors work on four continents in thirteen different countries. Their participation in this project tells us that peace history has earned a global recognition in academia that not so long ago was unimaginable. Their essays build upon prior scholarship, but they also introduce new research and new interpretations. As a whole *A Cultural History of Peace* highlights our humanity, something that has been for too long overshadowed in history by the inhumanity of war and other forms of violent conflict. Pursuing answers to new and seldom asked questions, these collected essays expand our knowledge of when, how, and why people in the past pursued peace within their own societies and peaceable relations with people from other societies.

The South African novelist Nadine Gordimer wisely observes, "The past is valid only in relation to whether the present recognises it." (2007: 7) In other words, what happened in the past is not necessarily history. History is made when scholars produce meaningful answers to the questions they ask about the past. The past cannot change, but history can and does change when scholars ask new questions, and when they use previously undiscovered or ignored evidence to develop new interpretations of the past. Evidence of what people said or did, or said they did, are basic materials out of which scholars shape answers to questions like "Does peace have a history?" Of course, to answer this particular question about the past, we must have in mind some definition of peace. Like most people we probably immediately think of peace as *not war*, a classic definition that describes peace in negative terms, as an absence of the type of violent conflicts that still loom so large popular histories and stories about the past. The American psychologist and peace activist William James succinctly summed up this common way of framing of the past, simply stating, "History is a bath of blood" (1910: 1).

James' description of history still plays well in a world that during the last century experienced the massive casualties and devastation of two world wars, genocides, and numerous civil wars, as well as the fears created by transnational terrorism and still-threatening nuclear arsenals. And significantly, a bath of blood framing continues to shape the priorities of most mainstream reporting of the news from around the world—"if it bleeds it leads"—when, in fact, most people today live in zones of peace where their lives are not threatened by violent political conflict. A human being's chances of dying in war have been historically low in this century, and in striking contrast to the peaks of worldwide violence reached during the global conflicts of the twentieth century (https://ourworldindata.org/war-and-peace). Yet so accustomed are we with framing history *and* the present as a bath of blood, most of us have difficulty comprehending these facts. Steven Pinker recently noted this problem in the preface to *The Better Angels of Our Nature: Why Violence Has Declined*, saying "Believe it or not—and I know that most people do not—violence has declined over long stretches of time, and today we might be living in the most peaceable era in our species' existence" (2011: xvi). It is not just a coincidence that the rapid growth and globalization of peace studies has happened since the end of the Cold War. Undoubtedly, some of the questions raised in *A Cultural History of Peace* have been influenced by the extraordinary recent decline of interstate warfare and resolution of many long-standing civil wars.

A Cultural History of Peace demonstrates that for several thousand years peace has been regarded as a highly desirable social condition, perhaps most especially when the violence and cruelty of war have been in the ascendency. Describing this collection of peace history essays as a cultural history—rather than social, political, diplomatic, or international history—is appropriate because throughout history peace has emerged from the cultures of groups, societies, and nations that developed practical ways to peaceably settle serious conflicts. Here I employ the broad environmental definition of culture that psychiatrist and classics scholar Jonathan Shay uses in his brilliant book, *Achilles in Vietnam*: "Our animal nature, our biological nature, is to live in relation to other people. The natural environment of humans is primarily culture, not the 'natural world' narrowly defined as other species, climate, etc." (1994: 207). Surely no human culture is ever truly homogeneous or free from conflicts that arise from serious differences between individuals and groups. Murder and warfare are the bloodiest ways that humans have dealt with those with whom they have serious differences. Bath of blood history foregrounds these activities when we peer into the past. Peace history does something very different. It reveals the long unfinished task of making human cultures peaceable environments that encourage the expression of our most humane instincts: respect for all others who are human like us, and sympathy for those humans who are fearful and/or suffering.

In a remarkable book, *Humanity: A Moral History of the Twentieth Century*, philosopher Jonathan Glover describes respect and sympathy as "human responses" that although they are "widespread and deep-rooted" are often blocked. Frequently, aggressive and cruel instincts find expression in warfare and encouragement in cultures that reserve the highest honors for warriors and their blood sacrifices. Yet clearly, respect and sympathy have been absolutely necessary for the survival of our social species. Respect and sympathy are, in Glover's words, "the core of our humanity which contrasts with inhumanity." However, as Glover recognizes "humanity is only partly an empirical claim. It remains also partly an aspiration" (1999: 24–5). *A Cultural History of Peace* presents strong evidence for the empirical claim, as well as the aspiration. It focuses on the many people in the past who worked to establish peace within their own societies and peace with other societies by institutionalizing respect and sympathy; people who are unlikely to be highlighted as heroes in bath of blood histories.

As General Editor of this title in Bloomsbury Publishing's cultural history series, I have had to follow two major guidelines. The first one required six volumes of essays that follow the same chronological order as other titles in the series. Accordingly, *A Cultural History of Peace* is presented in volumes focused on Antiquity, the Medieval Age, the Renaissance, the Enlightenment, Age of Empire, and the Modern Era since 1920. This chronology order is Western-oriented and something of a barrier to producing a truly global history of peace. Nonetheless, some of the essays in the first five volumes of *A Cultural History of Peace*, and all the essays in Volume Six present peace history in a global perspective. Indeed, those essays show that envisioning a more peaceful interconnected world and finding ways of realizing that vision is a crucial component of the complex of historical processes we call today "globalization."

Bloomsbury's other major guideline required the eight topical essays in each volume of *A Cultural History of Peace* to concentrate on identical themes in peace history. My first task as General Editor was developing the eight major themes for these collected essays. Developing the major themes was difficult particularly because I recognized that a kind of "translation" problem arises when applying modern ideas about peace to the study of peace history in earlier eras when those ideas, or at least modern formulations of them, were absent. I only started doing peace history in 1998 after two decades of teaching and writing concentrated almost exclusively on American history. Not surprisingly, I remained focused on the modern era when preparing my first peace history courses and new research projects. That focus on the modern era was reinforced by what I learned in a peace research seminar at the University of Oslo in the summer of 2007. Thus I knew that my initial selection of themes for this collection could be criticized as present-oriented. Many hours of discussion with my colleagues in Dartmouth's History Department convinced me that this "translation" problem was not insuperable, and that after significant revision my original ideas would be viable focal points for *A Cultural History of Peace*.

These six volumes validate this conviction. Each one contains an introductory overview of the historical era written by its editor and eight thematic essays written by specialists. They develop the following themes: Definitions of Peace; Human Nature, Peace, and War; Peace, War, and Gender; Peace, Pacifism, and Religion; Representations of Peace; Peace Movements; Peace, Security, and Deterrence; and Peace as Integration. This structure facilitates long views of key subjects in peace history. Anyone interested, for instance, in putting together a chronologically ordered history of how peace has been defined from antiquity to the modern era can achieve this goal by reading in order each of the first chapters in the six volumes of *A Cultural History of Peace*. When they do so, they will discover the distinction between "negative" and "positive" definitions of peace that are commonly used in peace research today is useful when formulating questions about pre-modern definitions of peace. But they will also see that the modern distinction between negative peace and positive peace is a simple model that may hinder understanding the variety and richness of what people since antiquity actually meant when they spoke and wrote about peace.

How people in different times and places have understood what we usually call "human nature" has deeply influenced what they said and did about making peace and war. Human nature is, of course, a tricky term. Does it even exist? If it does, is it an endowment of fixed characteristics, or malleable and evolving? And if by human nature, we mean "instinctual," does this mean "inevitable," or are instincts better understood as potential behaviors that have been repressed or expressed depending on environmental influences produced by particular cultures at particular times in the past. The essays in this collection that develop the theme "Human Nature, Peace, and War" make clear that prevailing beliefs about human nature, whether faith-based or secular, have always played an essential role in how people understand what kinds of peace are possible in their imperfect material world.

Peace and war are among the most clearly gendered historical categories, as Chapters Three in *A Cultural History of Peace* make abundantly clear. It has been common all over the world for women to be regarded as "life-givers" and men as "life-takers." Of course there are deviations from this global historical pattern. The Trung sisters of Vietnam and Joan of Arc are among the most famous transgressors of the male monopoly of military power. However, women like them have been exceptional. More commonly, women have provided material and psychological support to male warriors. And perhaps most significantly, some of them have been peace thinkers and peacemakers. Indeed, the widespread idea that peace is feminine has been a source of political legitimacy for women, not just a barrier to achieving political power.

Although pacifism in Western democracies is now usually understood as a principled and often religiously inspired refusal to engage in violence, in other historical settings people who could justify certain violent actions and some wars were still considered "pacifists" whenever they opposed militarism or an ongoing war. On such occasions the deeply subversive cultural implications of nonviolence—its resistance to the idea that history must be written in blood—have been manifest. The essays herein that develop the theme "Peace, Pacifism, and Religion" enable readers to better understand the ambiguous role of religious faith in peace history. They describe religious traditions that link faith and peace, but also ancient and enduring traditions that link religion to the promotion of war.

Since antiquity, countless artists, sculptors, composers, poets, playwrights, and writers have produced representations that reflected, but also shaped, understandings of peace in their cultures. Ancient symbols of peace like the olive branch and the dove that were incorporated into religious iconography have never lost their currency, even when used by secular peace activists. Many other representations of peace created during the last two millennia have also survived. Chapters Five in this collection present a long history of these representations of peace. These representations have often been of peace imagined because their creators could not find real peace in contemporary political cultures. The accumulated representations of peace now form a vast and priceless cultural reservoir, much of it easily accessed via the Internet. Currently, new representations of peace are being deposited in this cultural reservoir every day, while old ones are revived and reconfigured by peace activists around the world.

Peace and anti-war movements have always produced and deployed representations of peace, but they have not been a constant presence in the past. Chapters Six of *A Cultural History of Peace* describe collective efforts to prevent wars, or to stop them from continuing, as well as organized opposition to militarism. Throughout history peace movements have been condemned as subversive, especially when they resisted ongoing wars authorized by political authorities. And even when they have failed to achieve peace, as they have frequently done in the past, peace movements extended the contemporary cultural bases for challenging militarism and the glorification of warfare. Peace movements have over the long run produced traditions of anti-militarist thinking that in this century are mobilized by peace activists whenever interstate warfare threatens global peace.

Today, most global peace activists regard the achievement of security via the threat of force as itself a problem, partly because this kind of negative peace has so frequently broken down in the past. The six essays in this collection that explore the theme "Peace, Security, and Deterrence" nonetheless demonstrate the strong and enduring appeal of this approach to peace. Although the perception problem modern political scientists call "the security dilemma" has been recognized since antiquity, the political practicality and immediately recognizable results of deterrence has almost always prevailed in the face of building threats made by military rivals. Enshrined in the modern era as a form of political realism, deterrence policy shaped the nuclear arms that saw rival superpowers each deploy tens of thousands of nuclear weapons that if used would have certainly destroyed civilization. Yet today, most national governments still equate peace with security and produce deterrence policies that create military alliances and threaten adversaries with war.

The last chapters of each volume of *A Cultural History of Peace* address a theme that many people mistakenly identify as a modern phenomenon: peace through integration, as if it must be something resembling the European Union. These chapters show that the social order imposed by expanding empires, kingdoms, and nation-states has long been proclaimed as a form of peace, even when peace was not the reason for the warfare that preceded it. Moreover, its principal beneficiaries often have often identified their empires as an expanding civilization, most famously Pax Romana and more recently Pax Americana. Yet since the medieval age another kind of peace achieved by nonviolent agreements built upon shared characteristics of identity has been imagined, and occasionally implemented.

Christianity's claim to be a universal church that could bring all people together in a brotherhood of Christ opened the door for identifying "humanity," a word first used during the Renaissance. Then science, especially eighteenth century taxonomy, provided a secular path to a similar end: the recognition that all humans are in very important ways, a single unique species of life. In the modern era, threats to the continued existence of this humanity in the form of global catastrophes such as nuclear warfare and climate change have contributed to an unprecedented "species consciousness" and the claim that all humans have rights that must be respected. Unprecedented communications technologies that today allow us to see and hear people from all over the world in real time have facilitated the expansion of global peace and human rights networks. Although during the five years that *A Cultural History of Peace* has been in the making, politics that divide people into hostile groups have gathered strength in many countries, the long history presented in this collection suggests the cultural foundations for peace, so long in the making, will weather the present storm, and humanity will continue to make itself a global reality.

Introduction

ISABELLA LAZZARINI

> It is obvious that ever since the Roman Empire, more than a thousand years ago, weakened mainly by the corruption of ancient customs, began to decline from that peak which it had achieved as a result of marvelous skill and fortune, Italy had never enjoyed such prosperity, or known so favorable a situation as that in which it found itself so securely at rest in the year of our Christian salvation, 1490, and the years immediately before and after. The greatest peace and tranquility reigned everywhere; the land under cultivation no less in the most mountainous and arid regions than in the most fertile plains and areas; dominated by no power other than her own, not only did Italy abound in inhabitants, merchandise and riches, but she was also highly renowed for the magnificence of many princes, for the splendour of so many most noble and beautiful cities, as the seat and majesty of religion, and flourishing with men most skillful in the administration of public affairs and most nobly talented in all disciplines and distinguished and illustrious in all the arts.
>
> —Guicciardini, *History of Italy*, 1969: 3–4

Introducing his famous narrative of the Italian Wars at the end of the fifteenth century, Francesco Guicciardini pointed out in the first chapter of his *Storia d'Italia* that the Italian peninsula was submerged by calamities (*calamità*) when its condition (*stato*) was the happiest since the end of the Roman empire. Such an edenic state was the result of peace, and peace in this context included tranquillity, abundance of merchandise, money and resources, freedom from any external domination, magnificence of cities and princes, growth of aristocratic and merchant elites, religious prestige, and splendor of art and culture. In a word, peace (*pace*) meant not only absence of violence, conflicts and war (*tranquillità*), but first and foremost a more complex mixture of good luck and well-being (*felicità*) and prosperity (*prosperità*).

Guicciardini wrote at the end of the 1530s: some sixty years before, Nicodemo Tranchedini from Pontremoli, one among the duke of Milan Francesco Sforza's closest political advisors and trusted ambassadors, compiled the first Italian-Latin lexicon of the later Middle Ages. He was an eminent diplomat, an experienced politician, and an educated man: his lexicon reflects his cultural and professional interests, and the choice of the entries is highly interesting for our topic. The word peace (*pace*) is translated into a string of ten Latin nouns whose meaning is highly revealing: *pax*, integrated by *ocium, tranquilitas*, and *concordia*, is followed by the entries related to the act of reaching peace (*pacificacio*; *conciliatio*; *reconciliacio*), the noun for pact (*fedus*), and finally the words for the absence of war and the truce (*belli feria, venia*). Some of these nouns, mainly related to the act of peacemaking, reconciling or stipulating pacts appear in the two verbs connected with peace (*pacificare*: pacify; and *pactezare*: get into an agreement with someone), while the absence of war alone appears only as the translation of the adverb peacefully (*pacificamente*: *absque cedibus et sanguine*, without massacres and blood) (Tranchedini 2001: 121).

FIGURE 0.1: Formerly Piero della Francesca, *Ideal City*, Galleria Nazionale delle Marche, Urbino (*c.* 1480–4). Wikimedia Commons.

These two examples, chosen among many, clearly show that the rich polysemy of the word peace was widely known in the Renaissance: peace as absence of war (or negative peace) was only a facet of a much richer notion, whose nuances constructed a family of discourse that came from many diverse traditions and whose use was hugely differentiated (Galtung 1990: 13). Renaissance and Reformation, stemming from—and deeply transforming—a wide range of various and interwoven medieval traditions, offer to the scholar of peace a distinctive field of research, particularly in these days in which not only peace, coexistence, and tolerance more than ever in the past decades have dramatically become crucial notions, but also peace studies have reached a critical point. As a matter of fact, in his recent synthesis on the *Glorious Art of Peace* from antiquity to the present day John Gittings underlines the "impressive growth of peace studies in the past half-century, which has led to alternative and more credible ways to look at conflict and conflict prevention, and has explored fuller and more 'positive' forms of peace which could deliver social and economic justice in a globalized world" (Gittings 2012: 14; Adolf 2009). As the general editor of the *Oxford International Encyclopedia of Peace*, Nigel Young, states in 2010, research has indeed developed "multiple approaches, cultural perspectives, definitions and concepts of peace: from the personal to the global; from peace through military strength to absolute pacifism and nonviolence; from secular and pragmatic to spiritual and other-worldly understandings of peace" (Young 2010: I, xxiv). Since 2001, however, criticism from within led to new, contrasting conceptions and views, and problems started to arise between scientific engagement and social commitment (Evans Pim 2010: III, 452; Lopez (ed.) 1989). On the other hand, peace studies and history are still at odds with each other: while specific historical contexts are increasingly investigated, there are not enough general overviews, and the more so if we consider a cultural approach to the history of peace. Likewise, peace studies seem only occasionally interested in historical research, at least on the pre-industrial age: among others, by linking the rise of peace advocacy to the spread and deepening of democracy, David Cortright chooses to ignore any potential antecedent of a culture of peace inspired by other protagonists than kings and princes before Immanuel Kant and the nineteenth century (Cortright 2008: 19). However, peace studies and the history of peace should meet midway: in analyzing complex social, cultural, and political phenomena we all need not simple models or specific case-studies, but rather "a finely graded lens that allows [us] to disassemble what we have come to see as necessary" (Sassen 2006: 11). In this sense, a focus on a "cultural history" of peace is most needed, provided that the notion of "cultural history" encompasses representations, images, gestures, and a material culture made of objects and spaces shared or bundled as well as ideas and texts, and their reciprocal crossings, borrowings, and exchanges.

FRAMEWORK

According to the general profile of the series, the present volume focuses on a Renaissance that starts with the fall of Constantinople and the end of the Hundred Years War in 1453, and the peace of Lodi in 1454, and culminates with the end of the Thirty Years War in the imperial territories and of the Eighty Years War between Spain and the Netherlands, the peace of Westphalia and the treaties of Münster and Osnabrück (1648). Undeniably, this timescale has a distinctively political and European character: its length overtakes the Italian Renaissance to include the early modern period in the West and Mediterranean, and crosses more than one disciplinary boundary between the Middle Ages and the Early Modern Age. The origins of the grand narrative about it are grounded on the "invention" of the Italian Renaissance by Jakob Burckhardt and its later classical interpretation by Hans Baron (Hankins (ed.) 2000; Baker and Maxson (eds.) 2015); the recent research has moved towards a reappraisal of the historical, social and cultural developments in Italy (Gamberini and Lazzarini (eds.) 2012; Ruggiero 2015), but Renaissance has been more than just Italian, and the spatial and conceptual scale on which recent research looks at it has hugely broadened (Ruggiero (ed.) 2002; Caferro (ed.) 2017). As with all chronology, it is not always effective nor universally recognized (Russell 1986); both intra-European political dynamics and extra-European cultures evolved at a different pace, and even in the same cultural context, as Sean Roberts argues for instance in the chapter on representations of peace, the impact of this timescale upon some aspects of social and cultural life (like, in this case, visual and material culture) could prove itself to be unpredictable. Moreover, issues related to peace do not form and develop according to convenient beginning and ending dates. However, as William Caferro has stated by quoting Paula Finden's pivotal work on the material world of the Renaissance, the importance of the Renaissance and its effectiveness as a concept "lay in what it tells us about making and remaking the past, as a 'testing ground for new approaches to history'" (Caferro 2011: 25; Finden 1998: 113). As a matter of fact, the 200 years between *c.* 1450 and *c.* 1650 represent a culturally recognizable framework: while they allow the historian to take a comprehensive look at a cultural history of peace from a Western perspective, they also allow him/her to work discretely on the West and to throw more than casual glances at the world beyond.

Another issue is crucial: the term "peace" refers at the same time to a state and a notion; the first derives from events, treaties, or agreements, while the second participates in a system of representations—an ideology, that is an image that a specific society constructs about itself (Duby 1974; Bély 2007). In this second acceptation, the notion of peace crosses the path of some other crucial concepts like justice, freedom, the common good (Kempshall 1999; Mineo 2009; Lecuppre-Desjardins and van Bruaene (eds.) 2010). Cultural notions like freedom, peace, justice were not only at the crossroads of various learned discursive traditions but also entered into the wider political language outside intellectual circles. They were invoked in official speeches, correspondence, and acts, printed in books and in leaflets, shouted in the streets and written on banners, seals, and walls. Even though we can consider them in various ways (as elements of an ideology, the spontaneous and disorderly expression of popular aspirations, or mere *flatus vocis*), they were nevertheless powerful words. Moreover, political keywords were often clustered into something like ideological constellations—together with non-verbal signs like gestures, images, or colors. The question is whether the use of such keywords and their more or less widespread connection with other ones influenced the common understanding of fundamental political concepts. In that case, such combinations can account for some of the shifts, the allusions and the ambiguities in the ordinary use of political concepts (Ferente 2007: 571–3). Moreover, the notion of peace assumed different meanings according to circumstances and contexts, and often metamorphosed into a second constellation of words closely related to its main significance. While concord, harmony, tranquillity may be reconnected to the complex conceptual frame of peace as the social result of equity, justice, and prosperity (see the passage from Guicciardini quoted above), some others such as tolerance require adaptation and interpretation (Fournel and Zancarini 2009; Genet 2011).

Political keywords not only play a pivotal role in daily social and political life but also represent the building blocks of the theoretical analysis of reality outlined by intellectuals and political authors. In this sense, they shape and influence many intersections in political discourse. As a matter of fact, powerful words, while themselves gathering in constellations of practice, at the same time foster the building of dynamic and often contrasting constellations of thought. Machiavelli, Erasmus, Vives, Vitoria, Montaigne, Gentili, Bodin, Grotius—among others—worked extensively on peace and its opposite—war—and on their crossings and reciprocal interferences, and their analyses echo one another.

FIGURE 0.2: Raffaello Sanzio, *The School of Athens*, Palazzi Vaticani, Stanza della Segnatura, Rome (1509–11). Wikimedia Commons.

In this sense, a cultural history of these key notions should aim not only at investigating their features and applications but also at deciphering the many layers of the diverse systems of interpretation which derived from their use and became in turn crucial components of a long-lasting narrative about Western ideals and values.

The present volume therefore considers the sometimes disparate histories and historiographical traditions around the notion of peace in the Renaissance, and aims at revealing their equally unexpected divergences and convergences.

TURNING POINTS

A long-lasting and prestigious tradition of studies on the Renaissance has seen the age from the mid-fifteenth to the mid-seventeenth century as the ideal backdrop for the building of the modern state in Europe and its first spreading to a wider world. In this conceptual framework, the discovery of the Americas and in general the so-called first globalization, the Reformation, and the prolonged confrontation with the Muslim world (mostly personified by the Ottoman empire) were crucial and complementary features of the process of state-building (Cassirer 1946; Tilly 1975; Wallerstein, I, 1974, II, 1980; Headley 2008).

Although such grand narrative retains some interest, the debate on statecraft all over Europe in the 1980s and 1990s started nuancing the teleological concept of the birth of a monolithic national, centralized and bureaucratic "modern State," and some challenging research programs within the frameworks of both the European Science Foundation and the CNRS provided important landmarks in such a revision (Elliott 1992; Genet et al. (eds.) 1985–90; *The Origins* 1994–9; Ortu 2003). In the past three decades, research on politics, culture, and society in the Renaissance has oriented the analysis toward practices of power, factions, and clientage networks, informal relationships of influence and authority, and focused on a whole world of various social bodies and political actors. Not only did the dynamics of state-building and governmental growth in the early modern West prove to be more pactist than authoritarian, more reciprocal than vertical, but it involved not just formalized forms of government and institutions that differed merely in scale and purposes, but also actors and practices that did not derive from the public sphere, like aristocratic clients or factions. This informal world faced the institutional frame, forming with it the *unicum* of politics, and using different languages and cultures of power to express both from above and below codes of communication to generate new realities (Watts 2009; Blockmans, Holenstein, and Mathieu (eds.) 2009; Kirshner (ed.) 1994; Gamberini and Lazzarini (eds.) 2012). Likewise, the impact of the Reformation, the discovery of the New World, and the Ottoman challenge have been partly revisited and investigated according to different perspectives (Kaplan 2007; Scott, Freist, and Greengrass (eds.) 2009; Safley (ed.) 2011; Abulafia 2008; de Vries 2010; Bentley, Subrahmanyam and Wiesner-Hanks (eds.) 2015; Kunt and Woodhead 1995; Brummett 2015).

Repositioned in such an articulated historiographical background, and from the point of view of a cultural history of peace, the 200 years from 1450 to 1648 experienced, among many other lesser changes, two main turning points whose consequences changed forever the ways in which lay and religious men and women saw the world around them, and talked about, and acted for or against peace.

The first major change was the irreparable rupture of the Christian world and its consequences both on a theoretical and a practical plane. The collapse of the medieval

FIGURE 0.3: El Greco, *The Adoration of the Name of Jesus (Allegory of the Holy League)*, Real Monasterio de San Lorenzo de El Escorial (late 1570s). Wikimedia Commons.

universal idea of peace amongst Christian polities, and the consequent weakening of the moral authority of the Church undermined the medieval Christian moral traditions, while the Christian bifurcation of the Western Church into Catholic and Protestant reduced the jurisdiction of canon law (Lesaffer 2004: 29–34). The idea of a common Christendom was therefore gradually replaced by the idea that Europe was divided into territorially discrete states ruled by sovereigns. Such a profound change involved the theoretical approaches to peace and war, and heavily influenced the ways of obtaining and preserving the first, and conceiving, declaring and conducting the second (Bellamy 1996). Moreover, as a consequence of the rupture of the unity of the Church and the collapse of Western Christendom as a whole, regions which remained almost monolithically Catholic found themselves at the borders of areas in which a variety of churches and movements—under the umbrella of Protestantism—believed and behaved quite differently, being also often at odds among themselves. In this context, peace meant at the same time the end of real war—of princes against princes, cities against cities—and tolerance, a word that took on different meanings according to time and place. For the first time, people and lay and religious leaders were forced to develop forms of coexistence and ways of peaceful living not outward- but inward-looking, not toward others abroad, but toward their own folk, at home. But early modern Europe was a contradictory setting for tolerance; on the one hand there was a range of factors that fostered uniformity; on the other there was "the emerging discourse of tolerance and accommodation and, more to the point, the actual practice of plurality, the "ecumenicity of everyday life" that made it possible for antagonistic religious communities to live in close proximity" (Scott Dixon 2009: 11). Recent research on early-modern multi-confessionalism has discovered that early-modern men and women were able to move back and forth between two apparent opposites—tolerance and intolerance. Confessional relations were ambiguous and pragmatic, shaped more by contingencies than the higher principles of the faith, and tolerance was bound up with the other dimensions of social and cultural life (Bajczy 1997; Bérenger 2002).

The second major turning point was the widening of the world. Early modern European contacts with the Far East had medieval, as well as classical, precedents, and East–West interactions intensified at the time of the Crusades, particularly during the Fourth Crusade, when European, Byzantine, and Muslim armies came into contact through the conquest of Constantinople. However, the so-called Age of Encounters not only extended a long-standing tradition of cultural contacts, exchanges, and negotiations between Europeans and other cultures around the world, but also changed the European self-image and perception, and in the long run transformed the whole Western theoretical vision of the world and its approach to the other (Todorov 1982; Subrahmanyan 2007; Marcocci 2014). At the end of the famous chapter 9 of the sixth book of the *History of Italy*, in which Guicciardini talks about the Portuguese travels to India and Columbus' discovery of America, the Florentine concludes his detailed description of the events and their consequences with a revealing consideration about the impact of the new discoveries on the sacred and profane knowledge of his time:

> These voyages have not only confuted many things which had been affirmed by writers about terrestrial matters, but beside this, they have given some causes for alarm to interpreters of the Holy Scriptures, who are accustomed to interpret those verses of the Psalms [Ps. 18.5] in which it is declared that the sound of their songs had gone over all the earth and their words spread to the edge of the world, as meaning that faith in Christ had spread over the entire earth through the mouths of the Apostles: an interpretation contrary to the truth, because since no knowledge of these lands had hitherto been brought to light, nor have any signs or relics of our faith been found there, it is unworthy to be believed, either that faith in Christ had existed there before these times, or that so vast a part of the world had never before been discovered or found by men of our hemisphere.
> —Guicciardini, *History of Italy*, 1969: 182

It is telling that this final paragraph of book six has been cut out of all editions of the *Storia* before 1774.

According to Elizabeth Horodowich, among others, "the Renaissance occurred as much because early modern Western culture stood on the threshold of an expanding world of multicultural contact and exchange as it did because of the rediscovery of the antiquity" (Horodowich 2017: 192–3; Horodowich and Markey (eds.) 2018).

The contacts with a wider world impacted European society dramatically. To integrate both concretely and theoretically the new discoveries into the framework of a Western society already shaken from within by the collapse of the universal Church and the appearance of a new and unforeseen religious and moral diversity, new forms of governance and new ideas of peace and integration had to be invented and put into place.

THEMES

To do so, many were the contexts in which old and new ideas on peace were tried out. The decades between the 1450s and the early sixteenth century were a turning point and introduced an important period of contestation and change among the different medieval traditions: as seen above, the decline of medieval governance structures, rise of new technologies, discovery of the Americas, religious debate, and development of new methodologies that challenged scholasticism and introduced secularism contributed to a more open intellectual climate. Erasmus, Machiavelli and Guicciardini, Vitoria and the so-called "Spanish school," and Gentili refined both scholasticism and the theory of the just war. Realism, legalism, and reformism enhanced a profound revision of the account of the just war, which was in turn transformed in different ways by Bodin and Grotius in

FIGURE 0.4: Diego Velazquez, *The Surrender of Breda*, Museo del Prado, Madrid (*c.* 1635). Wikimedia Commons.

the context of the worsening of warfare and the near-constant state of open conflict which afflicted late Renaissance Western Europe.

Against the backdrop of such a theoretical framework, some major themes could be outlined. Ideas did not only foster change in theoretical analysis, but also influenced the concrete development of negotiations, the stipulation of partial or universal peace treaties, and the summoning of religious councils. In the negotiation processes, principles and ideas, as well as political notions and religious or moral values, were finally moulded to suit concrete political and social purposes. Learned discursive traditions therefore got tangled up in institutional developments and ordinary political language. Political treaties and religious councils represent key moments in such a complex process of definition of peace. The 200 years from 1450 to 1648 saw the growth in shape and scale of European political agreements. From the so-called peace of Lodi in 1454 to the treaties of Osnabrück and Münster passing through the many sixteenth-century treaties (among which Augsburg in 1555 and Cateau-Cambrésis in 1559), general agreements became more and more key events in an increasingly wider scenario full of old and new political actors and protagonists.

General treaties, agreements, and leagues therefore set the pace for defining both who could sit at the negotiating table, and what were the aims—or even the values – at stake (Lesaffer 2004). Although the grand narrative of the birth of modern diplomacy—that is,

FIGURE 0.5: Sebastian Dadler, *Medal of Emperor Ferdinand III with the Allegory of the Peace of Westphalia*, National Museum, Warsaw (1649). Wikimedia Commons.

of a diplomacy driven by nation states and performed by professional diplomats and permanent embassies—has been recently questioned and revised not only for the early Renaissance but also for the age of Westphalia, scholarship maintains that the great political and religious Renaissance agreements became crucial laboratories for defining both the standards of interaction and the constellations of the political notions in use (such as peace, friendship, fraternity, tranquillity, and repose) (Christin 1997; Rivère de Carles (ed.) 2016). If the agreements preceding the Reformation—like the peace of Lodi—were mainly political in content, the changing nature of sixteenth- and seventeenth-century wars and the relevance of religious factors in European conflicts imposed on almost all the peaces and truces (Kappel, 1531; Augsburg, 1555; Amboise, 1563; St.-Germain, 1570; Vervins, 1598) a strong religious content (Roberts 2013; Foa 2015). Such a change emphasized, on the one hand, the practical use—and thus the definition and re-definition—of "moral" notions in the process of peacemaking by lay "practitioners," and, on the other hand, the evolution of a new ideological framework for sovereignty which justified both the centralization and rationalization of the use and control of violence, and its transposition onto a political, rather than religious, plane [Phillips 2010]. The peace of Westphalia (1648), in which more than a hundred diplomatic delegations took part, finally and fully imposed the principle—obvious to us today—that the European system of states should be regulated by international law (*ius gentium*) and not by theological concepts.

In the same direction, the close relationship between religious choice and political autonomy (since the first was also a political matter, heavily interfering with the latter), enhanced the importance of religious councils such as the council of Trent. Religious councils in the Middle Ages intended peace as unity: the great councils at the beginning of the fifteenth century sought to end the Schism, at the same time aiming at redefining the Pope's authority and the balance of power among the different components of the Christian world (Black 1998; Oakley 2003), while the council of Ferrara–Florence (1434–8) aimed at recreating the original union between the Catholic and Greek Orthodox Churches (Viti (ed.) 1994). As for the diet gathered in Mantua in 1459 by Pius II, its nature was mixed (the pope and the cardinals went to Mantua to meet the lay princes of Europe) and its main scope was the crusade against the Ottoman conquerors of Byzantium (Baldi 2006; Weber 2014). At Trent, prelates played a crucial role in defining peacemaking between different confessions and its practical implementation in daily life, but the outcome was more an effort to build a religious peace and coexistence between different faiths to enable the community, the state, and society to survive, rather than an effort to reunite the fractured body of the Church. As a matter of fact, the council contributed to the construction of clearer boundaries between orthodoxies: according to its first historian, the Servite friar Paolo Sarpi, the council of Trent, "desired and procured by godly men, to reunite the Church which began to be divided, hath so established the Schisme, and made the parties so obstinate, that the discords are become irreconcilable" (Sarpi 1620: 1). However, the hope that the council, as the supreme authority of the Church and thus superior to the pope, could bring peace back to Christianity after the divisions of the Reformation did continue after the council itself.

Apart from the formal sphere of negotiation, lay and religious men and women at a local level experimented with many attempts to work out a daily coexistence. People enacted peace on a daily basis and on a micro-level through diversity and dialog, by interweaving multiple relations between the communities and by elaborating various strategies for surviving military wars and religious conflicts, forced integration and cultural clashes. Religious peace at a local level was not, according to Elena Bonora, "a doctrinal compromise, but a political and legal agreement, by which the civil authorities organized the coexistence of various religious beliefs and the conditions for public worship in a single political entity" (Bonora, ch. 4). While in royal and princely courts, private chapels were left for the use of the ambassadors of different faith, in European villages and towns people increasingly negotiated the sharing of places of worship, cemeteries, religious public spaces, and even seats in the local councils, and sometimes, as in France, worked out localized coexistence through "pacts of friendship" [Kaplan 2002; Foa 2011: 241]. Often such a prolonged and risky negotiation developed unexpected solutions, like the imperial "shared churches" or the "hidden churches" of Dutch origin, but widespread around Europe (Kaplan 2007; Mayes 2015). In a totally different context, that is in Spanish America, coexistence meant integration, and integration implied a governance strictly linked to religion (Hanke 1965). On a local basis, such a policy produced interesting experiments like the Spanish *reducciones*. Created by the Franciscans and the Jesuits, the *reducciones* were Christian settlements in which Amerindians were relocated, gathered, and instructed in *policía* (civility), which consisted of Spanish religion, language, customs, lifestyle, and culture. Coercion was at the basis of such a policy: however, their foundation was based on the legal, moral, and political theory of the world conceptualized by the School of Salamanca, according to which a range of non-European societies with a diversity of cultures and customs could be incorporated into the Christian world (Matsumori 2011; Anghie 2004; Fisch 1984).

Finally, the range of individuals controlling a quota of agency and using it to enhance peace was increasingly multifarious: recent research has been investigating gender, and both female and male agency in acting belligerently, abstaining from conflicts or openly fostering peace. The range of peaceful agency has proved itself to be more multifaceted than expected (Watkins 2008; van Gelder and Krstic 2015; Lazzarini 2015). Peace-making, both on a formal and general and on a local and specific level, included not only male rulers and formal ambassadors, but also male and female agents, and individuals and groups of "artisans of peace" (jurists, but also local councillors or priests) that operated locally to enhance daily coexistence. As Brian Sandberg argues in his chapter, the methodological issues generated by gender and cultural history have allowed scholars to enlarge their views on diplomatic and political agency, and "revealed new dimensions of female participation in European international relations in the early modern period" (Sandberg, ch. 3). Not only women—at all levels of society and almost in all cultures—partly, occasionally or regularly shared their male counterparts' power in peacemaking and in war, but they took part in negotiations in many ways, deeply influencing their outcome (Dixon (ed.) 2002; Sluga and James (eds.) 2016: 30–45).

* * *

The present book faces—in many ways—a difficult task. On the one hand, the volume on the Renaissance shares the same difficulty of the other volumes of the series devoted to a cultural history of peace. In fact, peace seems to be less interesting and appealing than war, because people instinctively prefer the bellicose and bloody, more eventful and passionate, to the calm and quiet, and such an attitude is hardly a modern invention. Therefore, working on peace is a patient quest, and scholars have to put together case-studies, elusive primary sources, old and new readings, and disparate second-hand research. Taking into account this specific volume, as seen above, the age that we call here the Renaissance is difficult to define. There have been many Renaissances, and apart from Europe, in many regions of the world there has possibly been no Renaissance in a Western sense or timescale at all. Moreover, even the Western Renaissance circumscribed by the peace of Lodi in 1454 and the Westphalia treaties in 1648 hardly experienced some of the main and recurrent phenomena treated as main themes in the series as a whole, while developing very distinctive features of its own. As a matter of fact, some of the general themes of the series are problematic at this period: "pacifism" has been deliberately eliminated from the title of the chapter on peace and religion (ch. 4), while peace movements (ch. 6) and integration (ch. 8) have been contextualized and partly reconsidered in order to adapt them to an age that did not invent nor know such notions in our modern sense.

It should not come as a surprise that some of the main themes of the volume appear in more than one chapter. The theoretical works of the likes of Erasmus, Machiavelli, or Grotius, the idea and practical settings of religious peace, the role, gender, and agency of ambassadors and agents, and the features of a diplomacy which was undergoing a profound change since the later Middle Ages re-emerge in the various chapters from different angles and perspectives. Chapters 1 ("Definitions of Peace") and 2 ("Human Nature, Peace, and War") deal with some of the major theoretical themes and authors, following the evolution of constellations of notions and theories about the bionomy of peace and war from the articulated but unitary late-medieval framework of a universal Christendom dealing with different but known cultures, to a much broader and less defined world in which Christian unity was just a memory, and people had to deal with the otherness inside and outside old and familiar boundaries. Chapters 4 ("Peace and Religion"), 6 ("Peace Movements"), and 8 ("Peace as Integration") consider from different points of view the crucial role of religion in shaping the meaning and forms of peace as coexistence, irenism, and integration in a very fragmented and broad world. Chapters 3 ("Peace, War, and Gender") and 7 ("Peace, Security, and Deterrence") examine the general frame of war and peace in the context of real wars and difficult peacemaking processes by analyzing it through gender lenses or interpreting it according to the issue of political and economical security. Finally, chapter 5 ("Representations of Peace") investigates the huge field of the representations of peace by considering them in a broad sense, that is by including not only "traditional" visual artworks, but also the extremely rich Renaissance material culture, and by surveying exchanges and borrowings between different cultures.

There is inevitably a bit of overlap among the different chapters; issues related to peace—in all the above-mentioned meanings—do not reassuringly form and develop according to unitary patterns and coherent models. Moreover, while some of the chapters go back to the medieval roots of theories and systems of thought or of habits and customs related to peace and peacemaking, the central focus of the volume turns mainly around the sixteenth- and early seventeenth century. As a matter of fact, the major changes of this age, while starting in the second half of the fifteenth century, grew and fully developed from the turn of the century onwards. Likewise, the volume aims at a global perspective, but in more than one chapter the authors consciously adopt a Western point of view, throwing when possible more than casual glances at the world beyond.

Each chapter is an original work of synthesis and interpretation and presents quite a variety of viewpoints, even on similar topics. All the authors have explored deeply both the secondary literature and representative primary sources, aiming to offer to scholars and students at universities and peace research institutes the go-to reference work on the cultural history of peace in the Renaissance. Therefore, the authors have been invited to calibrate their chapters between some kind of broad overview for the whole of the considered period, and detailed discussions of specific developments. Of course, and reassuringly, the balance between case-studies and surveys is different in each chapter: while some of them offer very broad synthesis with a global perspective, others dig deeper on few, revealing themes and case-studies.

Finally, it's the editor's modest, but heartfelt hope that in our present and troubled times this book could offer to the reader some experiment to try, some example to imitate, and some danger to avoid in the name of a universal common good.

CHAPTER ONE

Definitions of Peace

FILIPPO DEL LUCCHESE AND ALASTAIR MORDAUNT

The period under our scrutiny is roughly delimited by two major treaties, the peace of Lodi in 1454 and the peace of Westphalia in 1648. The two tumultuous centuries that separate these events fundamentally shape future philosophical ideas and the political paradigms that establish Western Europe as the crucible in which modernity is formed. Of critical political importance to this process is the rise of nation states, especially in Spain, France, and England, and the corresponding diminution of the *respublica christiana,* the name given to a combination of territorial Christian unity and the corresponding reach of Roman Catholicism.

This paradigm shift in political organization creates new principles in the management of these emerging state's affairs, both internally, within the increasingly well-defined borders, and in their external relations. As our period progresses, nation states become more autonomous from Rome and more dependant upon their own resources to make and enforce agreements among one another. Consequently, a more complex "balance of power" across larger geographical areas influences how and why wars are fought and peace treaties negotiated.

In the early part of our period, the dream of Charles V and his heirs of a universal Hispanic-Habsburg Empire is undermined mainly by their confrontation with the Ottoman empire in the east, the French in Italy, and the rising Dutch commercial power in the North of Europe. In addition, from 1517, Christian unity in Germany starts to fracture due to the Protestant Reformation, the scope and reach of which is only restrained by a Catholic Counter-Reformation that in turn strengthens the national "sovereign" governments where Catholicism remains and thrives.

Economic changes manifest themselves rapidly in this period. In a relatively short period after Columbus "discovers" America in 1492, the Europeans explore and open up extensive trade with the rest of the world, creating new colonial empires and unleashing new wealth that begins to generate nascent forms of capitalist economic activity. Within this triad of new economic interests, the invention of modern sovereignty, and the Protestant Reformation, we can distinguish two approaches to the problem of peace— one distinctly religious, and one distinctly political.

The Protestant Reformation gains momentum and begins to resist the Roman Catholic attempt to recover its ideological and political supremacy. This conflict eventually results in the "peace of Augsburg," which introduces the right of German princes to choose between these two forms of Christianity. By the mid-sixteenth century, however, this peace has sown the seeds of a deeper religious animosity that results in religious wars across Europe during the early seventeenth century. The ensuing Thirty Years War is one of the most destructive conflicts in European history and the deadliest European religious war. Our period closes with the peace treaties, collectively known as the peace of Westphalia, from which a provisional and altered balance in the European physiognomy emerges.

When we make a distinction between the religious and the political dimensions of the problem of peace, we are not suggesting a material distinction between different domains. Rather, we are making use of a theoretical construction to help in analyzing authors' priorities and intentions, their concrete positions and their theoretical definitions of peace. Politics and religion are strongly intertwined, and the early modern mentality hardly distinguishes between them. It is therefore more correct to speak of the mutual influence of the early modern theological discourse on one hand and the discourse on sovereignty on the other.

The cultural background of early modernity is very rich. It is useful to establish a few coordinates in this context: in the Old Testament, the Hebrew term *shalom* (שָׁלוֹם) represents the harmony and reconciliation with God and Nature, as opposed to the chaos and conflict brought by enemies of the Jews. In the New Testament, Jesus brings peace to the human world (Jn 14.27, 16.33) and blesses the peacemakers (Mt 5.9). Paul appeals to the "God of Peace" (Rm 15.33). Inside and outside the community, peace is a universal value, mediated and made possible by Christ, and sharply opposed to the political peace of the Romans, the *pax Romana* (ex. Jn 14.27).

The most authoritative and influential position among the Church Fathers is that of Augustine of Hippo. Augustine is not the first philosopher to develop a theory of just war. However, he systematizes ideas derived from Aristotle, Cicero, and his master Ambrogius in a highly original way. Commenting on Paul's *Rom* 12:17 and 21 in the *Ep.* 138, and in the *Civitas Dei*, Augustine recognizes the possibility of using violence to resist wickedness. Peace is a universal desire of all creatures, and although war is evil, it is nonetheless necessary when caused by unjust enemies. They are also part of the eternal divine order and contribute to the realization of the ultimate end, namely universal peace among all creatures, who will reach their own and deserved place under the government of the wise Judge (*Civitas Dei* XIX. 12–13).

Thomas Aquinas's *Summa Theologiae* also enriches the early modern philosophical background on the concept of peace. The IIa IIae Q. 40 is a systematic discussion of the problem of war. Thomas builds upon Aristotle and Augustine to develop a theory of just war grounded on the criteria of rightful authority, just cause, and the right intention to use violence. Thomas discusses Lk 3:14 in which Christ does not forbid war, thus indirectly admitting just war, and from the just war theory, a concept of peace can be derived. Peace is the *tranquillitas ordinis*, a harmonious and peaceful disposition that society enjoys in both its internal order and external security: "pax ergo in hoc est quod omnes sua loca teneant" (1–2 q. 70 3 c; 2–2 q. 29). Thomas distinguishes the social and the international sense of peace, to which he adds the notion of an interior peace when man is in peace with God.

THE RELIGIOUS DIMENSION OF PEACE

The religious dimension of the discourse on peace unfolds according to three main problematics. The first is imposed by the rising power of the Ottoman empire in the eastern Mediterranean Sea and Europe[1] until its defeat at Lepanto in 1571. The second is dictated by the clash with Amerindian civilizations in the newly discovered continent.[2] The third is opened up by the Protestant Reformation and the conflict within Christianity,

FIGURE 1.1: Benozzo Gozzoli, *Triumph of Saint Thomas of Aquin over Averroes*, Musée du Louvre, Paris (1468–84). Wikimedia Commons.

with the social and political establishment of new Churches as centers of ideological and political power,[3] but also the proliferation of heresy and rebellious religious movements, sects, and individual forms of resistance.[4]

The question of peace becomes of paramount importance for several reasons: the urgency of the Ottoman threat and the consequent call for unity within Christendom to resist the infidel (military league promoted by Pope Pius V 1571 leading to the victory of Lepanto); the necessity of meshing the religious enterprise of Christianization of the native Americans with the proto-capitalist system based on extermination, slavery and the colonial enterprise (Burgos's laws of 1512, Valladolid debate between Sepulveda and Las Casas, 1550); the need to end the carnage among Christians across Europe (sack of Rome, 1527).

FIGURE 1.2: Anthon von Werner, *Luther at the Diet of Worms*, Staatsgalerie Stuttgart (1877). Wikimedia Commons.

CHRISTIAN HUMANISM

In the beginning of the period under our scrutiny, humanists are often reluctant to accept the social consequences of a radical pacifism and its political implications for the recognition of legitimate authority. Toward the foreign and infidel enemy, though, positions are more clearly defined. In 1453, the year of the fall of Constantinople, the neoplatonic philosopher and Catholic cardinal Cusanus develops a consistent treatment of the concept of peace in his *De pace fidei*. While cardinal Bessarione and Pope Pius II preach the crusade against the Turks, Cusanus opts for a radical religious ecumenism. All non-Christian religions, he claims, contains fundamental truths compatible with Christianity. Rather than offering a definition of peace, the *De pace fidei* is a fictional dialog in heaven between the representatives of religions that share the conviction that peace will be the universal outcome once all religions deeply understand themselves and their core values. The implicit superiority of Christianity is not completely absent from Cusanus's work, as his utopian ideal is perhaps a Christianization of the whole world through Catholicism.

The first early modern author to develop a consistent pacifism is the great Dutch humanist, Desiderius Erasmus. The unsystematic character of his theory, scattered through several works and probably the result of political opportunity and historical contingency[5] has produced two different historiographical interpretations. The first sees Erasmus as an uncompromising upholder of peace; the second underlines the ambiguity and ambivalence of his discourse, especially where it concerns the possibility and even necessity of waging war against non-Christians and infidels.

In the *Enchiridion militis Christiani* (*Handbook of the Christian Soldier*, 1503), Erasmus speaks strongly for preserving peace, as directed by the original message of Christ. The motive of inspiration is the neoplatonic idea of unity in Christ, which also resonates in Marsilius Ficinus and Giovanni Pico della Mirandola, who promote a congress of scholars around the theme of ecumenism, religious, and philosophical peace.

In his most systematic writing, the *Querela pacis* of 1521, however, Erasmus explains that his call for peace is intended for Christians, not universally. "Cedo bona!" (I renounce to my former opinion!), he repeats in the *Utilissima consultatio de bello Turcico suscipiendo* of 1530, arguing again for the necessity of waging war against the Ottomans.

Erasmus thus moves between his initial radical and unconditional pacifism on the one hand, and the more classic limitation of pacifism within the boundaries of Christianity (Juan Luis Vives, *De Europae dissidiis et bello Turcico*, 1526, in J.L. Vives, *Opera omnia* (1529)). This ambiguity aside, during the early modern period Erasmus develops some of the theoretically and theologically strongest arguments for peace.

In the *Querela*, Erasmus focuses on the ideological and always unsubstantiated claims that one's own war is just. He asserts that whatever the alleged reasons for waging a just war, they are always a smokescreen for the real reason, i.e. discord among the powers that be. Erasmus is unafraid to confront the unchallenged authority of Augustine and Thomas Aquinas. Like the skeptic Carneades who thought just war was nothing but a cover-up of one's own interests, Erasmus powerfully asks "Cui sua causa non videtur justa?" (Who does not think his own cause is just?) (Erasmus, *Dulce Bellum Inexpertis,* Adag. IV. i. 1). In the *Institutio Principi Christiani*, written in 1516 and published in 1532, Erasmus contrasts Christ's and Augustine's authority, pointing out that their positions on peace seem impossible to reconcile. Regardless of Augustine's long-held authority, Erasmus is interested in revitalizing the original Christian message of unconditional peace.

In the same period, the Valencian humanist Juan Louis Vives writes *De concordia et discordia humani generis* (1529) as well as its sequel *De pacificatione*. Maintaining peace, Vives claims, is the emperor's duty. Following Marsilius and classic sources such as Plato, Aristotle, and Stoicism in an eclectic yet systematic way, Vives praises the superiority of concord over discord. Underlining the power of reason and morality as uniquely human virtues, Vives nonetheless chastises the ignorance, pride, and vice that lead men to conflict and war. With the help of Christ, men can avoid moral failure, choosing instead concord and friendship.

Vives lives during the early stage of the theological conflict within Christianity, and strongly blames erudite theologians (but also humanists like Poggio and Valla) who are responsible for endless disputes about irrelevant matters. Vives provides a description of an ideal (but not utopian) portrait of a good ruler, whose moral standing accords with models inspired by Platonism and Stoicism. But peace is not the exclusive duty of the sovereign: every citizen is part of the community and must contribute to concord and the common good.

Martin Luther accepts the classic distinction between just and unjust war in the *Treatise on Good Works* (1520). He speaks again about this topic in the *Temporal Authority* (1523) and in *Whether Soldiers, Too, Can Be Saved* (1526). Peace is the highest good on earth containing all other goods. Although reason must prevail and the sovereign must use his wisdom to avoid violence, war is permitted when needed to defend and protect Christians. On these grounds, Luther advises the Duke Maurice and the Elector of Saxony John Frederick to avoid war in the Holy Week of 1542. If mediation fails, however, a defensive war must be undertaken. In his approach to the religious question, Luther's position is original. Against the Turks, for example, war is unavoidable, but it is wholly political and not religious: the emperor defends the land and the subjects, but not the faith itself. It is not Christianity that wages war, since religion's weapons are the word and the spirit, not arms. Further, infidels are a tool God uses to punish corrupt Christianity. Like Catholics, infidels are the enemies of Christ, and must be resisted with the weapons of the spirit, i.e. repentance and prayer.[6] However, the war against the infidels is ambiguously twofold, since their power is also the eschatological sign of the end times. Against the Antichrist's force, the Christian fights to obtain the final victory. The war against the Ottomans is therefore a defensive war against a foreign power, but also an apocalyptic war against the forces of evil.

John Calvin also claims that the magistrate has the right to wage war and is in the wrong if he fails to defend his subjects. However, Calvin is more reluctant to admit just war, given the horror, chaos, and confusion that war produces, which he depicts clearly. Man is, after all, created in the image of God, and destroying man is thus a sin and a mark of inhumanity and bestiality (*Sermon on Deut.* 20: 16–20). Every possible means must be sought to avoid war, which is the last and ultimate resort to the problem of conflict. Also, in war not everything is permitted, but only a careful use of force that avoids cruelty of any kind. And like Luther, Calvin does not conceive war on religious grounds.

The problem of violence and pacifism is touched by two representative documents of the Protestant Reformation: the Augsburg Confession and the Helvetic Confession (both the First and Second versions). Article 16 of the Augsburg or Augustana Confession (1530) claims that Christians are allowed to wage a just war, without incurring sin. It moreover condemns Anabaptists who forbid this practice together with other *civilia officia*. The First (1536) and Second (1566) Helvetic Confessions express the belief of the Swiss Reformed Churches. Heinrich Bullinger, author of the Second Confession, claims that although the duty of the magistrate is to preserve peace and public tranquillity as well as to seek peace by all means, war is authorised in the name of God (art. 30). The Confession explicitly denies the Anabaptist refusal of war and obedience to the magistrate.

RADICAL REFORMATION

Beyond Lutheranism and Calvinism, the Reformation develops into a multifarious proliferation of groups. Radical reformers share with Luther the belief in the distinction of two kingdoms, the earthly and the divine. Against Luther, however, they refuse the political core of Protestantism, namely the legacy of Constantine and the Christianization of civic institutions and magistrates.

With his edict of Milan in 313 AD Emperor Constantine had established tolerance toward Christians. Formerly persecuted and harshly oppressed, Christians were now favored and walked a path that brought them to the top political posts of the empire. The edict is a real line of demarcation between two different approaches to peace. Christians were previously bound to the absolute principle of *pugnare mihi non licet* (I am not allowed to fight) as St. Martin tells the emperor Julian, according to Jacopo da Varagine's *Legenda Aurea*.[7] After the edict, Christians come more and more to distinguish between the peace of the citizen, whose duty is to defend the state, and the peace of the faithful, whose aim is to avoid war and defend human life above and beyond politics. The *Decretum Gratiani*, compiled by Gratian around 1140 and part of the *Corpus Juris Canonici*, reiterates this principle.

Religious movements during the Middle Ages had already begun to question the orthodox view about war's legitimacy. The Waldensian movement, founded by Peter Waldo in the twelfth century, holds a radical position in the history of pacifism. Although late Waldenses, moving away from their original source, allowed more flexibility on the principle of non-violence, Waldo's preaching and the early Waldensian practice is uncompromising in supporting a radical pacifism. Waldensian pacifism later has an influence on Lollardism in England, the Brethren in central Europe and, more specifically, the prominent self-taught fourteenth-century theologian Petr Chelčický, who denies the existence of such a thing as a "just war."

Immediately preceding the council of Constance (1414–18), which was called by the antipope John XXIII to end the Great Schism of 1054 between the Eastern Orthodox and the Western Catholic churches, the Czech theologian Jan Hus writes the *Sermo de pace*. Strongly influenced by John Wycliffe, who had been declared heretical in 1377, Hus's sermon speaks to a divided church and describes the way that the lack of true peace in "God's house" leads people to abandon God's justice. Hus employs the traditional scholastic definitions and orthodox distinctions between *pax Dei* and *pax mundi*. He also relies heavily on Church authorities like Bernard, Jerome, Gregory, and Wycliffe's master Robert Grosseteste. Against the authority, however, Hus does not fail to denounce the Antichrist who is responsible for the current situation. If, after all, Jesus came on earth to bring the sword, not peace, he intended to replace the world's peace and bring forth God's justice.

The sixteenth-century Reformation also moves toward a radical and unconditional pacifism. Conrad Grebel's thought, for example, is not inspired by Erasmian humanism, but rather by a theology of martyrdom that focuses on the idea of patience and suffering as a testimonial of salvation. In a 1524 letter to Thomas Müntzer, Grebel condemns the use of violence against the lords and testifies to an autonomous pacifist development of the some Protestant movements.

The Anabaptists' pacifist turn comes after the Peasants' War and the fall of Münster. Anabaptists interpret their defeat eschatologically, as a divinely ordained stage leading to the Final Judgment. Their pacifism was seen as coupled with anarchism and, ultimately, the lack of engagement in wordly affairs.

The Schleitheim Confession, approved in 1527 in the eponymous Swiss city, represents the Anabaptist theological core. The sixth and longest article of the document states that violence must be rejected by any means. Although the presence of violent punishment in

FIGURE 1.3: Ford Madox Ford, *The Trial of Wycliffe*, Manchester Town Hall (1886). Photo by The Picture Art Collection/Alamy Stock Photo.

FIGURE 1.4: Thomas Fairland, *George Fox*, Library of Congress (1915). Photo by Apic/Getty Images.

the Old Testament is acknowledged, the New Testament sets a different example through the peaceful figure of Christ. This position was perceived as a threat even by reformers and a potential danger for the Reform as a whole, given the aggressive attitudes of the Catholics.

Peace is also a major preoccupation for the German mystic and radical reformer Sebastian Franck. Franck begins within Lutheranism but, guided by an uncompromising ideal of religious tolerance, he soon moves toward more radical positions. Fiercely opposed to Catholics and Protestants, he does not spare even the Anabaptists from criticism. The civic institution as heir of the primitive Church is for him inappropriately authoritarian. His 1539 *Das Kriegsbüchlein des Friedens wider den Krieg*, published pseudonymously, is a theologically inspired text with arguments drawn by Erasmus's *Querela*. In this work, Franck attacks the magisterial chaplain who defends warfare.

In Poland, the "Controversy over the sword" of 1572–5 reveals the different levels of radical pacifism between the Brethren and the Antitrinitarians. In this rural mileu, in which no social movement like the German Peasants' Revolt takes place, pacifism is connected to the problem of social revolution. The Antitrinitarian Jacob Palaeologus strongly proclaims the duty of the Christian to take up weapons, since failing to do so always encourages the powerful and godless. Martin Czechowic's *Colloquia Christiana* (1575) develops, on the contrary, a radical pacifism that claims that the Christian must not wage war.

The strongest heritage that the radical Reformation leaves in terms of pacifism can be found in the pioneering positions of the Historic Peace Churches—the Mennonites and the Quakers. Although many Quakers serve under Cromwell's New Model Army, pacifism becomes the doctrine of the sect from the early 1660s, and in what later becomes known as the "Peace Testimony," its founder George Fox commits himself to opposing the use of force because it is contrary to God's will. In 1693, ardent Quaker William Penn, a friend of George Fox and the founder of the colony of Pennsylvania in 1682, writes *An Essay towards the Present and Future Peace of Europe by the Establishment of a European Dyet, Parliament or Estates*, often seen as the founding idea of a European Parliament.

THE POLITICAL DIMENSION OF PEACE

Early modernity is forged in the fire of very violent conflicts, tragically represented by the etchings of Jacques Callot and Urs Graf. In the period under scrutiny, and as an outcome of these conflicts, the political structures that characterize modernity, such as the nation state and sovereignty, arise. Political philosophers reflect on the progress of these institutions, and although their works' main focus is war, they also write about peace. This takes the form of a realist reflection, embedded in the major political works on sovereignty of this period, underlining the virtues and merits as well as the limits and difficulties, of obtaining peace. The discourse of peace also develops in utopian political literature, a stream of thought strongly intertwined with the mainstream works on sovereignty, but opposed and often critical of the realist theories of sovereignty on the ground of the superiority of the *ratio boni* to the *ratio veri*.

PEACE AS UTOPIA

Utopia has a long tradition beginning in Greek thought with the works of Theopompus, Euhemerus, and Iambulus. Although there are individual differences among authors, the underlying utopian objective is to present an inspiring portrait of politics based on harmony, often reached via the peaceful distinction between and division among individuals and functions. In an implicit response to Menenius Agrippa's Roman-crisis-era defense of the divisions between classes and their resulting disharmony, utopians deem the state well governed when it removes differences and resembles a single individual, with each of its organs performing a function, just as a human individual's organs are harmoniously united in their difference. Inspired by the idea of Platonic unity, utopian literature sees the state as a family, centripetal and harmoniously ordered despite social or economic conflicts.

Thomas More is credited with coining the neologism *utopia* in his influential eponymous work published in 1516. In his depiction of the ideal state, the discussion of peace and war is marked by ambiguity, and it is difficult to distinguish between the author's sincere beliefs and the ideas claimed and supported by his utopians. They hold peace in great esteem, but they are not pacifists: if invaded, they are prepared for war, and they live according to Vegetius's motto *si vis pacem para bellum*, avoiding war by establishing their economic and military superiority against potential enemies. Furthermore, they offer an unexpectedly wide spectrum of justifications for war, including the defense of their friends against enemies and the delivery of other people from the yoke of tyranny. They calculate war's outcome, which is typically successful for them, as an economic enterprise in which gains are maximized and costs minimized, including the loss of life, which they avoid by hiring mercenaries. The utopian claim for peace thus is ironically close to the ideological reality of war in More's time.

The preparation for war has a large space also in Tommaso Campanella's *La città del Sole* (1602 for the Italian version),[8] whose citizens are trained for war both physically, by constant exercise, and mentally, by reading Moses, Caesar, Alexander, and Scipio. In the Lutheran theologian and philosopher Johann Valentin Andreae's *Christianopolis* (1619) the name itself upon which the utopian city is built, i.e. Capharsalama (כפרשלמה), is the Hebrew word for "village of peace."

Universal peace is also the goal of the Moravian philosopher Jan Amos Comenius, who sees it as a way out of the "labyrinth of the world" toward the promised "paradise." Man and world must be reconnected to God through a program of reform of both temporal affairs and the human spirit. Through the idea of a general consultation (*De rerum humanarum emendatione consultatio catholica*, 1666), Comenius suggests a peace tribunal as a court of justice above individual states, whose function is to settle social and political conflicts and resist absolute sovereignty. He calls as well for two other institutions, a spiritual tribunal concerned with matters of faith and morality, and an educational tribunal dealing with knowledge and schools. The educational dimension is of paramount importance, since man must be educated to a concept of politics that is finally detached and made independent from war. The platonic inspiration is evident: politics must become once again Truth, taking the pattern of peace and renouncing Mars. In the *Panorthosia* section of the *Universal Reform*, the peace tribunal's function is to give a concrete existence to the universal principle of human wisdom. Guardians are established who collegially exercises power in a harmonious form. The mission of the tribunal is to establish universal peace through the real union of humanity as a whole rather than through the mediation of individual states' positions and interests. Thus, in Comenius's project, love and morality have as much importance as law and politics. This is the real essence of natural right and of peace: peace is not only an end, but also a means, which rules out the very possibility of something like a "just" war as a way toward peace—thus Comenius offers an implicit critique of mainstream utopianism.

Early modern utopianism leaves a strong mark on subsequent pacifism, whose main expression is undoubtedly Kant's essay *On Perpetual Peace* (1795). Kant builds on Abbé de Saint-Pierre's *Projet de paix perpétuelle* (1713) which includes a proposal for a proto "league of nations." Arguably, Kant's well-structured proposals for peace are finally made real in the founding of the League of Nations and, then, almost 150 years after his essay was written, in the United Nations.

PEACE AND SOVEREIGNTY

In the early modern period, the religious problem collides with the political problem. The dissolution of the *res publica christiana* and the rise of the nation state accompanies the development of a new concept of sovereignty and, consequently, a specific discourse on peace, whose roots are found in the classic heritage. Along with *Eirēnē*, the personification and deification of peace, the classic Greek sources also offer the concept of Κοινὴ Εἰρήνη, the common peace, sworn not only among Greek cities, but also with the Persians. The concept of common peace becomes concrete in the two-fold idea of autonomy and mutual assistance. In the Hellenistic period, however, the shared peace becomes the symbol of the hegemonic power of the Macedonians and thus loses its original strength. The Latin *pax* merely signifies the absence of war and the outcome of a conflict that leaves a winner and a loser, whose new relationship is sanctioned by a treaty. In the early centuries A.D. peace is identified with the *pax Augusta*, the era of internal peace under the Emperor Augustus, also celebrated by the *Ara Pacis* in Rome. More broadly, the *pax Romana* signifies the peaceful order imposed on the Graeco-Roman world that distinguishes the inner civilization from the outer barbarian world, and ensures security and the rule of law. Because the alternative to this order was the "war of all with all," both war and imperial expansion were seen as legitimate ways of maintaining and promoting peace.

Pacifism has an ancient tradition, exemplified by works of Aristophanes such as *Lysistrata* (411 BC), which called for panhellenic unity abroad and social unity at home; *Acharnians* (425 BC), which celebrated the happy life under peace against the harshness of war; and *Peace* (421 BC), in which Eirene, the personification of peace, is released from the prison in which Polemos had detained her.

Medieval thinkers and theologians such as Engelbert d'Admont also strive for such a universalistic concept of peace, interpreting it in various ways depending on their classic and Patristic sources and the concrete struggles they are engaged with. Dante Alighieri's project proposes the global reform of the Christian world as a way of overcoming the conflicts between Guelphs and Ghibellines and the crisis of the Church. His intellectual programme of reform is grounded on a moral conception of a global order that goes beyond every particularity (individual or national) toward the true realization and actualization of man in the world. Such an accomplishment is only possible through the kingdom of universal peace, which is in turn the highest good in view of human beatitude religiously intended.

A particularly original reflection on peace and war can be found in Siena, in Ambrogio Lorenzetti's (1290–1348) famous fresco, which owes its conception not to Christian or Aristotelian classical thought, but instead to pre-humanist (thirteenth century) Italian thinkers who were inspired by the late Roman republic, particularly Cicero. Seen from this perspective, peace is not just the absence of discord or conflict, but instead the triumph over discord and war-forces that, unless consciously opposed, will destroy all well-being. The key to creating civic peace, a concept central to these writers and faithfully depicted in Lorenzetti's fresco, is to ensure that government works in the interest of all citizens. If one group is favored over another, any chance of government for the "common good" is lost. Government must ensure equality and act on behalf of all its citizens. In this way Lorenzetti's fresco makes peace the outcome of a government that rules for the "common good" by a fair application of legal justice and equality.

Marsilius's *Defender of the Peace* (1324) is a strong defense of peace, presented by an acute philosopher and competent theologian who was exceptionally aware of the social and political reality of his time. Marsilius considers the Church's claim for political power the main cause of unrest, and his book against the papacy advocates the return to the original values of poverty and peace within a democratically organized ecclesiastical community. To this end, he abandons the traditional teleological conception of the State based on Aristotelian ethics in favor of a sharp distinction between the secular and the sacred spheres: the former is in charge of the peaceful organization of human life and depends on human reason, while the latter is concerned only with the eternal life and depends on faith. The distinction between human and divine law, Marsilius argues, is the condition to obtain peace on earth.

A concrete attempt to reach a stable and consistent peace is also found in the *Tractatus pacis toti Christianitati fiendae*, the plan presented in 1462 by George of Kunštát and Poděbrady (Podiebrad). Podiebrad is king of Bohemia and a follower of Jan Hus. In his pioneering text, he abandons the medieval idea of a universal empire to pursue the more realistic idea of a multilateral agreement among equal forces. Podiebrad's proposal takes shape in the wake of the fall of Constantinople and the concretization of the threat the infidels pose to Christianity.

Although aiming at concrete political reform, both Marsilius's and Podiebrad's attempts to theorize peace rest on the assumption of ideal values as targets far removed from the "effectual reality" of things. The "effectual reality" is the expression coined by Niccolò Machiavelli in *The Prince* (1513), ch. XVIII to deny universal consistency to any value, whether moral, religious, or political.[9] The fragmentation of the medieval universal political structures of the Church and the Empire into a multitude of nation states is sharply reflected, in theory, by Machiavelli's discovery of the necessary fragmentation of interests and positions both inside and outside of the nation state. Whereas medieval theory grounds its concept of political stability on the classic ideal of *bonum commune* or common good, largely derived from Aristotle and Cicero, Machiavelli's most original conclusion, reached through the study of the ancient history of Rome and the modern history of Florence, is that such a thing simply does not exist or is an illusion: politically speaking, the good cannot, by definition, be common, since someone's good is always someone else's harm, disadvantage, loss, and ruin. The conflictual dynamic of social classes in Rome described in the *Discourses on Livy* (1513–19), just like that of political factions analyzed in the *Florentine History* (1520–5), clearly shows that peace has always been a provisional balance of forces, guided by different ideological, political, religious, and economic interests, often irreconcilable.

Although he is not a pacifist, Machiavelli is certainly aware of the importance of peace and stability for the development of political entities. Machiavelli thus develops his philosophy of war—or, better, of war's necessity—against both conditional and unconditional pacifism, not to deny that something like peace can be reached, individually or collectively, but rather to reveal that peace is necessarily unstable and provisional, always subordinated to the natural phenomenon of violence.

Machiavelli's thought is grounded on realism and materialism. This approach derives from his original reading of the ancient historians who narrate the concrete realities of war and peace, including Thucydides, Polybius, Livius, and of the ancient philosophers claiming the material one as the only ontological reality of nature, mainly Lucretius. Machiavelli does not deny the existence or importance of the *idea* of peace. On the contrary, peace can, and sometimes should, be a legitimate political aim: Machiavelli praises the Roman dictator Cincinnatus who, after having defeated the enemy and saved Rome goes back to his peaceful life. Still, Machiavelli knows that peace is no more than an idea, always necessarily subordinated to the material reality of a political world that is shaped first and foremost by force. A peaceful balance among political forces within the state or among nation states is an illusion only when preached by "unarmed prophets." Peace, and with it, security and well-being are possible, but they must be imposed by a prince who is strong enough to resist those who do not want them.

War is thus not better than peace, in Machiavelli's view. War is necessary, because others always seek to impose their interests, whether through peaceful means or through war. Thus, it becomes necessary to abandon the ancient utopia of a universal peace and take a side in the concrete political arena. Machiavelli consistently takes the side of the people against the great and the nobles and of the prince who supports the people and secures their peaceful existence by any means necessary, including war. Warfare is actually the most secure way, in Machiavelli's time, to grant strength and power to the people

FIGURE 1.5: Lorenzo Bartolini, *Statue of Niccolò Machiavelli*, Loggiato degli Uffizi, Florence (1845). Wikimedia Commons.

because, as the Romans knew, he who wants to be secure must be ready to make war, and that readiness means giving weapons and power to the people.

It is with the St. Bartholomew's Day massacre (1572) in the background that Jean Bodin writes *The Six Books of the Republic* (1576), one of the most important works delineating the relatively new idea of state sovereignty. Bodin has been read as claiming that the state is absolute, but his reflection actually recognizes the important role of the social and political forces within the State that offset the monarch's power. Bodin grants a considerable importance to the concept of social peace, reworking the Aristotelian idea of friendship. Friendship, however, does not perform a revolutionary function for Bodin, since it is grounded on the recognition and justification of differences among subjects, as well as their harmonious organization, rather than on equality as a social, political, or economic value.

Italian republican political thought also strongly influenced James Harrington, who draws inspiration from the classical world, but is particularly attracted to the city of Venice. Institution building and liberty are his central concerns, but unlike some English republicans such as Algernon Sidney, he seeks solutions for peace and stability in the aristocratic Venetian model. For Harrington, war is a sign of weakness caused by poor constitutions that are unable to manage the tendency toward the imbalance of power. Peace, therefore, is made possible by balancing the power of social groups, in particular the aristocracy and the people. In line with early Italian humanists such as Brunetto Latini, Harrington considers that peace must triumph over the forces of discord. Within this framework he advocates an important innovation, no doubt inspired by Machiavelli, that government be organized in a way that allows conflict to be harmlessly dissipated so that it does not have to use its power to suppress dissent or make hollow appeals to humanity's "better" nature. Like Francesco Guicciardini and against Machiavelli, however, Harrington praises the pacific republican model of Venice rather than the tumultuous and conflictual one of Rome and Florence.

Thomas Hobbes' *Leviathan* (1651, with a revised Latin version published in 1668), written in the midst of the English revolution, is an attempt to impose political peace despite the divisive ideological and material forces that operate in society. Man, for Hobbes, is diverse, and the different ways he is affected by ideas, issues, and problems necessarily bring him to conflict. This realistic portrait, stemming from the society of Hobbes' time, is projected onto a hypothetical state of nature in which the war of everyone against everyone is at the same time the only possible outcome and the means to move beyond this state, to enter civil society by way of the deliberate construction of the political sphere. Only in the political domain[10] can and must peace be realized if man wants to achieve his primary impulse toward survival. Absolute sovereignty thus becomes the premise and the promise of peace within the State, defined as the preservation of individual's life at its most basic and physical level.

Although peace is not the natural state of humanity, and is subordinated to the human creation of politics, seen here as artificially conceived rather than as man's natural state, as claimed by Aristotle, it is too often forgotten that to seek peace and follow it is also the first and fundamental law of nature (*Leviathan*, ch. 14). Moral virtues and laws of nature incline people toward peace and although one can never trust other men (and thus must occupy oneself in the state of nature not only by preparing for war, but by actively waging preventive war), seeking long-term self-preservation through consistent peace is still logically required. This logic is different from the classic attitude of the ancients, since for Hobbes, the law of nature does not rely on any transcendent authority. Peace is thus conditional on the successful establishment of a sovereign who leaves as little space as possible for the potential areas of risk to fall back in the state of nature.

THE SUPRA-NATIONAL DIMENSION

Whereas sovereignty is the main preoccupation of political theorists of the nation state, a new dimension of the problem of peace characterizes this epoch. Beyond the nation state and, more concretely, the European boundaries, peace becomes a global problem and opens up ideas for projects of supra-national and international balance among equal powers.

The Basque theologian and law of nations theorist Francisco de Vitoria is one of the most important authors of the Spanish Golden Century. Educated in Paris, Vitoria brings a humanist spirit to his scholastic culture. Especially in his *De Indis* of 1532 and in the *Relectiones theologicae*, lectures given at the University of Salamanca between 1537 and 1539 and published posthumously in 1557, Vitoria develops an idea of a community of all humanity forming, in a way, a true *Respublica*. This conception is inspired by the Aristotelian and scholastic idea of man as a social animal, yet projected beyond every particularism toward a stoic and Christian universalism that encompasses all people. The concept of organized people is paramount, and prevails over the rights of the individual person, pointing to the idea of an international society of nations. This society is at the same time natural and positive, namely established by man and warranted not just by nature, but by the law. This double character is essential to Vitoria's aim vis-à-vis peace. He argues against sovereignty by claiming that nations and peoples cannot withdraw from this universal community and solidarity, as it belongs to their nature. Sovereignty is thus not absolute, but rather limited by the fundamental exigencies of the *jus gentium* (the law of nations) and the aim of seeking peace among nations.

Among the important concrete implications of Vitoria's position is that he links the right of Europeans to preach the Gospel among the natives to the prohibition against imposing it against the natives' belief. On a more general level, Vitoria praises the idea of a distributive social justice in international relationships that helps build peace through exchange, communication, and interaction. Such a notion has a strategic interest for Vitoria, since the international community has neither the concrete tools nor the force to prevent war, and war, for Vitoria, is a real threat. The way to overcome it is by obliterating its causes and making peace more convenient than war for the nations.

In France, Emeric Crucé thinks about political theory beyond the state, and argues for a strongly pacifist position. He delineates these ideas in the *Nouveau Cynée ou Discours d'Estat représentant les occasions et moyens d'establir une paix générale et la liberté de commerce pour tout le monde* (1623). Deriving the title from the name of Cyneas, Pyrrho's advisor who embodies the strongest desire for peace according to Plutarch, Crucé advocates an assembly of all States' sovereigns in which they can pursue peace just for moral reasons, but also for social and economic interests. Free exchange and commerce are at the heart of a commonly-shared economic sphere that does not grant any legitimate space to religion, one of the main divisive factors in Crucé's time. The universal order thus created ensures peace beyond ideological, religious, or geographical boundaries.

The South-Holland Humanist philosopher and philologist Hugo Grotius is certainly one of the major natural law theorists of this period. Directly involved in the politics of his time, first as commissioner defending the aggressive policy of the Dutch East India Company (1604) and then as Swedish ambassador to France between 1634 and 1645, he contributes to early modern political and legal theory with his work *De jure belli ac pacis* (1625). With the background of the synod of Dordrecht (1618–19) and the conflict between Remonstrant and Counter-Remonstrants in the Low Countries in mind, Grotius stresses the idea of concord and blames political and religious division for obscuring the fundamental unity among Christians. He advocates tolerance and peace among the churches, supporting his political theory with great erudition and knowledge of both revelation and philosophy, and asserting the strong unity of Christian and pagan culture. In his masterpiece, Grotius attempts to codify the *jus in bello* and the *jus ad bellum*. War is a savage way of settling conflicts, but its justice is recognized when war is waged to obtain peace. Although he is far from a pacifist, Grotius's work is of paramount importance in defining and organizing peace in concrete political and legal terms by developing instruments to establish and maintain peace. These include an international society of nations, justified by the claim of the sacred character of contracts and engagements (*pacta sunt servanda*), and the limitation of war to the subjects directly involved in the conflict. Grotius rejects the medieval vision of universal authorities such as that of the emperor or the Church. His universalism is closer to Vitoria's and based on a universal society of nations rather than of men, which he sees as the only way to promote and preserve peace on a global scale.

Early modern pacifism's strongest heritage can be seen in the development of theories of international law, the concept of balance of power, and the idea of peace through commerce. Strongly influenced by Christian Wolff, in 1758, Emer de Vattel publishes the *Law of Nations*, which codifies the conduct of nations in relation to one another. George Washington, the first President of the United States, was one of the many influential politicians affected by this seminal work. Although early modern thinkers agree that trade brings peace and prosperity to nations, the history of this period shows that the link between commerce and peace is far from straightforward. Early mercantilism pursues the establishment of a favorable balance of payment surpluses in relation to other nations. To this end, the seventeenth century Navigation Acts passed in Britain legalize exclusive and monopolistic trade. This type of economic competition foments conflict between states in the early modern and modern period, since each nation uses military enforcement to gain and maintain trade surpluses.

Early modernity sees the disintegration of the universal values and institutions of the past. It also experiences some of the most violent conflicts of European history. These conflicts are crucial in determining the new political, legal, and economic structures of the modern world. The discourse of peace, although varied, constantly resurfaces in authors as diverse as those belonging to Christian humanism, the radical Reformation, utopianism, political realism, and international legal thought. Although these authors rarely give a theoretical definition of the concept of peace, their works testify concretely to the attempt to make a political use of philosophy and history in the establishment of peace, or at least in avoiding war through a better understanding of its causes and reasons. Subsequent pacifism is thus largely indebted to this period's attempts, both on theoretical and practical grounds.

CHAPTER TWO

Human Nature, Peace, and War

ANDREA GUIDI

The task of explaining those human instincts which generate war and aggression is one which has troubled countless generations and cultures. War, conflict, and violence are a recurrent feature in the images that human societies create of themselves. Racial, ethnic, and religious perceptions and thinking have all played strong roles in how one "imagined community" (us) understands and deals with another (them). War is inconceivable without the concept of "enemy," the natural corollary of these two images (Rieber (ed.) 1991). They exert a huge influence on the ethical purposes which justify the waging of war (Coates 1997: 210). The traditional concept of peace, as the achievement of the common good of a society, clashes with the perceived danger which the interaction with other societies or individuals (*me* or *him*, *us* and *them*) is capable of creating (Finnis 1996: 16).

There is also a more sociological aspect to our formulation of the concept of war and peace. Every human society shares a general abhorrence toward violent behavior, but at the same time is fascinated by war. According to this interpretation, human nature appears twofold: on the one hand it is respectful—that is, with a natural instinct for respect and sympathy—on the other hand it is aggressive. In essence, there is a tension between two moral inclinations at the core of the secular debate on war and peace. In fact, over the course of European history, such tensions have typically been relieved by means of philosophy, politics, and religion; in particular, the doctrines provided by canon law. However, the structures and ideologies which necessarily underpin large scale outbreaks of violence, such as the propaganda and technological advances which facilitated the horrors of twentieth-century warfare, also precipitated substantial cultural shifts, as we will examine in this chapter. To comprehend the increasingly extreme means of warfare which characterized the beginning of the early modern era, philosophers, historians, and other prominent thinkers developed a new cultural and political concept of the relationship between war and peace. This chapter will show how the medieval cultural attitude toward war and peace was replaced during this period by a new concept, based on novel ideas on the nature of man.

In Europe, medieval Christendom was characterized by a cultural identification between the community and their ruler, which lessened the need for recourse to a coercive power or force in order to control society. According to a concept originally formulated by Jürgen Habermas, Christendom was a "common life-world," one which shared a cultural and social background of behaviors and beliefs (Habermas 1990: 135). This shared world of beliefs helped to form a moral authority which mitigated the effects of violence and disorder in societies of similar values, and has been a requisite condition for the historical processes which lie at the heart of any international order among nations and peoples (Phillips 2010: 23, 64–5). According to this interpretation, an authoritative rather than a coercive power acquires its persuasive force through collective identity, shared purposes and an agreed moral framework (Phillips 2010: 20). Such a framework also influenced the ethics of war itself, by limiting the use of violence during conflict.

These factors can also be identified in geo-political entities outside of Europe, such as the Confucian world. As with Latin Christendom, the Sinosphere was a purposive rather than a merely practical association. It too had a collective identity, shared purposes and an agreed moral framework (Phillips 2010: 20). In Confucian thought, there was no differentiation between legal and moral order. The political community was linked by ritual bonds of benevolence and obedience between the emperor and his vassals. This fundamental structure of political bodies and institutions was based on an ideological unity supported by a complex of norms and religious beliefs and social imaginary, which tended to regulate the use of violence in concordance with the order of Confucian ethics. So, for instance, war and violence were permitted by customary law (*fa*) in order to rectify error, such as in the case of a vassal state or region violating rules or refusing to obey commands (Chen 1991: 53–4, 60), and to restore the temporal state of harmony (*ping*) in concordance with the cosmic order (Phillips 2010: 28, 31; Chen 1991: 64–9).

In certain historical contexts, this shared world of beliefs and its influence on the ideas on war and peace, arising from a common theological and religious tradition, lasted for the entire period taken into consideration in this book. In the Jewish world, for instance, up until the late early-modern age and in contrast with the Christian's tradition, these concepts remained a matter of theology rather than politics; and the notion of peace in particular was seen from a utopian perspective within a strict theological framework (Solomon 2006: 123). The legislation and reflections on war are therefore to be found in both biblical texts and the works by the rabbis, beginning with *Deuteronomy* 20, which distinguishes war mandated by God against others which are not. According to this text, the former is unlimited in scope, whilst the latter is subject to several restraints (Solomon 2006: 108–9). (Walzer (1996: 95) argues that Jewish writers had tangentially discussed these topics since the late Middle Ages). Equally, for Islamic thinkers, war has long remained a struggle between Muslims (the community) and the non-Muslims (the enemy) (Tibi 2006: 131).

According to the message of these foundational sources, the distinction between just and unjust war, as conceived by medieval and early-modern European tradition, is unknown to the Islamic and Jewish tradition. Judaism, for instance, sees human nature as too fragile a basis for ordering such political, social, and ethical obligations (Last Stone 2006: 19). As in the case of Christianity, however, the Islamic and Jewish concepts of peace are indeed shaped by a definition of human nature arising from a particular theological and religious framework, which in turn influences the conduct of and the approach to war. To Islam as well as to Hebraism, human nature comprises body and soul, with each soul capable of both good and evil. Consequently, every aspect of life is important and, according to this belief, every human being must be protected. Renaissance Jewish thinkers such as the Spanish theologians Isaac Arama and Isaac Abravanel, who both commented on *Deuteronomy* 20, emphasized a Jewish commitment to peace by arguing that the *Torah* requires an obligation not to damage and destroy human beings (Solomon 2006: 117). Equally, as the objective of any war according to Islam is to force non-Muslims to submit to their faith, rather than to kill or destroy them, the conduct of war forbids pillage and destruction (Tibi 1996: 133). Hence the Qur'an, as well as the example of the Prophet Muhammad himself in regulating of the rules of war, forbids not only the fighting during certain months, but above all the killing of non-combatants.

However, if in these cases the concept of human nature continued to derive from a shared religious and theological framework throughout this long period, the political and social world of Renaissance Europe underwent a transition that eventually threatened the common life-world inherited from the Latin Christendom. In response to this, there appeared during the Renaissance a process which led to the formulation of new images and concepts of human nature, peace and war; which, as a consequence, facilitated the rise of a new international political order by the end of the period.

ANTECEDENTS: LATIN CHRISTENDOM

The problem of explaining, or justifying, the reasons that societies wage war had been at the very heart of political and philosophical thought across the centuries. In Renaissance Europe, there emerged various distinct yet overlapping areas of thought. Since antiquity, human societies have developed a strong need for defining means and norms through which to avoid violence. These reveal an ontological necessity for security, linked in turn to a continuing strive toward defining human nature and its attitude towards violent behaviors (Phillips 2010: 16). Latin Christendom, in particular, laid the groundwork for a series of normative restraints on violence and war that continued to hold Western Europe together. Augustine provided the first full attempt at a Christian ethics regarding war and peace; in effect, the first notable manifestation of the so called "just war" doctrine, in which conflict must have a just cause, be declared by a proper authority, and be conceived with a final goal of achieving peace (Finnis 1996: 17).

In this line of reasoning, moral concerns surrounding the concept of human nature take center stage. For Augustine, peace is a corollary of the ethical framework through which to reconcile the human condition: mankind is "perfect by nature, but corrupt by convention," and so these corrupt societies "must continually struggle, often violently, to achieve peace" (Christopher 1994: 36).

In the late medieval visual tradition—the decades immediately preceding the period taken into consideration in this volume—the disasters of war were contrasted to the benefits and virtues of peace. The Lorenzetti frescoes of the Palazzo Pubblico in Siena were an iconographic manifestation of such thinking. Their depiction of the outcomes of peace were presented in the context of a moral conception of mankind as united in Christian valor, and they exemplify the centrality of divinely-inspired justice as the crucial factor in maintaining peace (Nirit Ben-Aryeh 2001).

As Anthony Coates efficaciously explained, just war is characterized by the notion that the "enemy" remains part of a moral community that unites all belligerents; despite the conflict, there is still a sense of solidarity amongst them. The enemy, as such, still belongs to a community of shared behaviors, beliefs and culture, and is not imaged or seen as the "other." In the opposite case—unjust war, the absence of a perceived moral or psychological community—war descends into an abyss of hatred. When just war devolves into "the lust for power," as originally defined by the words of Augustine (*Libido dominandi*) (Augustine, *De Doctrina Christiana*, 1: 23; also *Civ. Dei* 1.30; 3.14; 5.13; 14.15, 19, 28; 19.15. See Capizzi 2015, 55), the enemy is dehumanized or even demonized, and thus becomes the "other." The lust for war and domination, seen as a foundational human impulse, substitutes the notion of just war with public hatred: as a result, moral inhibitions

FIGURE 2.1: Ambrogio Lorenzetti, *Effects of Good Government in the City*, Palazzo Pubblico, Siena (1338–9). Wikimedia Commons.

fall away. A just war intended as a last resort turns into an ethic of harshness, according to which the destruction of the enemy is a moral duty (Coates 2006: 216–18). Just as each man faces an internal struggle to control his passions, so too does the fallen nature of our earthly world struggle to contain the inherent passions of human and international relationships.

According to scholars such as James Turner Johnson, Christian ethics and norms arising from the Roman juridical tradition came together to form the "classic just war doctrine." This doctrine reached its full theoretical and juridical expression in the sixteenth and seventeenth centuries, yet fell apart soon after (Johnson 1987: xii–xiii). However, on a cultural as well as on a political level, the early Renaissance had already introduced new beliefs and circumstances that broke with the previous traditions of medieval canon law and scholasticism. In fact, the breakdown of Christendom over the course of the sixteenth century was accompanied by the rise of new monarchies and nations. This, alongside the new Renaissance emphasis on humans as individuals, brought to the fore a sense of moral self-sufficiency amongst rational agents, in stark contrast to the centrality of the community in the moral life of individuals during the middle ages (Coates 2006: 215–16).

THE CRISIS OF THE EARLY RENAISSANCE

The conflict between the papacy and the Holy Roman Empire in the late Middle Ages, followed by the secular and territorial ambitions which drew the late medieval and Renaissance papacy into the Italian Wars, started a process which would eventually lead to the collapse of the medieval universal idea of peace amongst Christian nations. This process was accompanied by a weakening of the central moral authority of the church and papacy, upon which the medieval approach to the restraints of conflict depended. This diminishing authority of a universal church compounded the loss of influence of earlier moral traditions.

On the one hand, Erasmus's doctrine rejected war as a political instrument by emphasizing an ideal of peace for Christendom. This line of reasoning stressed the role of man's irrationality—in his own words, the "irrational decision of the battle"—in its explanation of war (Erasmus 1917). As the latent aggressiveness of man was an unchangeable fact, any aspirations toward societal order relied upon a search for the most effective way to limit this destructive factor, and particularly within the religious sphere: "Even if we allow that some wars are just, yet since we see that all mankind is plagued by this madness, it should be the role of the priests to turn the minds of people and princes to other things" (Erasmus 1997: 108).

A distinct sector of northern Renaissance art was particularly influenced by such a pessimistic view of human nature, which, in the words of Erasmus, "for the most part [. . .] inclines towards evil" (Erasmus 1997: 8). In Hieronymus Bosch's paintings such as *The Mocking of Christ*, or *Christ Carrying the Cross*, the faces of the persecutors of the Christ reveal a very negative view of man.

Man was thought to have had a dual and conflicting psychology—from which peace relied on reconciling appetite and reason. To Erasmus, one inclination struggles with another inclination: piety versus cupidity. Good and evil, or reason versus appetite, in any case, both personal happiness and social behavior depended on the capacity of dealing with and consequently well ordering these two aspects of the human nature (Hale 1971: 13).

FIGURE 2.2: Hieronymus Bosch, *The Mocking of Christ*, also known as *The Crowning with Thorns*, National Gallery, London (*c.* 1510). Wikimedia Commons.

FIGURE 2.3: Hieronymus Bosch or follower, *Christ Carrying the Cross*, Museum of Fine Arts, Ghent (1500–35). Wikimedia Commons.

On the other hand, the turn of the sixteenth century saw the classical notion of "just war," which had previously dominated medieval culture, become the subject of new controversy, as the theological and religious norms which had regulated social and political life for centuries were challenged by political thinkers such as Niccolò Machiavelli and Francesco Guicciardini. These argued that only political realism could both explain (on theoretical grounds) and validate (on practical grounds) any kind of war or peace. At the center of any conception of war, the theory goes, is not only the human aptitude for aggression, but also and above all the necessity to consider the inclination of every human being to act in his own self-interest.

THE HUMANIST CHALLENGE

There were several intervening elements in the formulation of these new theories. Firstly, the early Italian humanists launched a philosophical and political challenge to the medieval international order and its doctrine of just war (Skinner 1978: 245). The rediscovery of ancient philosophical texts led to a re-evaluation of the prevalent teachings of Augustine and Thomas Aquinas on war and peace. The histories and philosophical writings of antiquity were spread not only through rediscovered, retranslated, or newly popularized texts, but also through compendia and commentaries. As John Hale explained, these latter volumes were circulated "far wider than the nucleus of scholars," with readership extending instead to politicians, military chiefs, and a general public interested in—amongst others—books on the art and on the law of war (Hale 1971: 5–6). As a result, humanist thinkers abandoned the scholastic doctrine of just war, and favored the Stoic philosophy of war-as-fratricide over the attempted justifications of Augustine and Aquinas (Copenhaver and Schmitt 2002: 273; also Cailes 2012: 15). According to Quentin Skinner, early humanists such as Petrarch stigmatized "any appeal to *vis*, i.e. force, intended as brutish or beastly quality, at the expense of a concept of *virtus* as civic virtue." They also were much less interested than the scholastics "in arguing about the relations between warfare and government." Their general claim, in essence, was that "as long as the ruler is a man of *virtus*, the goals of peace and security will be adequately secured" (Skinner 2002: 123–4. Cf. also Skinner 1978: 246). Thus, in the Italian peninsula of the late Quattrocento, Platonic Humanists insisted on a new form of education, based on the restoration of the classics, to serve as a tool for creating a new generation of rulers and citizens, capable of restraining the irrationality of evil through their own *virtus* and therefore governing for the good of the community.

GUNS, MONEY, AND MATERIAL TRANSFORMATIONS

Other aspects of this period also contributed to the aforementioned shift in cultural attitudes toward human nature, peace, and war. At the end of the fifteenth century, technological innovation, alongside the emergence of new methods for waging war, rendered conflicts crueller, more brutal, and far more pervasive within society itself (Johnson 1987: 133ff). The introduction of artillery in early-modern warfare was followed by a greater emphasis on offensive tactics on the battlefield. Francesco Guicciardini described the artillery used by the French army that invaded Italy in 1494 as a "new plague"; "so frequent and so violent was their battering that in a few hours they could accomplish what previously in Italy used to require many days" (Guicciardini 1969: 49–50). Ludovico Ariosto's famous condemnation of handguns in his poem *Orlando furioso* also mirrored this kind of thinking:

> How, foul and pestilent discovery,
> Didst thou find place within the human heart?
> Through thee is martial glory lost, through thee
> The trade of arms became a worthless art
> And at such ebb are worth and chivalry,
> That the base often plays the better part.
> Through thee no more shall gallantry, no more
> Shall valour prove their prowess as of yore.
> Through thee, alas! are dead, or have to die,
> So many noble lords and cavaliers
> Before this war shall end, which, Italy
> Afflicting most, has drowned the world in tears,
> That, if I said the word, I err not, I
> Saying he sure the cruellest appears
> And worst, of nature's impious and malign,
> Who did this hateful engine first design (. . .)
>
> —Ariosto 1910: 11, xxvi–xxvii (cf. Valleriani 2011)

The longer distances between enemy combatants permitted by this new kind of weapon, which so upset Ariosto, contributed to the formulation of a new concept of war as a mean of total destruction, in which there was no room for any of the moral restraints—such as honor and chivalry—that had previously regulated forms of combat and fighting amongst men (Bellamy 2006: 4).

The group most directly and significantly impacted by this new means of waging war, however, was civilians. Guicciardini's contemporary observation was that many local populations: "... saw nothing but scenes of infinite slaughter, plunder and destruction of multitudes of towns and cities, attended with the licentiousness of soldiers no less destructive to friends than foes" (quoted in Hale 1998: 179). Modern scholars such as John Hale have outlined the particularly bloody nature of the Italian Wars, and the moral descent that consequently influenced the cultural perception of warfare during that period (Hale 1962).

The introduction of firearms on such a large scale contributed to the formulation of a pessimistic view of mankind also in Northern Europe, as well as within Renaissance art and visual culture. Like Ariosto, Erasmus too commented on the evil power or firearms, highlighting the effects of such violence on the culture of his day:

> God made man unarmed. But anger and revenge have mended the work of God, and furnished his hands with weapons invented in hell. Christians attack Christians with engines of destruction, fabricated by the devil. A cannon! A mortar! No human being could have devised them originally; they must have been suggested by the evil one.
>
> —Erasmus 1917

Similarly, the title page to the 1489 Basle edition of Augustine's *De civitate dei* shows devils shooting with guns at the inhabitants of the city of God (Hale 1962: 29).

NEW MONARCHIES: PROVIDING AN ALTERNATIVE TO THE UNITY OF CHRISTENDOM

The early modern dissolution of Christendom gave rise to a more confrontational framework, of individual states battling for supremacy. This was accompanied by a more secular conceptualization of political authority, encouraged by the recovery of classical heritage, which also contributed to the weakening of Christian unity (Phillips 2010: 73ff; also Cailes 2012: 77). Such circumstances required a new set of political explanations and solutions for the realities of conflict and violence; a more realist approach to politics and warfare which intersected with the previous codes of conduct for waging war. Canon law had lost its previous influence and normative force in restraining the conduct and means of conflict, whilst chivalry had lost its ethical suasion with the passing of feudal social systems and values—another development decried by Ludovico Ariosto's aforementioned poem in its condemnation of modern warfare. Christendom entered the sixteenth century in a fragile state, beset by more violent offence-driven conflict and no longer supported by the institution of the feud. At the same time, the multiplicity of political authorities created by this dissolution only served to accelerate the fracturing of moral authority, and thus the undermining of previous interpretations of the causes and intention of war and violence (Elias 1982: 1ff, 131ff).

For Christian thinkers such as Savonarola, a medieval mind at the close of the fifteenth century, repentance and divine assistance was needed to bring individuals closer to a state of original "grace," or *prima forma* (first nature) (Pocock 1975: 136). Such divine inspiration was also considered necessary in the relationships between states, and it was common for medieval contemporaries to both perceive and conduct interstate relations in the same framework as the Christian ethical code for interpersonal relations. Breaches of trust, for instance, could tear them apart. However, the insecurity of the composite monarchies resulting from the schism in Christian unity constituted a new political reality (Phillips 2010: 108ff), in which it was now assumed that "princes needed to be skilled as war leaders and that all states had to be prepared to fight for survival" (Hale 1971: 22). A new reflection on human nature was thus put into focus, as the declining model of Christian ethics was accompanied by a reconsideration of the interplay between rational and emotional human nature within interstates relations. Renaissance historians often stressed the link between physiology and behavior, and made direct links between specific historical events and particular human drives. As pointed out by John Hale, Guicciardini's portrait of Pope Clement VII, much like Shakespeare's of Iago, was a psychological description and explanation of behavior in the light of the individual's life experience. Similarly, many writers of the time looked to human behavior in order to identify psychological explanations of violence (Hale 1971: 12–13), based on the "complex levels of (sometimes displaced) rivalry, competition, and even aggression that structure all dialogues and all friendships" highlighted by writers such as Erasmus (Najemy 1993: 55). At the beginning of the sixteenth century, the Florentine chancellor Niccolò Machiavelli examined the coexistence and interplay of two psychological forces—"the desire to have more and the fear of losing what is possessed"—in shaping the fortunes of entire states as well as the relationships between social groups (Cesa 2014: 5). Where medieval thinkers had considered interstate relations from the perspective of Christian ethics, it was now the more temporal, psychological and behavioural nature of man as an individual which was seen to govern the affairs of state.

GUICCIARDINI AND MACHIAVELLI ON HUMAN NATURE: MORAL SUASION AND POLITICAL SANCTION

In his *Memories*, Guicciardini elaborated his own particular, pessimistic view of human nature, one which inevitably tended toward evil rather than good. According to Guicciardini, men are only interested in their own *particulare* ("particular good"), with each individual thus seeking their own pleasure and wealth, the fulfilment of their own aims, without considering anything else. This would often result in acts of supreme cruelty, as such aims are more likely to be reached through evil means than good. This line of thinking, predicated on the assumption that human nature is both immutable and dominated by self-interest, is often referred to in the literature of international relations as realism (Mapel 1996: 54). It is a tradition dominated by a general moral skepticism, and thus one which refutes the application of ethics to war and politics (Coates 1997: 17). In Machiavelli's view, politics is dominated by the interaction between the man's consistent nature—which transcends the variations of civilization or society—and the vicissitudes of necessity and fortune (Webel 2014: 92). Although Machiavelli does not necessarily share Guicciardini's pessimism, to him too is human nature essentially selfish, driven by self-interest, and above all ambitious of wealth, honor and power ("For this may be said of men generally: that they are ungrateful, fickle, feigners and dissemblers, avoiders of danger, eager for gain": Machiavelli *The Prince*, XVII (1988: 59). Thus, the internal conflict between evil and good, which was at the very heart of the previous theological explanations of war and peace, was of no relevance to Machiavelli, as the only appropriate behavior for a ruler is that which would ensure the political survival of the community. For, Machiavelli, the rational mind simply cannot control the irrational. They are indissoluble. Even the theme of education, so central to humanist political theorists and predicated on the analysis of each statesman as individual, was therefore no longer the focus of Machiavelli's political thought (Pedullà 2004: 329). As Isaiah Berlin explained, his political proposal was "a game of skill, an activity called political, which is not concerned with ultimate human ends" (Berlin (1972) 2013: 54). His perception of mankind was political rather than metaphysical (Giorgini 2014: 633–4).

Despite rejecting Christian ethics and its previously dominant conception of human nature and just war, Machiavelli is not in favor of an absence of morality. The good of a community must sometimes require immoral behavior. To reconcile both fortune and human nature—which to Machiavelli is not inherently evil, but nonetheless more prone to do evil than good, and above all to follow one's own interest at the expenses of the political community—necessity sometimes forces the Prince to commit evil; including the waging of war or the use of violence against political opponents:

> how men live is so different from how they should live that a ruler who does not do what is generally done, but persists in doing what ought to be done, will undermine his power rather that maintain it. If a ruler who wants always to act honourably is surrounded by many unscrupulous men his downfall is inevitable. Therefore, a ruler who wishes to maintain his power must be prepared to act immorally when this becomes necessary.
>
> —Machiavelli, 1988: ch. XV, 54–5

This new conception of the politician is embodied in the image of a centaur: half beast, half man, a twofold symbol of the two opposing behaviors which must be alternatively embraced at appropriate times in order to maintain political order and safety (cf. Hale 1971: 14; Phillips 2010: 19; Rispoli 2015: 190–203):

> You should know, then, that there are two ways of contending: one by using laws, the other force. The first is appropriate for men, the second for animals; but because the former is often ineffective, one must have recourse to the latter. Therefore, a ruler must know well how to imitate beasts as well as employing properly human means. This policy was taught to rulers allegorically by ancient writers: they tell how Achilles and many other ancient rulers were entrusted to Chiron the centaur, to be raised carefully by him. Having a mentor who was half-beast and half-man signifies that a ruler needs to use both natures, and that one without the other is not effective.
>
> —Machiavelli 1988: ch. XVIII, 61

As a result, pre-emptive war and aggressive expansion are sometimes considered a wise course of action, not only in internal conflict but also in international relations amongst nations and states. According to this interpretation of human nature, there is no dichotomy between the first state of mankind, bestowed with divine grace in accordance with the Christian tradition, and a second, more corrupted nature. Although twofold, human nature is seen as a single, complex entity.

Nevertheless, Machiavelli issues clear caveats to the justification of violence and conduct of war. In a well-ordered republic, only citizens, sacrificing their private interests for common good, can be good soldiers (Pocock 1975: 201). Similarly, the Prince should legislate only in the interests of the community. Well-regulated political conflict benefits the state and provide security. Tyranny, by contrast, leads to inequality, which in turn leads to political behaviors which trigger civil war and violence. In a corrupt society, distorted relationships amongst individuals create open conflict and unregulated violence.

SIXTEENTH-CENTURY IDEAS OF INTERNATIONAL RELATIONSHIPS: FROM ETHICS TO POLITICS (MACHIAVELLI AND GENTILI)

In his *Discourses on Livy*, Machiavelli offers his views on war and peace among states from a new perspective. Far from being an inherent evil in Machiavelli's eyes, war is—and should remain—a regulated phenomenon (Fournel and Zancarini 2014: 675). So, if, on the one side, the doctrine of conquest and empire asserts the right of a particular state to rule by the use of force, on the other Machiavelli's solution favors making alliances instead of simply waging war. Machiavelli holds both of these beliefs. In the ideal republic outlined in the *Discourses*, external relationships and peace treaties should be regulated by political, cultural, and judicial practices which, rather than simply encouraging the invasion of new territories, aim toward the formation of alliances through an asymmetrical yet just and inclusive peace between nations. It is a solution which illustrates the author's deep understanding of the political motivations, religious attitudes, and cultural behaviors which shaped the Roman understanding of war and peace.

The importance of Machiavelli's observations was in fact recognized by the sixteenth-century legal scholar Alberico Gentili, who drew much inspiration from this source for his *De iure belli*. Although not a proponent of Machiavelli's political realism, Gentili too approached the issue of war from a secular perspective, as a contest between equal sovereign entities based on the same Roman tradition of thought. As there is often no one party with the sole just cause for conflict, it is necessary that both observe the same code of conduct in their engagement with the other (Reichberg, Syse and Begby 2006: 372). Following the Machiavellian reading of classical Roman history regarding the meaning, causes, and the consequences of warfare, Gentili's *De iure belli* prepares the ground for a juridical interpretation of war and peace, one which is grounded in the empirical study of historical precedent rather than the ethical or religious ideals which once dictated the medieval doctrine of the just cause. For Gentili, "just war" is not solely an ethical issue, but one which answers to both necessity (*necessitas*) and expediency (*utile*) (Koskenniemi 2010: 301). In this line of thinking, in which war is a calculation of convenience and necessity rather than the product of a corrupted human nature, the notion of just cause may well be identified on both sides of the conflict. Thus, the traditional distinction between just and unjust war should be made along juridical lines, taking into consideration the need for security as well as the strive towards power and conquest (Panizza 2010: 53–84).

VIOLENCE AND DISORDER IN RENAISSANCE EUROPE

The state of permanent war and insecurity which first struck Italy during the early to mid-sixteenth century, before spreading across Europe in the following decades, was accompanied by acts of supreme and outrageous cruelty, both on an individual and collective scale. Even beyond the European mainland, Muslim raiders terrorized the Christian coasts of the Mediterranean. In 1480, for instance, Turkish ships attacked the city of Otranto in Southern Italy, followed by the mass execution of hundreds of captives, in an episode that created large concern amongst public opinion of the time (Setton 1978).

Corsairs and pirate vessels, outside the jurisdiction or instruction of any government, now occupied the seas (Hale 1998: 80–3), while the land witnessed the brigandage carried out by groups of local bandits or military style units.

During this time, both local lords and the emerging standing armies of early modern states had to recruit from societies in which violence often prevailed over the rule of law. It is not surprising, then, that the question of military discipline eventually began to preoccupy both political and military thinkers such as Machiavelli, and in turn began to influence the conduct of war itself. If early humanists were obsessed with an abstract concept of discipline as part of the education of a good citizen-warrior, thinkers such as Machiavelli and Guicciardini placed their doctrine within a more pragmatic context, in keeping with their own perceptions of human nature. According to Guicciardini, the nature of man—which, as we have seen, tends toward avarice and evil—can be altered, but only through a gradual campaign of customs and habits. In particular, the traditions of a communal militia could train and encourage men to pursue the common good rather than personal ambition (Pocock 1975: 137, 144). For Machiavelli, military discipline was above all a practical and necessary tool for controlling violence and rebellion within military troops, a problem which he experienced firsthand at the siege of Pisa in 1499 (cf. the notes by Walker 1950, vol. 2: 69). However, according to his conception of man as driven solely by self-interest, he believed that the only way to develop a motivated infantry was to foster a sense of inclusion within a collective identity, whilst also encouraging good habits by rewarding the brave and punishing the insubordinate.

Along with this line of thought came a growing sense of repulsion toward mercenaries. For Machiavelli, only a national army, composed by the people in arms stimulated to defend himself, can be well disciplined as well as efficacious. Mercenaries, as Machiavelli says, could match neither the strength nor the determination of troops serving their own country ("there can be no more faithful, truer, or better soldiers," as he writes in *The Prince*). Through military discipline, the patriot warrior learns to be a citizen and to display civic virtue (Pocock 1975: 201). This kind of warrior, therefore, is on the one hand created by the positive influence of discipline, and on the other is encouraged by political and civic inclusion, e.g. by benefits to subjects, and—possibly—by the eventual conferral of citizenship, or, however, by creating the sense of benefitting one's *patria* (cf. Guidi 2009: 168–85, 259–77; Guidi 2017).

PACIFISM AND UTOPIA: FROM THE ANABAPTIST COMMUNITIES TO ERASMUS AND MORE

Whilst the shifting political, cultural, and social landscape led thinkers like Machiavelli toward a reassessment of war as an inherent evil, taking instead a more pragmatic approach to its occasional necessity, other contemporary writers opted to reject outright the notion of war as a rational and political instrument. In its place, there emerged a new cultural paradigm which emphasized instead an ideal of peace.

According to Johnson, there were two distinct branches to this new line of reasoning. The first had its origins in the egalitarian tradition of early Christianity, in which peace can only be achieved by those communities which set themselves apart from, or else took little political and social participation in, the wider world. Such reasoning could be found in both the Waldensian movement of the Middle Ages, and the Anabaptist sect of the sixteenth-century Swiss Brethren communities (Johnson 1987: xiii). The second branch is based instead on the belief that it is possible to create a new form of community in which violence and war are banished altogether. Writers such as Erasmus introduced this ideal into the ongoing debate regarding the causes and consequences of waging wars. Wars conducted for questionable and trivial ends, he argued, including the whims of an ill-meaning Prince, may only result in social deprivation (Johnson 1987: 158). Even where there is a supposed just cause, misery, destruction, and all other forms of evil will prevail, and thus he believes that they should be avoided at all costs. Peace, by contrast, sows the seeds of benevolence in every man, and so Erasmus formulates in his *Complaint of Peace* a strong appeal towards those elements of Christian and classical cultural tradition which tend towards the rejection of war:

> Be it granted that the suggestions of nature have no effect with a rational being [. . .] yet, as the suggestions of the Christian religion are far more excellent than those of nature, why does not the Christian religion persuade those who profess it, of a truth which it recommends above all others, that is, the expediency and necessity of peace on earth, and good-will towards men; or at least, why does it fail of effectually dissuading from the unnatural, and more than brutal, madness of waging war? [. . .]
>
> I appeal to all who call themselves Christians! I urge them, as they would manifest their sincerity, and preserve their consistency, to unite with one heart and one soul, in the abolition of war, and the establishment of perpetual and universal peace.
>
> —Erasmus 1917

For Johnson, this kind of reasoning amounts to a form of communal idealism—based upon a cosmopolitan brotherhood of Christendom—that is fundamentally "utopian" and directly contrasted to the notion of just war (Johnson 1987: xiii, 154, 162). Despite this, however, Erasmus also conceded the occasional necessity and just nature of conflict under certain circumstances. Erasmus condemns man's wrathful and warlike nature, but also fears internal unrest and dissent, and so according to Fernández-Santamaria he accepts "the lawfulness of the magistrate's sword, [which] necessarily implies acceptance of the prince's; and from there on there is no stopping" (Fernández-Santamaria 1977: 144). Although a pacifist by conviction, and despite genuinely despising war, Erasmus' conception of human nature as twofold and corrupted leads him to accept it as the final necessary option (Cailes 2012: 13).

NEW DISCOVERIES, ANTHROPOLOGICAL EXPLANATIONS OF VIOLENCE AND THE SIXTEENTH-CENTUARY RENOVATION OF MEDIEVAL SCHOLASTICISM

The ongoing debate regarding the causes of war and violence received further impetus from the discoveries of new civilizations and peoples during the sixteenth century. As John Hale noted, the second half of the sixteenth century saw the compilation of new accounts of the inhabitants of the new world discovered by European travelers, which provided an unparalleled abundance of anthropological and ethnological material. Amongst these were the Jesuit newsletters, which began to describe the lives and background of indigenous Americans (Hale 1971: 22–3). The subsequent result of these new observations was that Spanish Jesuit theologians began to augment the classical doctrine of just war by proposing a philosophical and juridical legitimation of war in terms of natural law as an expression of natural justice.

It is often assumed that the tradition of just war started with Augustine, and was then developed by scholars such as Aquinas in the late Middle Ages before continuing on into the early modern period. Yet the theory of just war also reached its own definitive form with the Spanish thinkers of the mid-sixteenth century (Johnson 1984: 43), first formulated in works such as Francisco de Vitoria's *relectiones* of 1539. First published as *De Indis* and then as *De iure belli* in 1557, Vitoria's ideas soon circulated all over Europe (Geuna 2012: 143), and were intended to justify the Spanish occupation of America whilst also defending the Christian ethics of natural law. To reconcile the two, whilst protecting the notion that every human being is born free and equal, Vitoria and other thinkers of the so-called School of Salamanca developed a theory of legitimate power under which could be justified both the emerging absolutism of monarchical regimes and the near-constant state of brutalized warfare.

According to this particular school, the antediluvian ideal of a universal society was now colliding with the contemporary needs of sovereignty. Whilst the Indian societies discovered at the end of the fifteenth century better mirrored this kind of ideal community, a modern society must deal with the grim realities of conflict in order to establish a new international order. As the two worlds collided, the inherent rights of the Indian republics, and by extension those of all other nations and societies (*ius gentium*), were placed at odds with the modern realities of the sovereign states (Fernández-Santamaria 1977: 97ff). Vitoria's solution is to consider the *ius gentium* not as natural law, but as human law. As examined earlier, contemporary Catholic thinkers such as Erasmus held a conception of war which considered man as an ethical being, predicated on the dual assumption of man's imperfect nature and his enmity toward other men. In this regard, Erasmus believed that it is impossible to fully translate the concept of just war into the political realities of his day, and so damned war as intolerable reality—albeit one which could be accepted as a necessity—and remained a pacifist until the end. The School of Salamanca shifted this balance. Vitoria elaborated a political ideology, based upon the principles of natural law, which simultaneously served to modernize, through secularization, the law of nature (Fernández-Santamaria 1977: 121–3), whilst transforming it into a scientific form of political theory. According to this ideology, the prince has the right to wage just war, yet Vitoria also argues that war is an exclusive prerogative of the state. Vitoria's philosophy marks the appearance of the modern state as conceived from a juridical perspective: a transition from the notion of war as hostility between two individuals to one understood as the exclusive prerogative of the state. It is a line of reasoning that spread all over Europe, and which marked the political and cultural development of a conception of the state as the only entity entitled to use violence.

WARS OF RELIGION IN LATE RENAISSANCE EUROPE

Both the Protestant and Counter-Reformation ignited a process of cultural, religious and social change which further precipitated the collapse of a united Christendom already threatened by the political and social insecurity of early modern Western Europe (Phillips 2010: 89). First the French Wars of Religion, then the Thirty Years War, created a crisis within the previous international order, which in turn led to its redefinition; a new set of cultural and ideological conceptions of the nature of peace and war (Phillips 2010: 130). The continuous state of conflict and revolt which characterized this period generated a new style of warfare based on "the calculated use of terror and atrocity to subdue civilians" (Phillips 2010: 132). As a result, the use of violence and dehumanizing practices became widespread, especially as the fall of universal Christendom created a vacuum of effective ethical restraints, and the lack of stable institutional authorities had severely weakened the rule of international law.

A MODERN THEORY OF SOVEREIGNTY: BODIN AND HOBBES ON HUMAN NATURE AND VIOLENCE

Such profound changes in European culture, warfare, and politics eventually contributed to a modern theory of sovereignty, one which attempted to remove all previous justifications for aristocratic, sectarian, and religious violence by bestowing the prerogative of force exclusively upon the (increasingly absolute) monarch. Political theorists such as Jean Bodin had a particular influence over this cultural and political shift, in which rulers were given a new ideological framework through which to justify their centralization and rationalization of the use of violence (Phillips 2010: 124–6). In the hands of the sovereign, war and violence, then, was perfectly conceivable.

This line of reasoning culminated in the clearest repudiation yet of civil war as a corollary of the belligerent nature of man, formulated by Thomas Hobbes. Hobbes threw himself into the contemporary debate on the state of mankind—whether violence was an inescapable facet of man's inherent bestial brutality, or the artificial product of the societies in which they lived—by stressing that human nature tended toward war and conflict. In contrast to Vitoria and other Spanish writers of the School of Salamanca, Hobbes and his contemporaries approached the notion of brutality through the child-like aggressiveness which they believed characterised more primitive societies (Hale 1971: 16). For Hobbes in particular, the state of nature is a state of war. To him, it was a mistake to predicate laws on the idea that men seek a mutual co-existence, one which "proceeds from a superficial view of human nature":

> Closer observation of the causes why men seek each other's company and enjoy associating with each other, will easily reach the conclusion that it does not happen because by nature it could not be otherwise [. . .]

Such an approach clearly derives from the realism of Machiavelli:

> By nature, then, we are not looking for friends but for honour or advantage from them [. . .] So clear is it from experience to anyone who gives any serious attention to human behaviour, that every voluntary encounter is a product either of mutual need or of the pursuit of glory
>
> —Hobbes 1998: 21–31 (quoted in Reichberg, Syse and Begby 2006: 443–4)

Hobbes' conception of human nature leads him to reject the efficacy and relevance of the medieval ethics of just war. Instead, he formulates a materialistic theory of war and peace, in which only the mechanisms of law and the politics of fear replace the ethical codes of previous centuries (Reichberg, Syse and Begby 2006: 441–3).

The fractious impact of the wars of religion, which sits at the very foundations of Bodin and Hobbes' thinking, are also visible in Renaissance painting. Images promoting peace, such as the works of Peter Paul Rubens, call back to the devastation caused by the Thirty Years War, whilst also advocating the same absolutist notion of wise, monarchical statecraft as a means of preventing the threat of future conflict (Rosenthal 2005: 5). At the same time, Rubens' depiction of the *Consequences of War* illustrates the emerging

FIGURE 2.4: Peter Paul Rubens, *The Consequences of War*, also known as *Horror of War*, Palazzo Pitti, Florence (1638–9). Photo by Peter Willi via Getty Images.

FIGURE 2.5: Peter Paul Rubens, *Minerva Protects Pax from Mars* ("*Peace and War*"), National Gallery, London (1629–30). Wikimedia Commons.

view of human nature in the modern age, in the form of a furious and destructive Mars failing to be controlled by a desperate and frustrated Venus (Cailes 2012: 11–12).

These two elements are symbolically brought together in another of Rubens' most famous painting by, in which Minerva, the goddess of wisdom, is shown protecting Pax (Peace) from Mars and Alecto, the raging ciphers of war.

GROTIUS AND THE FOUNDATION OF INTERNATIONAL LAW

Whilst Bodin and Hobbes' responses to the near-constant state of war which afflicted late Renaissance Western Europe were more greatly concerned with domestic affairs than international relations—although whilst espousing a more universal philosophy of war, peace, and human nature—their contemporaries were also constructing a new line of reasoning with regards to the legal regulation of conflict between states. Hugo Grotius is generally recognized as the founder of the new discipline of international law, which brought together the emerging concept of natural law with the medieval just war tradition. By promoting the notion of a natural legal order for mankind, states, and nations, his approach eschewed the complications of political realism. Grotius argued that there existed a common law across the nations, of which he was able to find traces in the cultural achievements of humanity: i.e. in a variety of sources, from philosophers, theologians, and Roman lawyers to poets and historians. By the end of the Renaissance, therefore, a new philosophical interpretation of human nature and human society was beginning to set the foundations for a new form of jurisprudence, according to which the natural law was to regulate war and peace (Reichberg, Syse, and Begby 2006: 386).

CHAPTER THREE

Peace, War, and Gender

BRIAN SANDBERG

PEACE AND POLITICAL CULTURE IN THE RENAISSANCE

Over the past two decades, a "new diplomatic history" of the Renaissance has arisen, fueled by interest in court culture, ambassadorial households, diplomatic language, and cultural intermediaries in Europe, the Mediterranean, the Atlantic world, and early global empires (van Gelder and Krstic 2015; Carrió-Invernizzi 2014; Fletcher and DeSilva 2010; Watkins 2008). Historians are investigating diplomatic practices and peacemaking processes using discursive and cultural practice approaches to political culture. Recent histories of peacemaking in the Renaissance also draw on insights from modern peace and reconciliation processes in Northern Ireland, ex-Yugoslavia, Rwanda, and other war-torn regions.

There is a certain irony in the choice of applying the "new diplomatic history" to the Renaissance period, since historian Garrett Mattingly used the term "new diplomacy" to describe the innovative diplomatic practices that emerged in Renaissance Italy (Mattingly 1955). The historical concept of the Renaissance has broadened considerably from an exclusively Italian phenomenon holding strong associations with art, architecture, and humanism to embrace European, Mediterranean, and global contexts (Ruggiero 2002). The Renaissance and Reformation movements are now considered as part of a broad "early modern" period stretching from about 1400 to 1800, although no precise periodization is accepted by historians. Despite the growing acceptance of the early modern designation, the notion of the Renaissance continues to captivate the public imagination, and world histories have sometimes adopted the concept of "Renaissance worlds" to capture the breathtaking pace of changes as global contacts and early empires developed in the late fifteenth and sixteenth centuries (Ruggiero, ed. 2002; Brotton 2002; Jardine 1996).

This essay examines peace, war, and gender in Renaissance worlds from approximately 1400 to 1650. The chapter will explore Renaissance women who engaged in warfare and diplomacy in societies around the world. This synthetic analysis of women and gender issues in warmaking and peacemaking necessarily relies on academic works in Renaissance studies, early modern history, and gender history. I will attempt to address global contexts of peace, war, and gender in the period, but the scholarly literature in gender history remains stronger for Europe and the Mediterranean at this point, so many of the specific examples will be drawn from those regions. Contemporary artistic and literary tropes often constructed neat, binary oppositions of war and peace, but the realities of warmaking and peacemaking were completely intertwined in Renaissance worlds. I argue that women were integral to the practices of both war and peace in the Renaissance and that the cultural history of peace was highly gendered.

SOVEREIGNTY AND FEMININE POWER

Gender histories of Renaissance women have focused on issues of gender and power, examining female rulers and fears of feminine power. The *Salic Law* famously banned women from sovereign power in France and the Holy Roman Empire, but many other Renaissance states permitted women to inherit dynastic titles and sovereign authority. John Knox's infamous *The First Blast of the Trumpet Against the Monstrous Regiment of Women* (1558) attacked both Mary Stuart and Mary Tudor as ungodly and illegitimate rulers. Merry Wiesner-Hanks points out that "the word 'monster' was used to describe female rulers by other authors as well, echoing Aristotle's notion that the female sex in general is monstrous" (Wiesner-Hanks 2002: 31). These fears also fit neatly into broader early modern discourses of monstrosities that seemed to threaten the body politic and its social foundations (Knoppers and Landes (eds.) 2004).

Concerns about feminine power seem to have been provoked partially because an unusually high number of women actually ruled imperial and royal states in Europe during the sixteenth and seventeenth centuries. Fourteen European queens ruled with full sovereign power between 1400 and 1650, and many more Renaissance women governed European states indirectly (Monter 2012: ix–xvi). Annette Dixon argues that during this period, "women's rule brought to the fore long-standing disputes about the appropriateness of women wielding control over their own destinies, along with newer concerns about the suitability of women exercising authority over others—whether in the state or the household" (Dixon 2002: 119). Female rule frequently represented a temporary pause in a prevailing pattern of masculine dominance of monarchical authority, however. Jeroen Duindam argues that "women held full sovereign power mostly when the dynasty could not provide males for the throne. They rose to power on the basis of their pedigree, as an interim solution safeguarding dynastic continuity. Most often the throne reverted to male successors in one generation" (Duindam 2015: 95). Nonetheless, ruling queens formulated policies and exerted a powerful presence in European political culture during their reigns.

Whether or not they ruled directly, queens and empresses were crucial to dynastic monarchies, since their bodies carried and conveyed sovereignty to their children. Early modern notions of the body politic relied on elaborate theorizations of monarchy that involved divine selection, legitimate procreation, and blood transmission of inheritance. For this reason, the bodies of princesses and their inheritances represented crucial negotiable elements of diplomatic treaties, which often constructed marriage alliances through multiple bodily exchanges. Even non-ruling queens could exercise enormous influence in patrilineal states because of their roles in transmitting sovereignty. Queens, queen mothers, dowager queens, and queens consort exercised indirect power through their bodily relationship to sovereignty and their positions within royal households, but their status varied in dynastic states around the world (Duindam, Artan, and Kunt (eds.) 2011).

Renaissance authors and artists held up ancient and medieval empresses and queens as providing exemplary models of *femmes fortes* (strong women) and women worthies for female rulers in their own societies. Pierre Le Moyne's *La Gallerie des femmes fortes* (1647) included lavish illustrations of female worthies by Abraham Bosse (Le Moyne 1647; Dixon (ed.) 2002: 48–9).

Female rulers had decision-making power over questions of war and peace. Renaissance women similarly directed royal governments and their diplomatic initiatives. Female rulers were not the only women to wield significant power in Renaissance societies, however, and the idea of *femmes fortes* inspired other formidable women.

FIGURE 3.1: *Zenobia*, an illustration from Pierre Le Moine's *La galerie des femmes fortes*, by Abraham Bosse, Gilles Rousselet, and after Claude Vignon, Paris (*c.* 1647). Courtesy of the MET.

Princely women and noblewomen played important roles at princely courts, exercising political power and influencing policy formation. Some court women were able to act as strategic advisors to rulers or their ministers. Renaissance noblewomen could act as diplomatic intermediaries between princely courts, so it is not surprising that Renaissance treatises on politics and courtly behavior discussed feminine roles at court. Baldassare Castiglione's *Book of the Courtier* (1528) placed the duchess of Urbino at the center of a series of imagined discussions of the perfect Renaissance courtier. Although the character of the duchess intervenes intermittently in the conversation, her presence foregrounds the ideals of noble masculinity and gendered discourses of power (Castiglione 1967). *The Book of the Courtier* became one of the real "bestsellers" of the Renaissance, prompting through at least fifty editions and translations by 1550 (Burke 1995).

Princely women and noblewomen conducted political patronage, diplomacy, and social networking through kinship and friendship networks. Elite women learned formal reading and writing skills through tutorial education in their households. Once they were married, queens and princesses maintained connections with their birth families through their letter-writing activities. Isabella Lazzarini argues that female epistolary communications in the Italian peninsula intensified toward the end of the fifteenth century (Lazzarini 2015: 140–4). Elena Woodacre finds that "epistolary diplomacy within a royal kinship group therefore served two purposes: to maintain and reinforce family ties and to leverage these connections in order to achieve diplomatic objectives" (Woodacre 2016: 30–45). Women enacted power through their epistolary networks and their closely overlapping kinship, friendship, and clientage relationships.

WOMEN RULERS IN THE RENAISSANCE WORLD

Although images of feminine authority often focus on the figure of a solitary queen, Renaissance women could actually rule in a number of ways as sole sovereigns, joint monarchs, or regents (Monter 2012). Recent studies of royal states, feminine power, and dynastic politics allow us to construct a brief survey of women rulers in the Renaissance world. This comparative examination of female rule reveals some of the reasons for the remarkable number of ruling women during the early modern period.

Elite women had restricted roles within the governing institutions of the Florentine Republic, but as the Medici family gradually established itself as dynastic rulers toward the end of the fifteenth century, Medici women took on increasingly important roles in late republican and then ducal regimes in Tuscany (Fantoni 1999: 255–73). Cosimo I de' Medici married Eleonora de Toledo, who placed her stamp on Medici household arrangements and court etiquette. Although women never ruled directly in Florence, Christine de Lorraine and Maria Maddalena von Habsburg held sweeping power as regents following the death of Ferdinando I de' Medici.

Female monarchs and regents dominated the political landscape of the British Isles during much of the Renaissance. King Henry VIII of England justified his famous divorce from Catherine of Aragon and his marriage to Anne Boleyn in terms of a search for a male heir. Henry VIII's eldest daughter, Mary Tudor acceded to the throne upon his death, ruling England from 1553 to 1558 as a joint monarch. Queen Elizabeth I of England never married, constructing a powerful image of herself as a Virgin Queen and protector of Protestantism through artworks and literary texts.

In the famous painting, *Eliza Triumphans,* Elizabeth I is portrayed as "Gloriana herself encircled by her court, moving like the sun and planets in their courses, towards some unknown mysterious destination" (Strong 1977: 16). Yet, Elizabeth I also used gender ambiguity and to assert a masculine image, presented herself as a powerful sovereign and solitary naval leader in the *Armada Portrait*, which celebrated the defeat of the Spanish Armada of 1588 (Bailey 2008: 176–215). Mary Stuart became queen of Scotland as a child, but her mother Marie de Guise effectively governed Scotland as regent. Mary Stuart ruled Scotland in person from 1561 to 1567, when Scottish nobles forced her to abdicate. She fled to England, where she was imprisoned and eventually executed in 1587.

FIGURE 3.2: Anonymous, *Elisabeth I of England*, Österreichische Nationalbibliothek, Wien. Courtesy of Europeana Collections.

Despite the famous Salic Law, women often governed Renaissance France. Anne de Bretagne, duchesse de Bretagne, was twice queen of France through successive marriages to Charles VIII and Louis XII. Contemporary sources shed little light on her role in governing France during Charles VIII's invasion of Italy in 1494, but she seems to have managed political situations in the kingdom during Louis XII's campaigns in northern Italy. A recent gender history concludes: "Anne's case reveals that a queen could, despite . . . significant obstacles, exert an important political and cultural influence" (Wellman 2013: 109). Louise de Savoie carefully managed her son's accession to the throne as François I, and then she acted as his "full political partner from the beginning of his reign," according to Kathleen Wellman (Wellman 2013: 130). Marguerite de Navarre, sister of François I, quickly became a leading intellectual and cultural patron at the French court, but her encouragement of religious reform led to controversies and tensions within the royal family.

Religious conflicts and civil wars severely disrupted French society during the Renaissance, but also allowed new opportunities for female rule in France. When Henri II died in 1559 in a tragic jousting accident, his son François II became king, but he suffered from illnesses and died about a year later. Catherine de' Medici became regent for young Charles IX and attempted to manage the serious divisions between the Catholic majority and the growing Calvinist (or Huguenot) minority in France. Despite her efforts, episodes of crowd violence and military mobilization plunged the kingdom into the French Wars of Religion (1562–1629). When Charles IX reached his majority, Catherine remained a very active queen mother, participating fully in political and military decision-making at the Valois court. Catherine de' Medici became regent once again when Charles IX died in 1574, and his younger brother was recalled from Poland to be enthroned as Henri III. Catherine remained intimately involved in politics as queen mother until her death in 1589. Marguerite de Valois became estranged from her husband, Henri IV, who eventually remarried Marie de' Medici in 1600. After the assassination of Henri IV in 1610, Marie became regent for her young son, Louis XIII, as political instability and religious conflict continued to disturb the kingdom. The queen mother's political programs provoked serious opposition, producing a series of civil wars between 1615 and 1620 (Sandberg 2010). Marie de' Medici remained a dominating, but controversial figure in French politics until her flight into exile in 1631, following the Day of Dupes. When Louis XIII died in 1643, Anne d'Autriche became regent for a young Louis XIV and governed France along with Cardinal Jules Mazarin in France. Anne d'Autriche and the first minister confronted financial difficulties and military challenges in waging the Thirty Years War, which France had entered in 1635. The burdens of war helped produce the Fronde Civil War (1648–53), during which the royal family had to flee from Paris.

Several Francophone principalities had prominent female leaders during the French Wars of Religion. Jeanne d'Albret ruled Navarre as a joint monarch beginning in 1555, and then as sole ruler following her husband's death in 1562. Jeanne promoted the Calvinist reform in Navarre and actively supported Huguenots during the French Wars of Religion until her death in 1572 (Roelker 1968). Princely women in the Lorraine dynasty and its cadet Guise branch women became major leaders of the Catholic Leagues in the duchy of Lorraine and the kingdom of France. Anna d'Este, duchesse de Guise, became one of the leaders of the Catholic League, but later supported Henri IV. Lorraine duchesses and other family members used Imperial and French law courts to defend their princely status and manage their inheritance rights (Spangler 2009).

Princely women in the Holy Roman Empire confronted the religious divisions that fragmented Germany beginning in the early sixteenth century. Habsburg women frequently acted as regents of Habsburg landholdings scattered throughout the Holy Roman Empire and conducted politics at the Imperial court. Mary of Burgundy inherited the sprawling Burgundian territories in 1477, but quickly married Maximilian I von Habsburg and did not actively rule. Margaret of Austria served as regent for Emperor Maximilian I in the Netherlands from 1507 to 1531. Mary of Hungary, widow of Louis II Jagiellon of Hungary, acted as regent of the Netherlands for Emperor Charles V from 1531 to 1555. Mary gained a reputation as an able administrator. Margaret of Parma governed the Netherlands as regent for Philip II from 1559 to 1567, and confronted the growing religious tensions that produced the Dutch Revolt. Infanta Isabel Clara

Eugenia and Archduke Albert later ruled the Spanish Netherlands as joint sovereign regents from 1599 to 1621. Following Albert's death, Isabel continued to rule as governor, claiming credit for the victory at the siege of Breda in 1625 and pursuing peace negotiations (Sánchez 2009).

In northern Europe, Queen Christina of Sweden inherited the kingdom of Sweden as a minor when her father, Gustav II Adolf died in Germany during the Thirty Years War. Chancellor Axel Oxenstierna conducted royal policy until Christina reached her majority in 1644 and became sovereign queen of one of the most militarized courts in Europe. Christina was involved in the negotiations to conclude the peace of Westphalia and to extricate Swedish military forces from Germany. Swedish naval and military forces remained engaged in warfare in the Baltic throughout the rest of Christina's reign until her abdication in 1654 (Persson 1999).

A number of women ruled in the Iberian kingdoms of Portugal, Navarre, Aragon, and Castile during the Renaissance. Queen Catalina of Portugal was an assertive joint ruler with her husband, João III. According to a Spanish ambassador, she was "held in great esteem in the kingdom, and the king, knowing this, informs her about everything; there is nothing great or small that does not pass through her hands" (Monter 2012: 106–9). After João III's death in 1557, Catalina acted as regent for her grandson until 1562. Portugal constructed a vast maritime empire of fortified trading posts in the Atlantic and Indian worlds, exerting sweeping territorial claims. The kingdom of Navarre, which straddled the Pyrenees mountains, had three ruling queens: Blanca, Catalina de Foix, and Jeanne III d'Albret. Ferdinand of Aragon and Isabel I of Castile ruled as joint monarchs, establishing the Spanish monarchy as one of the leading royal states in Europe and the Mediterranean. Juana of Aragon ruled Castile briefly as a joint monarch with her husband Philip from 1504 to 1506. Juana refused to participate in Castilian political culture and effectively abdicated, leaving her in a curious position for the next five decades as Juana "the Mad". The Columbian voyages to the Americas in the 1490s launched a Spanish maritime empire that rivaled Portugal's global empire by the mid-sixteenth century. King Sebastião of Portugal's death at the battle of Alcazarquivir in Morocco in 1578 weakened the dynasty, allowing Philip II of Spain to annex Portugal in 1580.

Women engaged in politics in the Sunni regions of the Islamic world, and especially in the Ottoman Empire. Ottoman rulers and their diplomats negotiated *ahidnames* (capitulations) for Italians and other Europeans to establish merchant communities in Istanbul and other Ottoman cities (Goffman 2007). Ottoman household women took sides in succession crises, when a new sultan often acted to assassinate his brothers in order to eliminate potential rivals. The Ottoman political culture accepted these fratricidal struggles as necessary to preserve dynastic rule. Ottoman princely women lived in the *harem* within the Topkapı Palace in Istanbul. Hürrem Sultan (1500–58) was able to wield considerable power as *haseki*, or favorite of Süleyman I "the Lawgiver." His death ushered in a period of even more expansive feminine power from 1566 to 1656, that has been described as "the age of the Queen Mother" (Pierce 1993: 91–112). *Valide sultans* (queen mothers) such as Turhan Sultan and Kösem Sultan effectively governed the Ottoman Empire in the seventeenth century, since "the favourite (*haseki sultan*) could rise to the pinnacle of female rank when her son ascended the throne: as *valide sultan* she towered above the others" (Duindam 2015: 113).

Shia Islam did not sanction female rulers, but Persian elite women participated in the political and religious life of the Safavid Empire. Isma'il I had founded the Safavid Empire in 1501, launching a series of military campaigns of expansion in Iran and Iraq. Isma'il and his successors aggressively promoted Shia Islam, sponsoring public preaching and proselytization to men and women in communities across Iran. Safavid rulers began to confine their princely sons in the *haram*, allowing elite women to have extensive influence over political and military policy formulation. Some historians have condemned this practice as creating a "Sultanate of Women," but princes seem to have received a sophisticated education and a "*haram* upbringing did not necessarily produce incompetent rulers" (Dale 2010: 87–96, 187–95, 249–50).

In South Asia, women did not gain sovereign authority, but they could participate in policy formulation. The Timurid prince Zahir al-Din Muhammed Babur defeated the army of the Delhi sultanate at Panipat in April 1526, conquering much of northern India and founding the Mughal Empire as a Muslim state. Babur's son, Humayun, succeeded to the Mughal throne, but faced civil conflicts throughout his reign, in part because of

FIGURE 3.3: Anonymous, *Idealized Portrait of the Mughal Empresse Nur Jahan*, India (*c.* 1725–50), LACMA. Wikimedia Commons.

FIGURE 3.4: Anonymous, *Head of a Queen Mother (Iyoba)*, Benin (c. 1750–1800), Metropolitan Museum of Arts, New York. Courtesy of the MET.

Timurid partible inheritance practices that divided territory among male family members. When Humayan died, his wife constructed a monumental tomb and garden in his memory. Such symbolic acts may have been crucial in maintaining the Mughal Empire's identity and coherence. Emperor Akbar promoted religious pluralism and syncretism at the Mughal court, sponsoring diverse intellectual and cultural projects. Akbar married several Rajput princesses, bringing their male relatives into imperial service as *mansabdars* (ranking officeholders) (Dale 2010: 96–105). Empress Nur Jahan (1577–1645), wife of Jahangir, wielded enormous power at the Mughal court by gathering information, controlling access, and directing policy formulation (Findly 1993).

Feminine power took on different forms in East Asia. Mahayana Buddhism influenced Chinese culture, allowing some space for feminine spiritual power, especially by women who entered monastic orders. Buddhist lay religiosity sometimes clashed with Confucian principles of kinship, marriage, and order, however. The Chinese imperial bureaucracy promoted Confucianism as a ruling ideology through Confucian academies and state service exams. A masculine ethic of imperial service largely barred women from positions of power in Ming China. Women in the imperial household could assert power in succession struggles, as when Lady Zheng tried to convince the Wanli Emperor to favor her son (Brook 2010: 100–3). Japanese women in the families of *daimyō* (provincial elites) became closely involved in the civil wars of the *Sengoku* (Warring States) period from 1467 to 1615. The wives and daughters of *daimyō* often managed military logistics and defended castles when provincial armies were on campaign.

African empires used gendered rules of succession and sometimes had powerful women rulers. The Akiya dynasty of the Songhay Empire ensured male inheritance by using patrilineal rules of succession that allowed for brothers to rule in turn. The kingdom of Asante in West Africa created a system of joint rule of the *asantehene* (king) and the *asantehemaa* (queen mother) (Duindam 2015: 96). Many African states, engaged in raiding warfare, which targeted women, men, and children as legitimate captives. Queen Njinga established her rule over the kingdom of Ndongo-Matmba. Njinga "copied male polygyny by adopting polyandry" and then she "decided to 'become a man', turning her male followers into concubines, requiring them to dress as women and to live among the palace maids without touching them." Njinga presented herself as supreme military commander of Ndongo and "led her armies personally in battle, showing remarkable dexterity" (Duindam 2015: 93; Thornton 2006: 437–60; Thornton 1991).

Amerindian societies practiced diverse forms of warfare across the Americas in the Renaissance, although Amerindian women's roles in conflicts are not well known. The Tupis initially resisted Portuguese colonization in Brazil, but many Tupi women gradually intermarried with Portuguese soldiers and colonists. Tupi warriors later served as auxiliaries in competing Portuguese and Dutch colonial militaries (Meuwese 2011). In the Great Lakes region, Iroquois waged "mourning war" to avenge warriors' deaths through raids and captive-taking. Captives would be ritually tortured, and then killed or adopted into their captors' society based in part on the reactions of Iroquois women.

AMAZONS AND WOMEN WARRIORS

Some Renaissance women actually led military forces and engaged in warfare, often appearing in political culture as modern Amazon warriors. The idea of women warriors who led armies on campaign, and, occasionally in combat, has captivated the public imagination. Literary and gender studies scholars have examined armed heroines in ancient, medieval, and modern plays, poems, and novels. Images of women warriors and feminine violence could be provocative. The figures of Athena and Minerva provided powerful models for Renaissance artists and writers who wanted to depict women in arms and armor.

Jean Bethke Elshtain offers a useful model for moving beyond these images of violent women, which have helped to create the women warrior stereotype. Elshtain analyzes the gendered nature of representations of warfare and political discourses on war and peace, arguing that a "gender gap" has historically structured portrayals of life givers versus life takers (Elshtain 1987). More recent studies demonstrate that women were actually involved in many dimensions of Renaissance warfare.

Princely women participated in strategic planning and logistical preparation to organize military campaigns. Noblewomen often assisted their families in recruiting soldiers and mobilizing for war each campaigning season. When male family members departed, noblewomen maintained and defended their châteaux and urban residences, especially during civil wars and religious conflicts. Some of these elite women may have read military treatises and commentaries, and a few of them actually wrote military

FIGURE 3.5: Bartholomeus Sprangler and Jan Muller, *Minerva* (*c.* 1632), Metropolitan Museum of Arts, New York. Courtesy of the MET.

treatises of their own. Christine de Pizan's *The Book of Deeds of Arms and of Chivalry* was undoubtedly the most famous military treatise by a female author. Christine de Pizan studied Vegetius, Sextus Julius Frontinus, Valerius Maximus, and other ancient writers on warfare, incorporating passages of their texts into her own commentaries on the art of war and the laws of war (Christine de Pizan 2003). If Minerva offered Renaissance women a potent image of an armed woman, military treatises presented them with pragmatic discussions of the conduct of war that women could employ.

Women could occasionally take up arms and serve in military forces and bodyguard units. European noblewomen sometimes armed themselves when defending châteaux and urban women participated in siege defenses (Sandberg 2004). Women apparently served as palace guards in a number of Southeast Asian kingdoms. Female guards in Siam controlled the inner palace, while those in Java adopted firearms. Female palace guards in Aceh and Mataram "included a corps trained in the use of arms, who mounted guard on the palace and took part in royal processions" (Reid 1988: 166–8).

Peasant and urban women confronted war directly as Renaissance armies pillaged farmhouses and enforced contributions (extorted payments) on villages and towns. Soldiers inflicted physical violence, intimidation, and plundering on peasants and townspeople, who were often forced to abandon their homes as war refugees. Thousands of men, women, and children accompanied each field army as camp followers. Wives, daughters, sutlers, and prostitutes formed part of a broader "campaign community" in army camps, according to John A. Lynn (Lynn 2008). For camp followers, women's work included clothes washing, cooking, carrying belongings, selling goods, ditch digging, and other arduous tasks. Many women seem to have played a direct role in the pillage economy, either by plundering unfortunate civilians or managing and reselling goods taken by soldiers. Women and their husbands (or domestic partners) thus "were partners in the family economy of makeshifts that required entrepreneurship and pillage" (Lynn 2008: 163). The women who actually engaged in warfare and exercised violence may have actively challenged conventional gender expectations, but they also revealed gendered norms of military and diplomatic activity. Warmaking and peacemaking processes were closely intertwined in the early modern period and they both involved complex gendered constructions.

BODILY NEGOTIATIONS AND GENDERED DIPLOMACY

Renaissance women engaged in diplomatic activities and peacemaking processes. Diplomacy is often described as "soft power" in today's world, and Renaissance diplomacy has sometimes been discussed in these terms (Rivère de Carles, ed. 2016). Renaissance artists and writers often represented peace through personifications as Artemesia and Minerva Pacifera (Baumgärtel 2002). A cycle of paintings by Jacopo Tintoretto in the Palazzo Ducale in Venice depicts Minerva pushing Mars away, while embracing Peace and Concord. A seventeenth-century writer explained that Minerva here represented "the wisdom of the Republic in keeping war far from the state, from which is born the happiness of its subjects" (Carlo Ridolfi, quoted in Rosand 2001: 142–5). Feminine figures of peace (Venus, Artemesia, or Minerva) were normally juxtaposed against bellicose Mars.

Despite such gendered imagery, Renaissance peacemaking was normally closely linked with military force and warmaking. The permanent ambassadors in Renaissance states conducted constant negotiation, information-gathering, and espionage. There were violent dimensions to Renaissance diplomacy, which also had significant gendered aspects. Early modern notions of pacification could be harsh and peace agreements were often imposed through military force and judicial punishment.

The body of a queen always represented a crucial a site of power for dynastic, court, territorial, and international politics. Regina Schulte argues that "from the beginning, the body of the queen appears to have been incorporated into a political concept, that of the monarchy" (Schulte 2006: 1). Political cultures everywhere focused on elite women's bodies in terms of procreation and dynastic politics. Dynasties crafted various strategies for preservation and reproduction that relied heavily on marriage alliances and kinship structures. Legal and political languages guided the formation of marriage alliances through complex diplomatic processes centered on queen's bodies.

Queens and princely women often played crucial roles as marriage brokers, conducting negotiations for marriage alliances. "During the pre-modern centuries, when royal marriages defined the political map of Europe, it was inevitable that royal wives and their ladies-in-waiting were recognized by their contemporaries as major diplomatic actors. Marriage diplomacy was the means by which nobles from various regions, possessing great or small degrees of influence and wealth, were integrated into trans-European alliances and networks. It was also the way in which new rulers, with perhaps little claim to political legitimacy, improved their bloodlines while acquiring powerful allies that would help them to preserve their hold on power" (Sluga and James 2016: 3). Dynastic marriages involved complex negotiations about titles, precedence, households, inheritance, and territorial settlements.

Marriage alliances were often concluded as a component of broader peace settlements. Catherine de' Medici's marriage to Henri de Valois was negotiated as part of François I's alliance with Pope Clement VII. Catherine later negotiated the election of her third son, Henri de Valois, as king of Poland. She organized elaborate ceremonies in Paris as entertainment for the Polish ambassadors who arrived to escort Henri de Valois to Poland for his coronation in 1573. Another notable example of royal marriage negotiations is provided by Marie de' Medici's negotiations for a double marriage for her young son, Louis XIII, and his sister Elisabeth as part of a policy of *rapprochement* with Spain. The queen mother used her kinship ties to the Medici family in Tuscany to conduct negotiations and conclude the marriage alliance, despite strongly anti-Spanish public opinion and significant opposition from Huguenots. The double marriages were accomplished in 1615, but civil warfare broke out once again within the kingdom (Dubost 2009).

Dynastic households normally collaborated to plan elaborate marriage ceremonies in both courts, and sometimes at multiple sites along the queen's route toward the host court. New queens normally traveled with large entourages composed of members of both dynasties' courts, including numerous ladies-in-waiting who would take up residence in the queen's household. Once a queen arrived at a new court, she and her household acted as cross-cultural intermediaries between both courts. Queens and their households often became long-term diplomatic actors in the relations between their natal court and their adopted court, even if relations between the two states soured. When a male ruler died, the prospect of a widowed queen remarrying could seriously upset political relationships.

NEW DIPLOMACY AND RENAISSANCE PEACEMAKING

New diplomatic practices transformed peacemaking in the Renaissance. The gradual development of permanent ambassadors and residential embassies created sustained negotiations and more complex forms of diplomatic communication (Queller 1967; Mattingly 1955). One of the earliest examples of a permanent ambassador was the *bailo*, the Venetian representative to the Ottoman sultan at Istanbul. The Venetians established a *bailate* (residence) in Galata to house the *bailo*, his household, and an embassy staff including secretaries and *dragomans* (interpreters) (Dursteler 2006: 23–40). Other Renaissance states established permanent ambassadors in Istanbul and at other imperial or royal courts. Many ambassadors' households grew to include extensive embassy staff, arguably creating a new form of domesticity (Netzloff 2011). When empowered, resident ambassadors at distant courts allowed states to conduct near-continuous negotiations, rather than relying on periodic visits by envoys. Courts became sites of multilateral negotiations, since even bilateral talks were normally set within the multiplex conversations of courtly society. Meanwhile, the development of regularly scheduled courier and postal services in Spain, France, Italy, and other regions allowed for rapid diplomatic communication between courts. Ministers and ambassadors frequently engaged in an overtly public diplomacy in the Renaissance, engaging popular opinion in order to gain support for policies (Helmers 2016).

Historians have debated whether or not these changes constituted a recognizably "modern" form of diplomacy. The construction of bastioned fortifications and the proliferation of artillery pieces (both defensive and offensive) in the sixteenth century contributed to intensive siege warfare at fortified sites around the world. The rigorous demands of siege warfare and lengthy campaigning seasons produced conditions for frequent temporary truces, especially in civil and religious wars that resulted in protracted warfare and social conflict. Timothy Hampton points to "Shakespeare's depiction of the truce as something to which princes must agree for the good of their subjects but then break, 'when it your pleasure serves'" (Hampton 2016). The Reformation movements and confessional conflicts prompted large-scale religious migrations of dissenting and persecuted populations. In this context, resident ambassadors who were of a religious minority now needed religious protections to practice their faith within the confines of their embassies. Benjamin J. Kaplan argues that religious divisions in Europe during the Reformations forced states to accept embassy chapels for ambassadors of differing faiths and their staffs. These embassy chapels would later provide the basis for the legal principle of extra-territoriality (Kaplan 2002).

Peacemaking initiatives occurred frequently during the Habsburg–Valois Wars (1494–1559) that raged across the Italian peninsula, southern France, and Flanders. Female rulers and diplomats negotiated several of the truces and peace settlements during the successive wars. When François I was captured during the disastrous battle of Pavia in 1525, Louise de Savoie governed France for a year while seeking her son's release. Louise acted to ensure the kingdom's security and renewed a truce along the French–Flanders border with Margaret of Austria, governor of the Netherlands. Louise at first maintained a firm stance against Charles V's sweeping ransom demands, but then agreed to the peace of Madrid in 1526, to obtain the liberation of François I. The Valois viewed this peace as coerced and the Habsburg–Valois Wars quickly resumed (Knecht 1994: 216–48). The imperialists won a major victory at Saint-Quentin in August 1557, forcing King Henri II to negotiate. The peace of Cateau-Cambrésis of April 1559 finally ended the Habsburg–Valois Wars.

The negotiations for an end of the Schmalkaldic Wars (1546–55) produced a tentative religious compromise within the Holy Roman Empire. The continuing Protestant and Catholic Reformation movements had created a "cleavage of the sacral community" and a constitutional crisis within the Empire, which relied on rituals and a symbolic language to maintain its form, according to Barbara Stollberg-Rilinger (Stollberg-Rilinger 2015). The peace of Augsburg of 1555 articulated pragmatic guarantees that rulers could choose the confessional affiliations of their territories. The peace sanctioned the Lutheran and Catholic confessions, but did not legalize Calvinism within the Empire. The peace's provisions failed to address what would happen if a new ruler were to reverse his predecessor's religious determination for a territory. The peace of Augsburg nonetheless created conditions for a limited peace—but not coexistence—within the Holy Roman Empire, becoming a model for religious peaces in other areas plagued by confessional conflict (Christin 1997).

Many religious peaces and truces were produced during the long French Wars of Religion (1562–1629). The first religious war in France ended with the edict of Amboise of 1563, a religious peace which provided limited guarantees to Calvinists in the kingdom. Catherine de' Medici organized a royal tour of France in 1564–6 in order for the young Charles IX to greet his subjects, but also to calm confessional tensions and solidify peace in the kingdom. Huguenot nobles attempted to seize the royal family in 1567, sparking renewed religious warfare in France. Catherine helped broker a temporary religious peace with the edict of Saint-Germain in 1570—arranging a marriage for her daughter, Marguerite de Valois, with the Huguenot Henri de Bourbon, roi de Navarre. Continuing religious tensions led to the Saint Bartholomew's Day massacre of August 1572, when the royal family suddenly opted to eliminate the Huguenot nobles gathered in Paris. Thousands of Huguenots were killed in a brutal massacre that shocked contemporaries and prompted a resumption of religious warfare across the kingdom. Many observers blamed Catherine for ordering this episode of mass violence, but it remains unsure who really organized the killing (Diefendorf 1991). Religious peaces provided limited guarantees of religious worship for the Huguenot religious minority in certain areas, especially through the use of security towns (Roberts 2013). Jérémie Foa demonstrates attempts by villages and towns to work out localized coexistence through "pacts of friendship" (Foa 2015). Peacemaking initiatives were always very fragile, however, and the wars continued into an even more virulent and confused phase, as the Catholic Leaguers, the Huguenots, and the *politiques* fought in the 1580s and 1590s. Even the celebrated edict of Nantes of 1598 (and the linked peace of Vervins with Spain) failed to end the religious wars in France, which continued until 1629 (Sandberg 2010).

Heresy prosecutions, confessional tensions, and public preaching campaigns fueled a wave of iconoclastic destruction in the Netherlands in 1566. King Philip II of Spain expected his regent, Margaret of Parma, to respond forcefully to this outrage in his territories, but she instead attempted to diffuse the crisis. Philip II sent the duke of Alba and Spanish military forces to restore order in the Netherlands. Alva instituted a military government, prompting calvinist nobles and Protestant-dominated cities to mobilize in the Dutch Revolt (1572–1648). Frequent sieges and periodic truces, such as the pacification of Ghent (1576), were features of the Dutch Revolt. The duke of Parma led a series of brilliant military campaigns in the Netherlands that retook Antwerp and many other Dutch cities in the 1580s, but the failure of the Spanish Armada in 1588 slowed the Spanish military effort in the Netherlands. The long siege of Ostend captivated European audiences, but occupied Spanish military forces from July 1601 to 1604. The continuing Dutch Revolt drained Spanish royal finances and exhausted the Spanish Army of Flanders and finally forced Spain to begin negotiations with the Dutch. The Twelve Years Truce was finally concluded in 1609, providing for a lengthy truce until 1621, but without resolving the confessional issues or granting full recognition of Dutch independence (Allen 2000). Fighting would resume in the Netherlands in 1621, but with the Dutch Revolt subsumed within the broader European context of the Thirty Years War.

The changing practices of diplomacy during the religious wars clearly affected gender relations in several ways. Timothy Hampton argues that the nature and form of diplomatic language changed radically during this period (Hampton 2009). Barbara Stollberg-

Rilinger finds that symbolic communication became a key component of early modern state development as rulers and other political leaders staged events in the public sphere (Stollberg-Rilinger 2009). The rise of royal favorites as first ministers (or chief advisors) in the early seventeenth century emphasized masculine direction of war and peace, especially once the Thirty Years War broke out in 1618. Concino Concini, Charles d'Albert, duc de Luynes, Cardinal Armand-Jean du Plessis de Richelieu, and Cardinal Jules Mazarin all acted as powerful ministers for Louis XIII of France, while Gaspar de Guzmán, count-duke of Olivares coordinated the Spanish war effort during much of the Thirty Years War. George Villiers, duke of Buckingham, became royal favorite of King James I and led British naval and military forces in an attempt to relieve the siege of La Rochelle in 1627 (Elliott and Brockliss, eds. 1999).

The Thirty Years War (1618–48) began as a localized revolt against Habsburg power in the kingdom of Bohemia, but gradually expanded to engulf the entire Holy Roman Empire and much of Europe. Many German princes joined confessional political leagues and unions that mobilized their own field armies. Elector Johann Georg I of Saxony tried to pursue a policy of neutrality at several points in the conflict, but he was compelled to take sides. Confessional conflict and international military interventions made it difficult to negotiate peace in the Holy Roman Empire. The Thirty Years War gradually turned into a devastating war of attrition. An attempt to negotiate a general peace resulted in the peace of Prague of 1635, but it failed to end the conflict. The 1636 campaign in Italy showed how difficult it was to turn battlefield victories into firm territorial control and lasting political gains (Hanlon 2016). Amalia Elisabeth, Landgravine of Hesse-Cassel, assumed the regency of this small German state in 1637, after her husband's death during the Thirty Years War. Amalia Elisabeth confirmed Hesse-Cassel's alliances with Sweden and France, but she also pursued negotiations with the Holy Roman Emperor. Tryntje Helfferich argues that Amalia Elisabeth used a "strategy of delay" that ultimately aimed at forging a lasting peace and securing German liberties. Helfferich provides extensive evidence of "the continued importance of religion in the second half of the Thirty Years War" (Helfferich 2013).

A series of peace conferences, collectively referred to as the congress of Westphalia, assembled to negotiate a peace among all of the European states involved in the Thirty Years War. Imperial and Spanish leaders were especially desperate for peace in 1644, but the talks drug on as Anne d'Autriche, queen regent in France, and her first minister, Cardinal Jules Mazarin, pressed for total military victory against Spain (Sonnino 2008). Sustained negotiations proceeded at Münster and Osnabrück from 1644 to 1648, even as the armies continued to wage war. Although the direct peace negotiations were handled by male ambassadors, female rulers and princely women engaged in diplomacy. For example, Queen Christina of Sweden aggressively pushed her lead negotiator at Osnabrück, Johan Oxenstierna, to conclude peace (Croxton and Tischer 2002: 59–61). Peace was finally concluded among most of the warring parties in 1648. The peace of Westphalia was actually a complex series of separate treaties, but they collectively aimed to produce a "Christian, general and permanent peace" (Wilson 2009: 753). The agreements ended the Thirty Years War and brought peace to Germany and Central Europe, but the kingdoms of France and Spain continued to fight for another decade.

Gender history and cultural history methods allow scholars to re-examine manuscript and printed sources relating to peace processes, demonstrating the possibilities of Renaissance women as diplomatic actors and revealing new dimensions of female participation in European international relations in the early modern period.

CONCLUSION

We live once again in an age of powerful women. Prime Minister Theresa May of the United Kingdom, Chancellor Angela Merkel of Germany, Prime Minister Jóhanna Sigurðardóttir of Iceland, Prime Minister Sheikh Hasina Wazed of Bangladesh, and State Counsellor Aung San Suu Kyi of Myanmar currently serve (or have recently served) as heads of government. President Cristina Fernández de Kirchner of Argentina, President Dilma Rousseff of Brazil, and President Park Geun-hye of South Korea have held office as heads of state. A number of queens rule as titled monarchs, even if these are largely ceremonial positions because elected prime ministers and parliaments actually govern their states. Queen Elizabeth II has reigned for more than half a century in the United Kingdom, and Queen Margrethe II rules in Denmark. Female rule remains far from the norm, but women seem to have growing opportunities to govern in the early twenty-first century (Skard 2014). Female ministers, ambassadors, and envoys participate directly in policy formulation and conduct international diplomacy around the world.

The women of the Renaissance offer striking examples of feminine power for today's women political leaders and policymakers. Renaissance women were intimately involved in court politics, military policies, strategic planning, and international diplomacy. The roles that women have historically played in warmaking and peacemaking are still relatively obscure, but recent research is rapidly accumulating new evidence of women's active participation in military and diplomatic activity. Thus, the editors of a recent book on *Women, Diplomacy and International Politics since 1500* emphasize that "the recovery of female agency —'the lost and silenced contribution of women to international relations'—constitutes a methodological choice" (Sluga and James 2016: 9). The gendered dynamics of Renaissance military policies and diplomatic practices suggest that we need to rethink the role of gender in shaping war and peace throughout human history.

CHAPTER FOUR

Peace and Religion

ELENA BONORA

There are various possible perspectives for thinking about how peace and religion interact in the early modern age. Each of them would involve adopting specific periodizations and concentrating on different geographical spaces. If we interpreted peace as union, we might start with the failed attempts of the Greek and Latin churches to unite in the decades leading up to the fall of Constantinople (1453). If we looked at the area of the Mediterranean where members of the three so-called "religions of the book" (Christians, Muslims, and Jews) had been living side-by-side for centuries, we might examine the cohabitation between Christians and "infidels" that developed despite conflicts and religious antagonism, dwelling on the peace treaties, trading agreements, and cross-cultural exchange with the Muslim empire. From there we might move on to the world of the *pax Ottomana* ("Ottoman peace"), which held together the mosaic of ethnic groups and juridical-religious communities in the huge domain of the sultan. If we shifted our attention to the role of the peacemakers, we might analyze the action of those transcultural go-betweens across the globe who were the missionaries – the Jesuits in particular.

Instead, in the following pages I shall be considering Europe, starting from Luther's Reformation (1517), as that religious break radically changed how the old continent thought and lived, posing new problems. The European space then became the theatre of many practical attempts by various historical actors to build a religious peace and coexistence between different faiths that would enable the community, the state and society to survive.

EUROPE IN THE FORM OF A VIRGIN

In 1537 a woodcut map by the Tyrolese poet Johannes Putsch was printed. Putsch's map is an example of an embodied map. It shows the continent in the form of a queen standing: the Iberian peninsula is the head, France is her breast, her right arm extending into the Mediterranean is Italy, her left arm bent over the Baltic sea is Denmark, and her heart is Bohemia. The center of the scene is occupied by the symbols of imperial power: the crown set on the queen's head, the scepter and globe surmounted by the cross in her hands. This image is also known as *Europa in forma virginis* (Europe in the form of a virgin), referring to the myth of the virgin seized by Zeus, and is the archetype of a series of manuscript and printed adaptations that circulated in the late sixteenth century, in a radically different political context. It shows us how one might imagine the continent of Europe in the first half of the sixteenth century: as a political and religious body united under the Christian emperor (Prosperi 1999; Meurer 2008).

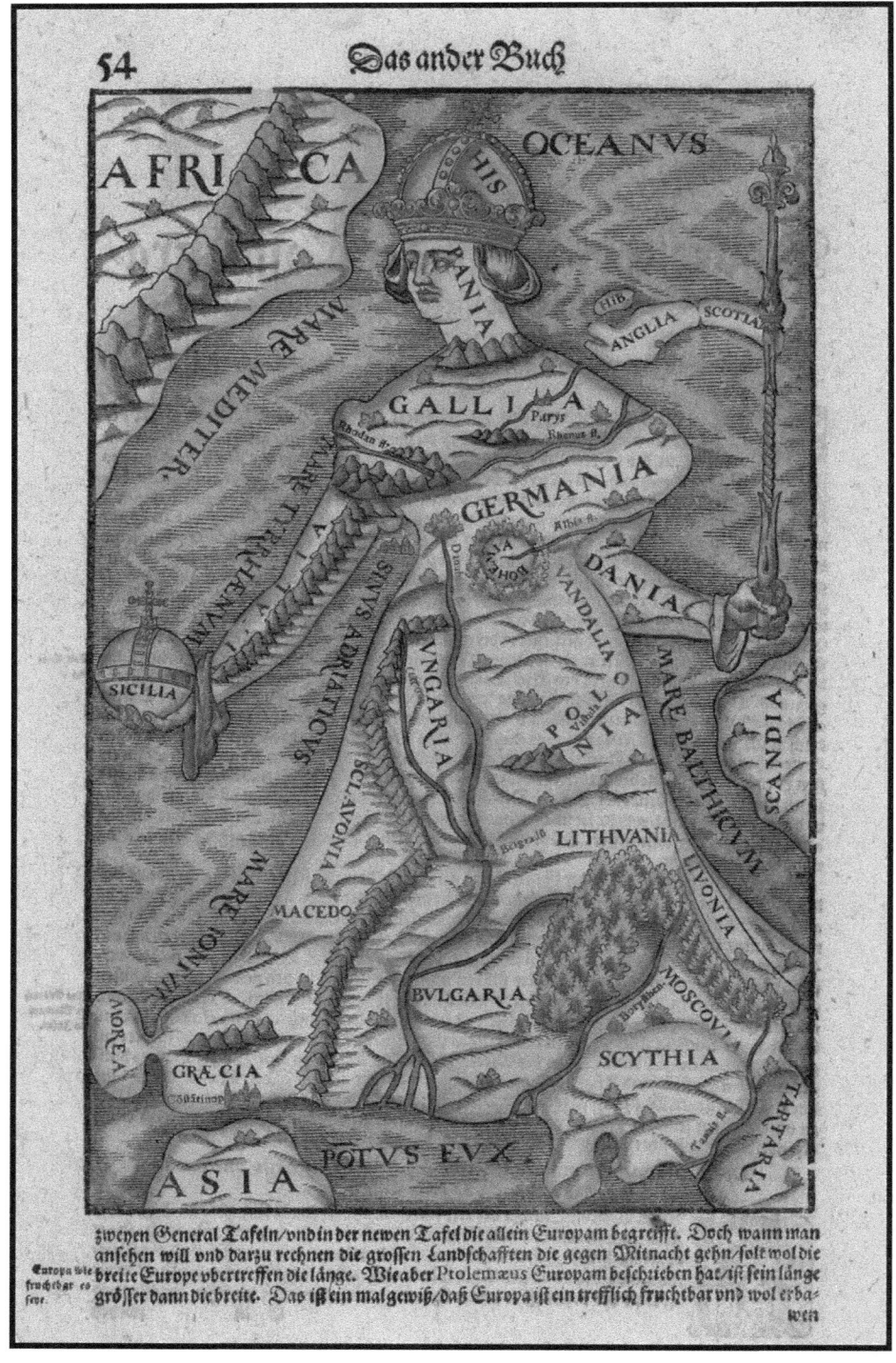

FIGURE 4.1: Sebastian Münster, *Map of Europe as a Queen*, in *Cosmographia Universalis*, Basel (1570). Photo by Fine Art Images/Heritage Images/Getty Images.

FIGURE 4.2: Heinrich Bünting, *Map of Europe Shaped as a Virgin* (Hannover? 1582?). Photo by ART Collection/Alamy Stock Photo.

This idea of unity was rooted in the Middle Ages, but made an emphatic return in Western culture in the early sixteenth century, after Charles of Habsburg had been elected emperor (1519). For almost two generations, and for the first time in seven centuries since Charlemagne, the name of emperor was no longer an empty title, but was associated with an immense territorial power. The emperor could now present himself as the supreme authority and guarantor of universal peace. It was not just propaganda, but a shared way of looking at reality, encouraged by the fear of the growing Turkish threat. Different figures in different parts of the continent, from Valladolid to Vienna, and from Brussels to Naples, began to use the images of the ancient myths to celebrate the return of the Golden Age of peace, prosperity, and justice. Not only reformers and prophets, but poets too, such as Ludovico Ariosto in *Orlando Furioso*, saw in Charles V the artificer of the renewal of Christendom and celebrated him through evangelical metaphors ("*Che sotto a questo imperatore/solo un ovile sia, solo un pastore,*" 15:26 ("That under this emperor/there may be only one sheepfold, only one shepherd"). Peace and justice were two concepts closely associated in Western culture— "Righteousness and peace have kissed each other" in the words of Psalm 85:10. The hope that they could finally be achieved was reflected even by the popular songs circulating in the public squares (Yates 1975; Niccoli 1990).

However, not only did Europe not enjoy peace, but it was in this very period that the reference points which for centuries had made it possible to think of Western civilization as an organic unity were lost. The medieval *Respublica christiana*, that religious background common to Dante Alighieri and Charlemagne, to Abelard and Eloise, to

Geoffrey Chaucer and Marco Polo, ended forever with the spread of the Reformation. Together with its religious unity, the ideal of the political unity of the West was swept away by the new Europe of states, political entities independent of any other law and power. It was precisely from the consolidation of their religious identity that they found the opportunity for development, since the religious choice was also a political matter. The German princes who adhered to the Reformation, for example, consolidated their own power at the expense of the emperor's, became richer because they confiscated Church property, and reinforced their authority within the state by acquiring control over the ecclesiastical institutions.

When, in 1556, Emperor Charles V, defeated and tired, divided his domains and abandoned power to retire to a monastery in Spain, Lutheranism was now widespread and Calvinism was beginning a period of powerful expansion. Half of Europe regarded the pope as the antichrist and the Church of Rome as the incarnation of the whore of Babylon in the Apocalypse.

In this framework, the rival Christian churches (Catholic, Lutheran, and Calvinist) entrenched their positions, like citadels fortified against each other. We should not forget that religion at that time was not just a matter of individual convictions and feelings. Religion shaped society. Birth, marriage, and death took on different meanings, according to whether one was Catholic or Protestant. But if the sense of these rites of passage changed, the meaning that was attributed to the individual, the family, and the relations between generations changed too. The clergy were different: among the Protestants, ministers were often married men, and there were no longer monks and friars. Teaching and education were structured differently in the respective schools and universities. Reading, too, had a different sense: in Catholic countries such as Spain and Italy there was a centralized system in the hands of the Church for the censorship and control of books, and not only those with a religious subject, but literature, university textbooks, and books of history and science. The word of God reached the faithful in a different way: the Germans could read it translated by Luther into their own tongue, while in Italy the Bible could be explained by a priest or read in Latin alone—reading the vernacular Bible was a matter for the Inquisition, and forbidden until the mid-eighteenth century. Even the forms of worship no longer resembled each other. Protestant faith had no use for images, rosaries, and candles, or the cult of the saints and the Virgin Mary—ways of relating to the sacred that gave help and comfort to Catholics. In this chapter we shall see how even small, apparently insignificant, daily gestures could become formidable obstacles to peace between Christians.

After the Reformation, new demarcation lines between different faiths were drawn within the same country, the same city, or the same family. These differences were accompanied by agonizing conflicts as we gradually enter what Henry Kamen has called the "iron century," the period running from the mid-sixteenth to the mid-seventeenth century (Kamen 1971). In this time-span, France was torn apart by wars of religion between Catholics and Huguenots, in Paris as in the most remote villages. In England, the Catholic Bloody Mary was succeeded by the Protestant Elizabeth, who was excommunicated by the pope. In 1649, under the Stuarts, a revolution in which religion played a central part cut off the king's head. The Low Countries, where Calvinism had spread, rebelled against the dominion of the Catholic Philip II in a long and bloody war with Spain. In Catholic Europe, in Spain, Portugal, and Italy, heretics tried by the tribunals of the Inquisition were burnt at the stake. The hardening of the opposing orthodoxies (Lutheran, Calvinist, and Catholic) led to a European war that lasted thirty years, from 1618 to 1648, and devastated Germany.

FIGURE 4.3: Peter Paul Rubens, *The Consequences of War*, Palazzo Pitti, Florence (1637–8). Photo by Art Collection 2/Alamy Stock Photo.

The image of Europe that circulated in the iron century was always that of a maiden—but one unlike the figure in Putsch's anthropomorphic map. We might take as an example the painting by Peter Paul Rubens entitled *The Consequences of War* (1637–8).

Both painter and diplomat, during his life Rubens took part in peace negotiations, witnessed dynastic marriages designed to consolidate peace, and attended baroque celebrations with fireworks and music designed to convey an emotional sense of the new-won peace to the people. He belonged to that world of international relations that was developing and increasingly professionalizing after the outbreak of the Thirty Years War in 1618. He died without seeing the end of that long war ratified in the peace of Westphalia in 1648.

Painted while the conflict was still raging, *The Consequences of War* shows a frenzied scene: the temple of Janus is open, leaving the god Mars (ineffectively held back by Venus) and the fury Alekto free to perform their work of devastation. They trample down the arts and charity, the Christian virtue *par excellence*, who, following classical iconography, is shown as a mother with a babe in arms. To the left, slightly to one side, stands Europe—a young woman in despair, dressed in mourning and with her dress torn, raising her arms to the heavens. The imperial globe has ended up in the hands of a terrified *putto* who seeks refuge in her robes. An illustrated German leaflet of the same period is entitled *Europa querula et vulnerata (Europe weeping and wounded)*. It is an anti-Catholic variation on the theme of a famous work published in 1517, Erasmus's *Querela pacis (Complaint of peace)*. The leaflet was printed during the terrible siege of the Protestant city of Magdeburg, and it depicts the young Europe dishevelled and barefoot, pierced by the arrows of a Catholic army that is raising the banner of the devil (a Jesuit can be seen among them) (*Deutsche illustrierte Flugblätter des 16. und 17. Jahrhunderts*, 1980: no. 223).

In this divided Europe, what meaning did the concept of peace have? Amid the clash of arms and the flames of burning heretics, what form could religious peace assume? The answer in this chapter will not be found in the history of ideas, or in the suggestions of such exceptional figures as Erasmus, Sebastian Castellio, Montaigne, or minority groups and movements like the Anabaptists and Socinians. All of them developed their ideas of peace and tolerance in opposition to the dominant values of the society and community they belonged to. It is with this in mind that we shall be asking other questions. What obstacles prevented everyone else—the majority of sixteenth- and seventeenth-century men and women—from sharing their ideas? What was the nature of these obstacles, and what was the soil in which they grew? What solutions were sought and tried out to make the violence cease, to prevent the self-destruction of society and the body politic, and to make religious pluralism possible in a city or a community? And finally: what did "live in peace" mean for individuals of different religions?

THE OBSTACLES TO RELIGIOUS PEACE

The positions of the theologians were one of the obstacles to peace. After the fracture of the Reformation, their voice acquired growing importance. Rival churches, each claiming to possess the truth, reinforced their internal unity and confessional identity by rigidly defining orthodoxy and controlling behavior. There was no longer room for either dissent or doubt—i.e. that form of the critical use of intelligence exercised by the non-theologian Erasmus and displayed in his writings. Returning the heretic to the straight and narrow of orthodoxy was more of a duty than ever, as it meant saving his soul. Tolerating his presence in the community was a sin against God. Concepts central to the Christian tradition, such as forgiveness and charity, did not apply to the heretic. The doctrinal reference point was St Augustine's *Compelle intrare* (Compel them to come in), based on Luke's Gospel (14:23): the principle by which it is admissible to force heretics to repent and return to the bosom of the Church. In line with this theological premise, from the mid-sixteenth century on, the Churches put in place practical and institutional mechanisms of coercion.

We cannot give an account here of either the history or the geography of intolerance in Europe. Depending on the context, it could assume different faces, as the Churches were not only the custodians of doctrine, worship, and liturgy, but were also historical institutions that produced laws and possessed the apparatus to apply them in society, within the framework of either cooperative or conflicting relations with civil powers. Intolerance could therefore manifest itself in many ways. It could assume the form of a personal attitude like the "charitable hatred" that in the complex religious situation in the

England of 1630 an Anglican pastor urged the faithful to display towards dissident neighbours (Walsham 2006: 278). Or it could be exercised by means of tribunals and the sentences of ecclesiastical judges, focusing on outward behavior in order to secure external conformity and obedience. Different again was the intolerance systematically exercised by the tribunals of the Inquisition in Spain, Portugal and Italy. They were genuine "tribunals of the conscience" (Prosperi 1996). They persecuted inner beliefs with the aim of making the guilty confess, repent and abjure before sentence was carried out.

Another obstacle to peace was the use of metaphors that were widespread and deep-rooted in the collective imagination. Those who strayed from orthodoxy were seen as tares to be uprooted, or a contagious sickness of the body, a form of "gangrene" to be cured with surgical amputation of the infected parts. Behind these botanical and medical metaphors was the idea that the heretic endangered the spiritual salvation of the entire community in the same way as a diseased limb could compromise the health of the entire body. Dire events such as epidemics, earthquakes and famines were seen as indicative of divine punishment for the sins of the community. According to common belief, there were essentially two ways of expiating and purifying the social body: celebrating collective penitential rites and cutting away the diseased limbs that caused the infection, which were usually identified among heretics, infidels and witches.

Another obstacle to peace was the different way in which Protestants related to the holy. The iconoclasm of the Calvinists in particular—their rejection of sacred images—clashed with Catholic tradition. The crosses at crossroads in open country, which for Catholics exorcized the dangers of the unknown, were unacceptable forms of blasphemy for Calvinists. Before the Reformation, space and time in cities and villages were marked in the same way by the sacred. Rites and devotions defined the order of daily life even at the level of the senses, through the sounds of bells, the smell of incense, liturgical chants, and religious images which were not confined to the interior of the churches. The community saw itself as a single body. When under threat, it turned to the patron saint and organized a procession along the city walls, where the sacred image or the holy relics were shown to the outside world that was the source of the danger. That is what the inhabitants of the French coastal town of Toulon did in 1543, invoking the Virgin protectress of the city while the Turkish fleet wintered menacingly in the harbor.

The people believed in the apotropaic functions—their capacity to ward off malign influences—of objects and practices. During the spring processions they recited the litanies, did penance, and carried the relics through the fields. All manner of beliefs and lore collected around these practices. They had propitiatory functions designed to guarantee a good harvest from God and procure peace before the arrival of spring, the season when wars were resumed. The rite was also supposed to ensure the control of the passions, and so of the humors circulating in the human body, for, as they could read in Varagine's *Legenda aurea*, the blood was warmer in spring than in other seasons. They were polysemic practices: the ritual processions in the fields also had the social value of establishing the confines and ratifying legal possession (Benvenuti 2006). The Reformation burst into this world of traditional devotions, stigmatizing them as papist, idolatrous, and superstitious, and set about constructing a different world of beliefs and customs.

The obstacles to peace were not only cultural, and did not just concern how "others" were perceived collectively or their relation with the sacred. The Church exercised a public function: its baptisms and marriages had a civil effect. Through baptism the ecclesiastical authorities gave an identity to the new-born baby in the eyes of the state too. The marriage that was legally valid for the civil authorities was the religious one celebrated in the parish church, the basic institution of religious life, which could legally define a village as such, rather than as a mere cluster of houses. In this framework, peaceful coexistence between different confessions required not only a change in convictions, ideas, and ways of feeling, but a reorganization of the system of relations between Church and State, as well as a sharper separation of their ambits (Brambilla 2006).

The lore concerning power was another formidable obstacle to religious peace. In the treatises of political theology and in the way ordinary people saw things, the legitimate sovereign was the guarantor of the religious unity that was necessary for the health and spiritual salvation of the body politic. The jurist Jean Bégat, who was against the legal recognition of two confessions in the kingdom of France, summarized his conviction like this: "The sovereign who thinks he can be the protector of two religions finds himself (in the words of the proverb) between two saddles, on the ground" (Christin 1997: 58).

RELIGIOUS PEACES

In the medieval and early modern periods the allegories of artists return again and again to the same figurative elements to symbolize the positive effects of peace. Cornucopias overflowing with fruit and flowers, children, jewels, musical instruments, and books symbolize the abundance, fertility and development of the arts in time of peace. With the Reformation this fundamental value came into conflict with that of religious unity. To preserve the peace, confessional division needed to be accepted. To prevent violence bringing down the state, some European countries found themselves forced to reconsider shared ideas, ways of thinking and feeling, and to fix new rules that allowed the peaceful coexistence of different faiths.

This did not happen in Catholic countries such as Italy, Spain, and Portugal, where the Inquisition's firm repression of heresy, with the participation (somewhat reluctant in Italy) of the civil authorities, prevented the peace of society and the continuity of the institutions being imperilled, as happened in Switzerland, the Empire, and in France. The history of the "iron century" is punctuated by these forms of more or less stable pacification: the peace of Kappel (1531) between the Protestant and Catholic cantons in Switzerland, the peace of Augsburg (1555) legalizing Lutheranism in the empire, the royal edict of Amboise (1563), and the later ones in France, culminating in the edict of Nantes (1598), which put an end to the civil wars and granted rights to the Huguenot (Calvinist) communities until it was rescinded in 1685. But the list should be extended to other religious agreements, such as the Warsaw Confederation (1573), in which the powerful aristocratic groups that governed Eastern Europe swore to live in peace despite their religious differences, and the pacification of Ghent, by which the northern and southern provinces of the Low Countries put aside their religious difference and united in revolt against the king of Spain (1576). At the end of the list, the peace of Westphalia (1648), concluded a European conflict lasted thirty years, and admitted Calvinism too to the empire.

Every religious peace has specific characteristics, depending on context, but Olivier Christin has shown convincingly both what they had in common and how important they were (Christin 1997). The religious peaces put an end to religious wars, but the term "religious" may be misleading: behind these peaces was a new idea—that the problem of peace was to be dealt with on a political, rather than a religious, plane.

This idea developed parallel to the process of forming the modern European state, and was fully affirmed in the peace of Westphalia (1648). No fewer than 109 diplomatic delegations, representing 140 German and sixteen European countries took part in the negotiations. It was a great event, which finally and fully imposed the principle—obvious to us today—that the European system of states should be regulated by international law (*ius gentium*) and not by theological concepts. The papal delegates walked away from the peace table in protest at the concessions granted to Lutherans and Calvinists. For the first time in centuries, the head of the Catholic Church abandoned the idea of presenting himself as the *Pacificator orbis Christiani* (supreme pacifier of the Christian world) and "common father"—a neutral arbiter of the conflicts between the European princes.

Who were the promotors and artificers of the religious peaces? They were the civil authorities, after other means of pacification, such as the "religious colloquies" promoted by the emperor (Regensburg, 1541) and the king of France (Poissy, 1562) had come to nothing, due to disagreement between theologians. The protagonists of religious peace were not theologians, but jurists. It was not a doctrinal compromise, but a political and legal agreement, by which the civil authorities organized the coexistence of various religious beliefs and the conditions for public worship in a single political entity (a confederation, a state or a city). The aim was to put an end to the violence that was destroying the state.

Religious peace, then, was neither by nature nor in its aims a chapter in the history of tolerance or the history of ideas. Freedom of conscience was more a corollary than the main objective. It was an agreement drawn up and implemented by various mediators—counsellors, functionaries, minor local notables, officials—who were not so much pacifists as "artisans of peace," for they were building peace, not on the basis of abstract principles, but by rules and procedures conceived as experimental and open to improvement (Christin 1997: 73). Christin has brought out how the language of the peace edicts in sixteenth-century France refers to subjects needing to regain "tranquillity" and "repose," to resume the ties of friendship against special interests under the protection of the sovereign pacifier (Christin 1997: 39, 49, 181). The word "tolerance" was rarely used, and certainly not in the sense that we usually give it today of a fundamental moral value for human society.

The peace of Augsburg, drawn up in 1555 after a dramatic period of wars between the Catholic emperor and the Lutheran princes, established Germany as a bi-confessional country, legalizing Lutheranism. It recognized the right of a prince who held sovereignty over a given territory to choose between the two confessions. Subjects of the other faith had the right to emigrate—a choice that had a very high cost. Emigrating meant leaving home and friends for the unknown, scraping together one's goods and selling off quickly what could not be taken with one. It meant leaving behind the cemeteries where one's forebears were buried. Nevertheless, it was a precious right, which refugees today do not have.

In this way, the empire as a whole became bi-confessional, containing mono-confessional Lutheran and Catholic states. However, there were places where Catholics and Lutherans lived side by side. These were the free or imperial cities, independent city-states where both confessions were allowed and representatives of both faiths sat on the town council. Rich and important cities such as Augsburg and Ravensburg became, as we shall see below, a place for experimenting new peace practices. The area of coexistence tended to extend, and continued to do so during the Thirty Years Wars, as a result of the conquests and dynastic changes that might set a prince over a given territory whose subjects followed a faith different from his own.

The first important religious peace in France was the edict of Amboise (1563), promulgated after the first war of religion (it had been preceded in 1562 by the short-lived edict of Saint-Germain). The king then officially recognized religious pluralism in his kingdom, devastated by conflicts between Catholics and Huguenots. The edict authorized the members of the high aristocracy (those who could exercise high justice) and their household to practice Protestantism in their homes. The peace of Amboise changed the religious geography of the kingdom so that it could be perceived by any traveler, modifying the rules of cohabitation, not only in the castles of the nobility, but inside and outside the city walls. Each royal administrative district (*baillage* or *sénéchaussé*), excluding Paris and its region, had to choose a locality where the Huguenots could worship outside the walls. In the cities where they had already worshipped publicly, the Huguenots could maintain one or two temples. France, too, became a sort of patchwork in which people of different faiths lived side by side. In 1564, the young King Charles IX made his triumphal entry in Lyons, presenting himself as a restorer of peace. He was welcomed by children of the city, marching in pairs—one Catholic and the other Protestant.

Every religious peace stirred up fierce resistance as, by nature, it represented a break with deeply rooted ways of thinking. The peace of Augsburg was severely condemned by the pope, but the attempt to transform religious division into a principle of pacification was a misguided idea for most people of the time. The result was an avalanche of speeches and anonymous pamphlets scorning and criticizing these first agreements.

At local level, the application of peace created endless conflicts over the choice and distribution of places of worship, the use of cemeteries, and the allocation of seats in the town council, down to the smallest questions, such as the right to sound bells. Hundreds of incidents could be set off in the sphere of daily relations in communities "divided by faith," to quote the title of Benjamin J. Kaplan's book (Kaplan 2007). Yet, despite the resistance and obstacles they met, religious peaces made it possible to construct a new legal framework and a new way of thinking. When problems cropped up at local level, violence was not always the response. Instead, justice was sought in the law courts, and people accepted and exploited the laws to their own advantage, reporting any violation of them to representatives and commissioners of the central power, who were sent into religiously mixed areas to resolve disputes and mediate or arbitrate conflicts.

In some cities of France, local actors were even more decisive and autonomous in drawing up what were called "friendship pacts." To forestall the danger of violence returning, believers of the two religions agreed to act from then on as "brothers, friends and fellow-citizens," setting down in writing that they wanted to live "peacefully and in accordance with the king's edicts" (Foa 2011: 241).

The "friendship pacts" show that the peace processes were multidirectional and not merely guided from above. The initiators were not humanist champions of advanced positions on tolerance, but local notables, merchants, artisans, and farmworkers who exchanged mutual vows to preserve the peace while civil war had set the rest of the kingdom ablaze. Fearing that discord might return to the cities, they swore to forgive and forget past wrongs. On a practical level, they promised to organize military defense together to protect the city day and night, help each other financially, and not foment discord with "false stories, false news and notices designed to stir up sedition and strong feelings" (Christin 1997: 125).

These documents describe the efforts to build up an extremely fragile peace from the bottom. They emerged from the legal and moral framework set up by the king's edicts of pacification, widely disseminated in printed, handwritten, and oral form, whose language they imitated. But what was used here was above all a specific modality of resolving social conflicts, great and small—one which was widespread in the early modern period.

This way of making peace, which goes back to the Middle Ages, made use of codified gestures (kissing, embracing, drinking together), not requiring any intervention by judges and tribunals. In Italy they were known as *paci private* (private peaces) and drew on the Christian values of charity and forgiveness. But it would be a mistake to regard them as no more than the expression of an inner moral disposition (Niccoli 2007). For the community and the civil authorities they were legally valid, thanks to the ritual gestures, which were still more important than the presence of a notary. I shall try to explain this with an example. In the past, the ritual gesture of a handshake constituted the validity of an agreement between two parties. Our custom of sealing a contract with a handshake is a pale echo of this way of seeing things. The difference now lies in the fact that the gesture has become only an accessory factor.

In the light of all this, we might conjecture that the friendship pacts between Catholics and Huguenots, who no longer shared the same church or the same religious rites, were accompanied by the exchange of ancient gestures: touching the other's hand and shaking it, embracing, kissing, laughing, eating from the same plate, and drinking together.

COEXISTENCE

In the late sixteenth century, the religious landscape of Europe had radically changed, marked as it was by areas in which different Christian faiths lived together. Montaigne recounts this Europe in his *Journal de voyage*, the diary of his journey from France to Italy. It was 1580. Before crossing the Alps and entering the mono-confessional area of the Italian peninsula, he describes the religious mixture of the French, Swiss, and German cities, scrupulously noting details of this cohabitation: the churches, the liturgies, the rites, and the mixed marriages. If Montaigne had continued on his travels across Europe instead of heading for the capital of the pope, he would have met other patterns of confessional coexistence: in the Dutch Republic, Britain, and even Eastern Europe, with its complex and fluid political boundaries, where religious sects flourished and various ethnic communities were concentrated—Orthodox Christians, Jews, Muslims, and others.

In all these places, peace was the outcome of daily practice. It was the result of a search for concrete solutions to many different concrete problems, which tended to occur when one confession occupied the public space with its gestures and rites.

Processions were a constant source of conflict. At Agen, in South-East France, a Calvinist one day encountered a priest, who, preceded by an assistant ringing a little warning bell, marched solemnly through the street to the home of a dying parishioner, carrying the viaticum. As he passed the Catholic crowd fell silent, knelt down, and the men raised their hats, but the Calvinist remained standing with his head covered. He barely escaped with his life from the violence of the furious crowd (Hanlon 1993: 232).

The cases reported to the civil authorities tell of Huguenots forced to kneel down and make the sign of the cross (Benoist 1693: II, 592), and of Catholic priests who silenced their bells before storming into the markets and streets crowded with Huguenots, or who assailed them with their fists or with the crucifix, as the victims reported to the king's commissars. Protestants who raised their hats also risked censure from their own churches. The Lutheran ecclesiastical authorities in the imperial city of Augsburg and the Calvinist consistories in France (judicial bodies that were half secular and half ecclesiastical, and that controlled customs) had to find a compromise. They decided not to punish their co-religionists for baring their heads as it was simply a gesture of good manners to those passing by and not to the Host, but forbade them to kneel down. Later, the ideal prevailed that it was better for the Huguenots to withdraw into the doorways or quickly slip away from the processions. Sometimes this was not enough, as is shown by the case of Toinette, which was heard before the Parliament of Bordeaux. She was a Protestant maidservant who had not knelt down, and who had been chased by the priest with the Host in hand as far as her master's house (Kaplan 2007: 80–6; Christin 1997: 108–17).

Calvinist iconoclasm against crucifixes, altars, statues, paintings, and sacred relics included burning, roasting, smashing, ripping, urinating, and defecating; such behavior might set off reactions, during which the bodies of those who had been killed were butchered, mutilated and dragged through the streets. The research of Natalie Zemon Davis and Denis Crouzet has encouraged other historians to give more attention to the ritual significance of these savage actions (Zemon Davis [1973] 1975; Crouzet 1990).

The efforts and compromises with which people tried to live peacefully together stand out against this bloodstained background. The edict of Nantes (1598) established that the Huguenots could refuse to decorate the façades of their homes on the occasion of a Catholic procession, but at the same time allowed Catholics to decorate them at their own expense. This does not mean that the regulation was always respected, as is shown by the case of a Huguenot who one day cut the strings of the tapestries that had been hung at the windows for the procession of the Most Blessed Sacrament (Plancher 1781: 564).

FIGURE 4.4: Frans Hogenberg, *The Calvinist Iconoclastic Riot of August 20, 1566* (1588), Kunsthalle, Hamburg. Photo by The Picture Art Collection/Alamy Stock Photo.

Time itself could become a threat to peace. In 1582, when Montaigne had now returned to France, Pope Gregory XIII reformed the calendar to solve some astronomical problems. Ten days were removed, and so that year there was a jump from October 4 to October 15. This measure had an enormous impact on people's daily lives. It was also an extraordinary pretext for affirming the authority of the papacy, not only over Catholics, but over Protestants and the many Orthodox Christians in Eastern Europe, the Balkans, and the Venetian Republic.

University professors and German Lutheran princes recognized that the Catholic calculations were correct, but they still preferred to argue with the stars rather than declare themselves in agreement with the pope-Antichrist. This difference in reckoning time continued into the eighteenth century and created enormous practical problems in cities where Catholics and Protestants were living together but on different days. The local authorities were forced to find compromises to solve a collective problem that risked paralyzing the city and its economic activities. The kings of England, who were also the heads of the Anglican Church, behaved in similar fashion to the pope when they invented a new calendar that was marked by feast-days based, not on the saints, but on events concerning the monarchy (Cressy 1989).

The peaceful sharing of the same time between different religions was difficult to achieve, even without the pope and the English kings intervening. In Dutch cities, Catholic housemaids complained that their masters prevented them from not working on Catholic holidays or observing fast days, while a Protestant servant in Haarlem reported his Catholic master to the magistrates for preventing him from working on saints' days, depriving him of his wages.

These stories of difficult coexistence have left written traces: we know them because one of the parties turned to the crown, local magistrates, or various lay and ecclesiastical intermediaries to have justice. This way of proceeding demonstrates that those involved had a sense of the limits of acceptable behavior. The arguments they used tell us what they expected to be persuasive to the judges. They show there was an imagined justice which made them feel authorized to demand that the rules be respected. Assurances and rules fixed from above and applied at local level by an array of mediators had been assimilated and become values of the community, even if they did not always lead to virtuous or peaceful behavior.

Divisions could also be resolved without recourse to the magistrates by simply crossing confessional borders. Reformed ministers were often distressed by their co-religionists taking part in dances, parties and the fairs that were held on Catholic feast-days (Sauzet 1979: 173–8).

Mixed marriages were another way of transgressing religious boundaries. Cross-confessional marriages are a sign of the confessional border's permeability. When Montaigne reached the imperial city of Augsburg, he did not fail to note how frequent they were: "Marriages between Catholics and Lutherans are common, and the more ardent of the pair submits to the laws of the other. A thousand such marriages have been celebrated" (Montaigne 1983: 126). This was all the more significant if we consider that marriage was then not just a union between two individuals, but more of an alliance between families. In evaluating cases of this kind, however, we need to go beyond the tempting but somewhat overworked image of the porousness of the boundaries between different religions or cultures. We need to examine the legal, social, and patrimonial aspects in the various contexts, follow the development of cross-confessional marriage in long time-span, consider gender distinctions, and, above all, reconstruct the incidence of conversion policies on the part of the Church toward one of the partners (Safley 1984; Seidel Menchi (ed.) 2016).

SPATIAL COMPROMISES

Peace was not merely the result of practical daily coexistence. It was also carefully negotiated and based on meticulously constructed agreements. Such agreements did not blur the confessional boundary. On the contrary, they defined in detail the rights of each group, dividing the civic space, starting from the churches (Kaplan 2007: 172–234; Te Brake 2009; Spicer (ed.) 2012).

"Shared churches" (*Simultankirchen*) began to appear in the empire even before the peace of Augsburg in 1555. As well as in the empire, they were to be found throughout Europe, wherever public worship by several confessions was allowed: in Poland, Moravia, Ireland, and Valtellina. They were places used in turn by Catholics and Protestants, following a painstaking division of the spaces by means of walls and galleries. Formal contracts governed the times of worship, the division of the sacred space, and the use of the altars and baptisteries. Decrees of the authorities laid down what architectural modifications were permissible, such as the opening of a new door, and even the number and arrangement of the benches.

FIGURE 4.5: The Simultankirche of St. Petri in Bautzen, from Johann Leisentrit's *Geistliche Lieder und Psalmen* (*Spiritual Hymns and Psalms*) (1567). The picture shows the Catholic mass in the foreground, the Lutheran Lord's sermon in the back. Wikimedia Commons.

Two centuries later, the Enlightenment would sneer at this kind of tolerance, which was not founded on the recognition of the equality of rights or on the growth of public opinion, but was more the result of a scrupulous division of quotas and officially imposed book-keeping. However, seen against its historical background, it was little short of sensational, compared with other situations and other ways of thinking. From the point of view of the Roman papacy, for example, these arrangements, which allowed the enemies of the faith to use the house of God, were regarded as unacceptably monstrous.

If the shared churches allowed various confessions to occupy the public space, *Auslauf* (walking out) shows that the problem of peaceful cohabitation of different faiths could find other solutions. This German expression refers to a new kind of religious commuting, which saw groups of dissenters crossing the city gates on Sundays, for all to see, so as to worship as they wished in another state, city, or estate. This practice was common throughout Europe, from France to Moravia. It fostered peace and stability among opposing religious groups down to the Enlightenment in the changing geo-political and confessional patchwork of the Empire. *Auslauf* allowed the authorities to give one faith a monopoly of public worship in the city and channel any possible tensions to the outside.

Another of the creative solutions that people of the early modern age found to guarantee peace inside the city walls was the *Schuilkerk* (hidden church). The *Schuilkerk* was a solution that lasted a long time in European history. Many synagogues and Jewish oratories survived in certain periods and contexts in this form, well beyond the reforms of the Enlightenment. Its name indicates its Dutch origins, although it extended throughout Europe. In the tolerant Dutch Republic, believers had freedom of conscience, but freedom of worship was limited to the domestic space, and applied to those who lived under the same roof. The Dutch Reformed Church was the only Church that was allowed to perform religious functions publicly and to intervene publicly in moral affairs. A traveler who had walked the streets of Amsterdam would therefore have come across imposing churches whose whitewashed walls had been stripped of sacred images, their interior purified of any idolatry, as we can see from the representations of them in seventeenth-century Flemish painting. But if that same traveler had penetrated the rows of houses and entered the secluded building in the courtyards, he would have found a *Schuilkerk* able to house as many as 150 people, where dissenters (Catholics, Lutherans, Remonstrants, Mennonites) worshipped in secret.

The *Schuilkerk* was a kind of ghost church, as it had renounced any sign of its presence in the public space. It had no bell-tower, no crosses, no bells, no external ornamentation, it had discreet entrances and the faithful too were expected to show discretion on approaching them. According to Benjamin Kaplan, these places of worship were an "open secret" (Kaplan 2007: 183). Both the local authorities and the neighbors were aware of their existence. In 1691, the city authorities of Amsterdam fixed precise rules for the new "hidden church" of the Catholics: an entrance set back from the road, no parking for carriages in the surrounding streets, no beggars, no groups of people or visible objects of devotion such as rosaries and prayer books. Sometimes these hidden churches were so little hidden that they appeared in travelers' guides. In this way, dissenting religious traditions were able to survive in particular periods and contexts, thanks to the tolerance of the city authorities, local officials and neighbours.

The legal context and the social fabric that allowed the development of hidden or clandestine churches dissolve if we cross the invisible border that divided multi-confessional Europe from Catholic, inquisitorial, and intolerant Europe. In the 1520s and 1530s, following the Reformation, various "*conventicole ereticali*" (clandestine gatherings

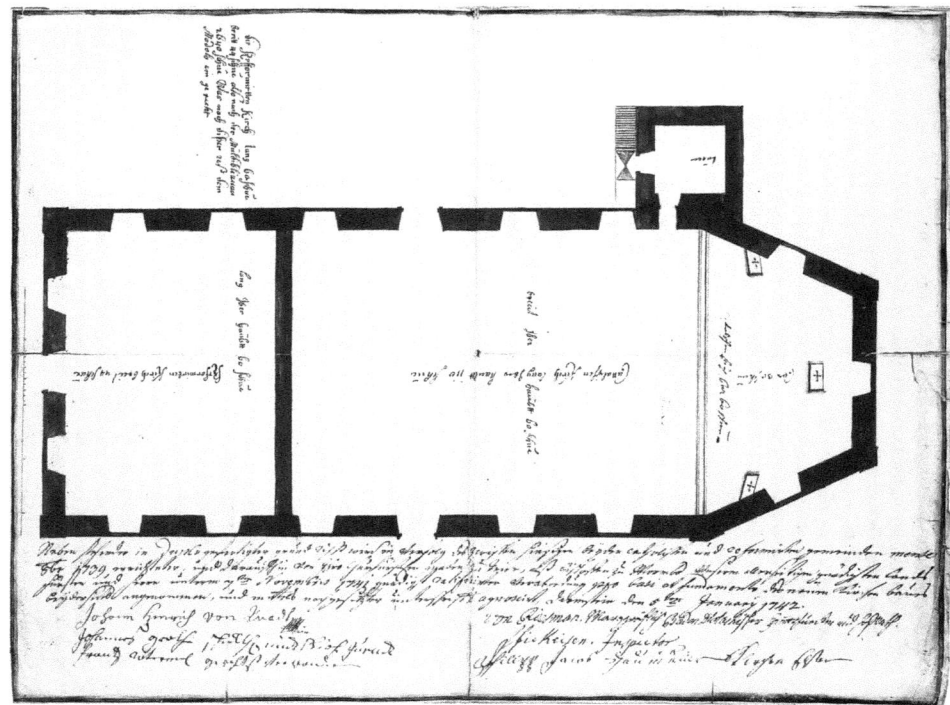

FIGURE 4.6: Ground plan sketch (1741) of St. Laurentius church in Dirmstein (Rhineland-Palatinate): Protestant part (left third) and Catholic part (right, including the tower). Wikimedia Commons.

and communities of dissenters) had spread in Italy, Spain, and Portugal. By the end of the century, these clandestine communities of "heretics" had now been uprooted, thanks to an intransigent policy that had banned any form of dissent, including freedom of conscience. Even the social relations on which community life was based had been modified by the sharpening of the policy of repression. Denouncing one's neighbor on suspicion of heresy had actually become a duty, and every good Catholic now had not only to answer to God for this, but also to the judges of the Inquisition.

CONCLUSION

This study has tried to describe a new concept of peace that gradually took shape after the Reformation. Peace was no longer seen as the consequence of the political and religious *unity* of Europe, as was the case in Putsch's anthropomorphized map, but was now thought of as the coexistence of different faiths, and so as the result of *division*.

After the fracture of Christendom, religious diversity was no longer limited to the familiar face of the Jew, the Muslim, or the Orthodox Christian. It no longer concerned a minority, which could be controlled. Religious diversity now had the aggressive features of a rival confession that threatened to become the majority and to invade the vital spaces, of a disease that could spread through the whole of society and the body politic. To prevent religious violence from destroying that body, some parts of sixteenth-century

Europe set up processes of pacification between different faiths. These processes were later implemented and constantly transformed by a great variety of mediators who made the enactment and enculturation of peace practices possible.

There emerged a leopard-skin Europe of mono-confessional Catholic areas and areas where Catholics, Lutherans, and Calvinists attempted a difficult cohabitation. It was a different Europe from that imagined by the early-modern pontiffs, who continued to act as supreme peacemaker in order to unite all Catholic princes in the "just war" against the enemies of the Church, the "infidels" and the "heretics" (Prosperi 2005; Visceglia (ed.) 2013). It was those same crusading ideals of the "just war" that had propelled an intolerant Spain to conquer the New World in the late fifteenth century. In the following century, the result of the combined action of conquest, evangelization and destruction of other cultures was called the *pax Hispanica* (Spanish peace).

But, returning to Europe, the peace that was constructed in everyday practice in specific places, not in the rarefied air of the world of ideas, did not develop straightforwardly. There were retreats and sudden advances, and a mixture of minor and major compromises, provisional rules and solutions, which, as time passed and contexts changed, might alter their meaning, set off new aggressive dynamics, or prove obsolete (David Mayes 2015; Roussel and Grandjean (eds.) 1998). Thus, for some Europeans, preserving religious peace became the result of compromises and negotiations, only a few examples of which have been given in the previous pages.

"Living in peace" was therefore an exceptional and precarious achievement in the contested space of Europe, where religion continued to be perceived as the "difference that makes a difference," and where tolerance had become a practice that placed clear boundaries between communities divided by faith. Despite the rise of contacts, interconnections, and circulations between the various regions, empires, and cultural areas of the world that occurred in the early modern period, religious identity continued to condition even trade and economic decisions (Burkhardt (ed.) 2007; Antunes, Halevi, and Trivellato (eds.) 2014). Those who traveled had the sensation that conflicts and tensions for religious reasons could break out without warning. A mere gesture was enough to spark them off, as the semantics of many gestures—even the most common—was religious in nature. In the 1550s, the printer Giulio Accolti ordered some boiled chicken one Friday in a German inn. He understood German, and had realized that the Lutherans at the next table intended to attack and kill him as a papist if he fasted. When he returned to Italy, he was put on trial by a papal court as a heretic. But, on the other side of the Alps, the act he was accused of had saved his life (Bonora 2011).

CHAPTER FIVE

Representations of Peace

SEAN ROBERTS

VISUALIZING AND MATERIALIZING PEACE IN EARLY MODERN EUROPE

The history of peace tends to be appended as a kind of footnote (or sometimes epilogue) to more commonplace narratives of politics, social change, and especially warfare. To be sure, treaties and truces like the peace of Lodi (1454) and the treaty of Münster (1648) which frame this volume are indispensable milestones in canonical studies of medieval and early modern Europe. Yet, such discrete events are easily gathered under the umbrella of conventional military and political history while "peace studies" remain a disciplinary rarity, often regarded as suspiciously leftist in its origins (Gittings 2012; Adolf 2009). Conflict and strife are routinely advanced as defining features of the early modern world, while peace plays the more circumscribed role of punctuating turbulent (and undoubtedly thrilling) tales. Indeed, one of the most influential recent synthetic histories of the Renaissance uses 'Violence' as a chapter heading and organizing rubric (Ruggiero 2015: 154–204). Likewise, Alexander Lee's sensationalizing, popular account *The Ugly Renaissance* promises to open readers' eyes to the "Sex, Greed, Violence, and Depravity" that characterized the period (Lee 2013). Peace has received little corresponding treatment.

For historians of art, this imbalance is, if anything, more striking. In stark contrast to the recent proliferation of studies on the visual histories and taxonomies of battle, punishment, and torture, those of peace have yet to be written (Wolfthal 2004; Terry-Fritsch and Labbie (eds.) 2012; Decker and Kirkland Ives (eds.) 2015). Art historians and their readers—like many of us—are hardly immune to fascination with the violent, gruesome, and even macabre (Loh (ed.) 2001). Perhaps most compellingly, the visual history of violence is a history of the body in action and pain. Peace, in contrast, quite literally lacks this sense of the visceral. Indeed, it is frequently—though hardly without controversy—regarded as an absence, defined as the static lack of conflict. When artists did furnish peace with a body, it was often that of the bloodless allegory or emblem. Andrea Aliciati's *Emblematica* (1550), the most popular book of its sort, provided a sequence of three pacific emblems; "Peace," "From War Peace," and "From Peace Plenty." (Alciati (1550) 1996; Alciati 2004). All are intellectualizing, textually dependent, and schematic. Aliciati articulates peace and its effects not through narrative but through the juxtaposition of static icons including an elephant, a helmet, and a kingfisher. Predictably, these emblems lack any trace of the emotive (and motive) qualities that made a composition like Leonardo da Vinci's equestrian clash at Anghiari (begun 1503) compelling for generations of artists and scholars alike.

This selective preference for the bellicose and gory is hardly an invention of modern scholarship. Rather, artists and patrons alike found themselves drawn to dramatic vignettes of warfare, whether in the service of local patriotism, as with Michelangelo and Leonardo's lost competing battles of Cascina and Anghiari (1503–5) or on the grander scale of Mediterranean political strife, such as the pitched naval engagement of Veronese's *Allegory of the Battle of Lepanto* (1572) (Cole 2015). So too, panoramic, martial landscapes like Albrecht Altdorfer's *Battle of Isus* (1528) allowed rulers like his patron Duke Wilhelm IV to visualize their own—and their illustrious predecessors'—strategic and active role in world events and to draw parallels between their martial exploits and those of an illustrious, classical past (Wood 1993). The study of artistic patronage is, to an extraordinary degree, the study of the vicarious exercise of power. So natural is the connection that one of the most popular textbooks on Renaissance art within university curricula bears the title *Art, Power, and Patronage* (Paoletti and Radke 2005). Yet it was not just the powerful who profited from and perpetuated this bellicose imaginary, especially within an Italianate tradition that came to exert tremendous influence over European artists generally. Paintings, sculptures, and all variety of the representational arts were often judged on their success (or failure) at meeting the challenges of showing the heroic body in dramatic motion (Alpers 1983). Facility with representing the body as initiator and recipient of violent action would remain the stock in trade of many artists through the early nineteenth century.

This volume, like many others, begins with the peace of Lodi (1454) which ushered in four decades of relative stability on the previously tumultuous Italian peninsula, and encompasses the turmoil of the Reformation and its varied responses. Most obviously, it includes the unprecedented threat to European unity presented by the wars of religion. It is bookended by the treaty of Westphalia (Münster) (1648) and with it the end to both the Eighty Years War between Spain and the Netherlands and the Thirty Years War in German territories. Nonetheless, my chapter follows this chronology only approximately and makes no attempt to provide a comprehensive consideration of the political ups and downs of these two hundred years. While the undeniable importance of such events have rightly shaped diplomatic and military history, their impact upon and relationship with visual and material culture was always and ever mediated and unpredictable. Neither do I stake any claim for the special coherence of these centuries beyond certain shared features of the pre-modern European and Mediterranean worlds. Likewise, my definition of peace and of pacific culture will prove unsatisfying for the philologist or the historian of philosophy. Competing terminology and literary models, including distinctions between *pax* and *concordia* are not discussed here (Borghesi 2012; Campbell 2008, 97–120). Instead, this chapter takes a broad look at activities and their material culture which sought the restraint and cessation of violence, hostility, warfare, and strife.

Some of the works considered require little justification. Gerard ter Borch's ambitious group portrait of the dignitaries responsible for the treaty of Münster is self-evidently pertinent to the theme and dramatic allegories like *The Return from War* (*c*. 1610–12) of Rubens and Jan Brueghel the elder directly confront the challenges of representing peace. Yet if it is tempting to provide an iconographical survey, this would be both necessarily massive and, more importantly, exclude a corpus of images and objects that both thematized peace and played active roles in its achievement and maintenance. For the history of peace is not only a history of emblems and allegories, but also one of a robust material culture. What follows, then, is not an attempt to trace a comprehensive iconography of peace. Instead, I will focus on a few case studies among a diverse body of visual and material

FIGURE 5.1: Gerard ter Borch, *The Ratification of the Treaty of Münster*, oil on copper (1648), Amsterdam, Rijksmuseum. Courtesy of the Rijksmuseum.

culture which shed light upon long-standing attitudes, to ask not only how peace was pictured, but also what role "things" played in shaping these concepts and practices.

One such object hiding in plain sight is a Florentine bronze candelabrum today in the collection of the Rijksmuseum. Candelabra served as fixed furnishings in domestic, ecclesiastic, and governmental interiors and were also carried in processions and parades throughout the period. Bronze casting was a highly specialized and costly artisanal activity; this example was produced by one of the most important workshops in Florence, that of Andrea del Verrocchio. Over one and a half meters tall, Verrocchio's all'antica candlestick is an imposing object for public display. On the sides of its triangular base are the words *MAGGIO* (May), *GIUGNO* (June) and the year 1468, in elegant, raised block capitals. As Andrew Butterfield has convincingly demonstrated, these inscriptions refer to the *Pace Paolina* (Butterfield 1996; Butterfield 1997: 81). Concluded on May 18, 1468 the agreement, named for the intercessory role played by Pope Paul II, ended the so-called Colleoni War. The conflict had seen anti-Medicean exiles enlist the services of condottiere Bartolomeo Colleoni to harry the Florentine republic, ultimately pitting that city and its allies Milan and Naples against Venice and threatening peninsular stability. The peace was an uneasy one, representing a military stalemate that could hardly be claimed as an unequivocal victory for Florence. Nonetheless, it ensured Medici hegemony and that the basic structure set in place by the peace of Lodi would continue to hold (Belotti 1933: 310–20).

FIGURE 5.2: Andrea del Verrocchio, Candelabrum, bronze (1468–9), Amsterdam, Rijksmuseum. Courtesy of the Rijksmuseum.

Though isolated today in the museum's collection, Verrocchio and his patrons—the Florentine Signoria—would not have expected his candelabrum to stand on its own. Rather, it represented one component of a rich festive culture that comprised processions, jousts, orations, and that generated an array of commemorative and spectacular objects to help mark diplomatic occasions. While some of these were ephemeral, including banners, temporary triumphal arches, fireworks displays, and elaborate culinary monuments, others, like this bronze, served as lasting reminders (Reed (ed.) 2015). Like all of the objects considered here, this monument to peace was motivated, in part, by personal interests. These included, of course, Verrocchio's own economic investment and the Signoria's desire to put the best possible face on the treaty. Equally, however, it served to punctuate the personal pride of the government's elected leader, the gonfaloniere Carlo di Nicola di Messer Vieri de' Medici, for securing peace during his tenure. Officers like Carlo were selected for what seem, by modern bureaucratic standards, exceedingly short terms of two months. The gonfaloniere may have played only a minor role in the lengthy negotiations that culminated in the peace, but as the records of both Verrocchio's shop and the Signoria demonstrate, Carlo took significant personal interest in the candelabrum (Butterfield 1997: 81, 212–13). Peacemaking was hardly the exclusive province of states but rather provided an opportunity for individual commemoration and self-fashioning.

Harmony between citizens and states (and for that matter between men), however, was neither the only, nor even the most fundamental conception of peace in many fifteenth- and sixteenth-century minds. Instead, it was the peace of God—Christendom's aspirational state of accord between humanity and the divine—which weighed most heavily on the hearts and minds of Renaissance women and men. And like earthly peace, this too frequently acquired material form.

GOD'S PEACE

The admonition to share God's peace with one's neighbor was familiar to every Western European Christian in the language and ritual of the mass. Within the liturgy, this took the performative expression of the kiss and embrace—the *osculum pacis*—initiated by the priest, and shared between congregants (along same-sex lines). Such gestures served as bodily extensions of God's peace. It comes as little surprise, then, that these most visible and physical signs appear with some frequency in the arts and form a distinctive iconographic tradition. In 1431, the monastic painter Fra Angelico (Giovanni da Fiesole) painted his *Last Judgement* for the Florentine chapter of the Camaldolese order to display in the church of Santa Maria degli Angeli (Hood 1993; Cohl Ahl 2008: 165–71). The center of the panel is dominated by a row of empty tombs, their stone lids cast aside by former inhabitants. To the immediate left, the righteous among the newly resurrected appear with their bodies gloriously restored. The blessed are warmly embraced by waiting angels, an unmistakable echo of the liturgy's peace offering, before being ushered into a paradisiacal garden. Joined hand-in-hand with their angelic counterparts, they dance in a circle, the rhythmic alternation of bodies serving as a poignant reminder that love for fellow men and women was an extension of God's love. Equally, the painter's choice of dance as an external

FIGURE 5.3: Fra Angelico (Giovanni da Fiesole), *Last Judgement*, tempera on panel (1431), Florence, Museo di San Marco. Wikimedia Commons.

expression of peace touches on the recurring motif of musical harmony—the balance of concord and discord—as a powerful cultural model for pacific relationships (Gilbert 2003: 46–7).

Peace, in Fra Angelico's picture, is a distinctly positive concept. It is not merely a cessation of hostility but an activity in the making, visualized through dance, embrace, and kiss. Yet, like so many other visualizations of peace, it equally plays upon negative characterizations through the unmistakable counterpoint of the damned at the right side of the painting. Here, in the characteristically spectacular style of the period, those who have rejected divine authority suffer the violent retributions consequent to the absence of peace. These vignettes reinforce a conviction that—despite liturgical practice—peace was only truly obtained beyond this post-lapsarian world, when creation was restored to its pristine and finally incorruptible state. Far from confined to Fra Angelico's Tuscan milieu, this basic iconography found fertile ground across Europe. The Antwerp painter Bartholomeus Spranger adapted the composition for his own beatific dance around 1570 (Cohl Ahl 2008: 167). It was also the familiarity of these bodily manifestations of God's peace that so effectively drove home the ironic parody of images of the kiss of death. In a tradition stretching from Giotto's prototype at the Scrovegni chapel (*c.* 1310) to Caravaggio's *Arrest of Christ* (1602), Judas' betrayal appeared as a forceful travesty of such liturgical affection, proffering the violence of the Passion with the outward signs of peace (Fried 2010: 287; Mormando 1999).

Though representations of these gestures were ubiquitous throughout Catholic Europe, they were not the principal embodiment of the invocation of peace. Thanks in part to changes within liturgical practices—including concerns about the regulation of intimate same-sex contact—a material intermediary for the kiss was developed. Increasingly, decorated plaques known as paxes were employed to convey the *osculum pacis* from the officiant to his congregation. Having kissed the altar (itself a stand in for Christ) the priest then kissed the pax which was carried to the congregation by a co-congregant. While these paxes originated in England, and are mentioned in church records there by the thirteenth century, their use spread rapidly throughout Western Europe. By the fifteenth century, a great many churches had at least one—and some quite a few (Duffy 1996: 388–90). Their ubiquity suggests both the importance of the pacific rite and the ways in which it evolved to meet changing needs of the faithful (Duffy 1996; Harvey 2005).

Most paxes were probably quite ordinary, fashioned from wood and painted with simple images. Predictably, like so many objects of daily use, the bulk of these quotidian paxes are no longer extant. By the mid-fifteenth century, however, a tradition of materially precious examples had developed, and some of these objects ranked among of the most valued possessions in church treasuries. In the Italian city-states of the late fifteenth and early sixteenth century, including Florence, Rome, and Bologna, metal plaques were the preferred form (Walker 1991; Palmer 2001). While some were made from cast bronze (often enhanced with gilt), many employed the distinctive technique of niello upon silver, in which lines engraved into a polished silver plaque were subsequently inlaid with a black mixture of copper, sulfur, and lead to create intricate motifs. Like an example today in the Walters Art Museum, these little plaques appear unassuming today. They are often tucked away with other decorative arts and are difficult to display since they are usually best seen in raking light. Surely too, many precious examples have not survived, for though silver was more durable than many other materials, it was also a target for reuse when times were tough or when fashions changed, a liability shared by metalwork in general (Wright 2005: 27–9). No fixed iconography was adopted for the pax, and surviving examples

FIGURE 5.4: Unknown Florentine smith, *Pax with the Dormition and Assumption of the Virgin,* silver, niello, gilded copper, and enamel (*c.* 1440–1500), Baltimore, Walters Art Museum. Wikimedia Commons.

include the Virgin and Child enthroned, the Baptism of Christ, episodes from the Passion, and—like the Walters' example—scenes from the life of the Virgin.[1] The majority of these plaques, however, were emblazoned with the less than pacific image of the crucifixion, often accompanied with St. John and the Virgin. Paxes served as a substitute for the altar (itself a substitute for Christ) and thus as visual reminders that peace was attained only on account of violent, atoning sacrifice.

From Paris to Rome to Nuremberg, the goldsmiths who produced these objects were positioned at the top of Europe's artisanal hierarchy. Consigned the most precious of materials by their patrons, the trustworthiness of a goldsmith was of paramount importance and they enjoyed especially public profiles in comparison to many other medieval and Renaissance craftsmen (Lightbown 1978; Stuard 2006; Smith, 2007). The highly visible role of paxes through their display to congregants meant that at least some goldsmiths were able to build their reputation almost exclusively on these objects. Benvenuto Cellini reported that the quasi-legendary smith and "maestro di disegno" Maso Finiguerra "pursued only the art of engraving niello, in which he had no rival" (Cellini, *Treatises*, 1898: 2) (Roberts 2014). Of course, niello was used to decorate a variety of metalwork, both secular and liturgical. But Cellini, himself a goldsmith, singled out one of Maso's paxes—produced for Florence's baptistery of San Giovanni—as the masterwork by which he was known some fifty years later. Cellini described a Crucifixion with the two thieves "and with many ornaments including horses and other things," which does not seem to have survived (Cellini, *Treatises*, 1898: 2) (Hind 1938: 3–8). An example depicting the *Coronation of the Virgin*, today in the Bargello, is almost certainly by Maso's hand. Only 20 centimeters in height, the silver plate is astonishingly intricate, convincing and subtle in its modeling, and rivals, even at this scale, the magnificent altarpieces of its day (Gregory 2012: 10). Their diminutive size might appear to make paxes an unlikely venue for artistic fame. In fact, the intimacy entailed by kissing these plates guaranteed that the faithful would have gotten a close look—much closer, indeed, than that afforded to today's museum goers who peer through Plexiglass vitrines (Randolph 2014: 217).

As these liturgical objects suggest, peace, for many medieval and early modern Christians was not only (or even principally) the absence of war but rather proximity to God. In contrast, alienation and estrangement from God were often understood as root causes of interpersonal and interstate violence and seen as the consequence of sin. War, even, could be seen as an epiphenomenon of the primary strife between humanity's disobedience and divine love. The extent to which this estrangement represented an omnipresent threat to peace is evident in the common attitude that the Ottoman conquests of the period must be one of its products. Preachers and laymen alike blamed a lack of Christian unity not practically but spiritually for such calamities as the conquest of Constantinople (1453), the sack of Otranto (1480), the Hospitaller's loss of Rhodes (1521), and the siege of Vienna (1529). The truly pragmatic (Machiavelli among them) certainly expressed skepticism. That the "Turkish menace" was recognized as a potential source of opportunistic exaggerations is clear from his *Mandragola* (published 1524). In the play's third act, a woman confessing to her priest asks in fright "Do you think that the Turks will invade Italy this year?" Her confessor sarcastically replies "Certainly, if you don't pray." (Machiavelli, *The Mandrake*, 1954: 67). Such impiety, however, was hardly the order of the day.

External threats to peace within Christendom were but one side of a coin whose reverse was emblazoned with an increasingly contentious confessional environment. While there were many, like Erasmus, who persisted in arguments for a Christian peace, the thin fiction of such unity was felled by the realities of Protestantism and sectarianism, the violent forces of iconoclasm, Tridentine reforms (including the now legendary abuses of the Inquisition), and the devastating wars of religion. So, too, moving beyond the aspirational realm of Christendom, the two centuries under consideration here were characterized by violence on an unprecedented scale directed toward Christianity's others. The expulsion of the Jewish populations of Spain and England and the culmination of the so-called *Reconquista* were, to a large degree, continuations of centuries-long attitudes and policies. Likewise, the brutal persecution of Jews in the German-speaking lands and Northern Italy, which generated a thriving visual culture of antisemitism encapsulated in the pan-European demand for prints of the supposed infant martyr Simon of Trent was, in many ways, par for the course (Hsia 1996; Katz 2008: 119–57; Kohl

2018). The same can be said for the savage conquest of the Americas. The abuses of colonial expansion, of course, were sometimes bent to sectarian ends, most notoriously in constructing the anti-Spanish "Black Legend." Their violence and even cruelty, however, are undeniable (Greer, Mignolo, and Quilligan (eds.) 2008). Yet if illustrations of such atrocities accompanying publications like those of Bartolomeo de las Casas stretched its credibility, notions of Christian peace remained extremely resilient as a cultural form in part because lapsarian thought predicted its own imperfection, unevenness, and disappointment.

GIFTS OF PEACE

Peace may have flowed from heaven but it required terrestrial means to achieve its ends. And while waging peace was not nearly as suited to the brushes of narrative painters as its bellicose alternative, it nonetheless made use of a vibrant material culture. Gifts, especially, played a pivotal role in maintaining and initiating interpersonal and interstate relationships, commemorating auspicious events, and smoothing over potential conflict. One occasion that demanded such material exchanges as signs of peace were weddings. Elite marriages, of course, often had the practical aim of uniting dynastic rivals and forging alliances between potentially hostile clans and factions. Nearly universally, these unions were hoped to have lasting, multi-generational consequences and their success or failure were understood to stem from God's love. Epithalamic objects thus provide another powerful material sign of the relationship between earthly and divine peace. To be sure, such gifts functioned on multiple registers; they competitively denoted wealth, projected status, and proffered moralizing (and frequently misogynist) instruction to newlyweds (D'Elia 2005; Baskins et al. 2008; Musacchio 2009).

One such gift was a manuscript produced for the 1518 wedding of Lorenzo II de'Medici and Madeleine de la Tour d'Auvergne (Shephard 2010; Lowinsky (ed.) 1968 vol. 1). Known as the *Medici Codex*, the book collects fifty-three motets by a veritable who's who of the period's most significant composers, particularly those associated with the court of Francis I. The product of Roman illuminators and scribes of the highest caliber, the codex is among the most lavishly illuminated music manuscripts of the Renaissance. Despite the prevalence of printed books by the second decade of the sixteenth century, manuscripts remained the overwhelming choice when it came to high profile gifts.[2] Music, of course, was a fitting choice for a wedding gift, connecting, as in Fra Angelico's paradise, sonic and kinetic harmony with union. Foremost among the wishes expressed within the collected compositions was that peace would prevail between the princes of Europe and, crucially, that such earthly peace anticipated God's peace in the world to come. Thus, a motet by the French composer Jean Mouton declared that "The glorious princes of the earth, as they loved each other in life, thus also in death they are not separated." The security of Lorenzo's domain in Urbino was likewise to be safeguarded by God who "strengthened the bolts of [his] gates" and "placed peace at [your] borders" (Shepard 2010: 111). The material history of peace is, in part, one of objects which both attempt to effect alliances in real terms while necessarily—and not, in all cases anyway, insincerely—attributing successful unification to God's love. This close link between divine and marital peace was emphasized not only by musical manuscripts but even more directly by the use of paxes as gifts for elite marriages, suggesting that their pacific meanings extended beyond the confines of the liturgy. The wedding of Giovanni Sforza, lord of Pesaro and Lucrezia Borgia in 1493, for example, saw the couple presented with a silver pax. The subject of the now-lost plaque is not recorded, but it was produced by the Bolognese smith and painter Francesco Raibolini (known as Francia) and was surely a splendid object (Williamson 1901: 10; Negro and Roio 1998: 113). Likewise, the arms of the Neroni and Pandolfini families emblazoned on the pax illustrated here (see figure 5.4 above) indicate that it too was intended to commemorate such a union.

Wedding gifts were but one category of objects which commemorated alliances. Undoubtedly the most significant category of gifts intended to represent and foster peace were those of a diplomatic sort. Precious and skillfully-wrought objects commemorated treaties and truces, served as tribute and bribes, and projected impressions of status, wealth, and allegiance. A carefully considered gift could be just what was needed to initiate favorable relations between previously isolated states and their rulers. Gifts also helped to smooth over crises and signaled good faith during the course of negotiations (McCall and Roberts 2017). So too, the material culture of diplomacy extended beyond gifts to embrace a host of objects essential to peace processes. Treaties, for example, were frequently transported and displayed within elaborate caskets, a practice widespread in Christian and Islamic lands alike (Soucek 1997: 411). Precious containers served exactly this purpose at Münster and are carefully described in ter Borch's visual record of the proceedings (see figure 5.1 above). An especially fine Spanish chest with silver inlay appears on the central table, a gathering of sealed documents placed suggestively at its side (McNeil Kettering 1998: 16–17).

This diplomatic culture hardly ended at the boundaries of Europe but extended across the Mediterranean and, by the end of our period, around the globe. Beginning in the later fifteenth century, and intensifying over the next hundred years, one principle target for gifts of peace was the powerful Ottoman state. The two centuries following Mehmed II's conquest of Constantinople (1453) saw a Mediterranean world in which even periods of relative peace were disrupted by skirmishes, trade disputes, and piracy, and in which outright war frequently loomed (Goffman 2002: 137–51). Scholars have often recounted the history of these hostilities and indeed of their visual representation. Throughout Western Europe, resurgent enthusiasm for holy war drew on humanist and chivalric ideals alike (Bisaha 2006; Meserve 2008). Despite common misconceptions, Renaissance zeal for classical revival hardly dampened the embrace of chivalry and noble masculinity across the continent (Sandberg 2010).

Yet if holy war possessed a certain glamor for Europe's elite, it found itself relegated increasingly to the realm of fantasy and even play. In 1637, Grand Duke Ferdinando II de'Medici wed Vittoria della Rovere, uniting two of the Italian peninsula's most powerful families. A printed quarto description of the festivities produced in the same year (*Descrizione delle feste fatte in Firenze per le reali nozze de serenissimi sposi Ferdinando II Gran Duc di Toscana e Vittoria Principessa d'Urbino* 1637) helps us to get some sense of the symbolic resonance of the occasion. The centerpiece of the event was an equestrian ballet, choreographed by Agnolo Ricci based on episodes in Tasso's *Gerusalemme Liberata* (Strong 1984: 57–8). This built upon a long Florentine tradition of festive, mock battle that pit Tuscan crusaders against "Saracens." Dozens of horses and their riders played out the ill-fated romance between Rinaldo and the Saracen enchantress, Armida. Tasso had toyed with several resolutions to the tale but settled on Armida's eventual salvation through conversion to Christianity (Cavallo 2004). It was this "happy ending," suited to the instructive tone typical of marital fables that greeted the ducal wedding's guests.

Armed conflict was undeniably costly—even ruinously so for those like the Venetian state and Dutch East India Company with vested interests in commerce. It is impossible to comprehensively assess the sincerity of would-be crusaders, but there is little question that de-facto peace was almost universally preferable for state-level actors. The collapse, for example, of Pope Pius II's ill-fated crusade upon his death in 1464 was a relief to many princes who had found themselves duty-bound to commit their assistance (Bisaha 2004). Moreover, the fifteenth and sixteenth centuries are replete with examples of European potentates and pretenders who sought amicable relationships with their Ottoman counterparts, from petty warlords like Sigismondo Malatesta of Rimini to the French kings (McCall and Roberts 2017; Heath 1989). Further, a desire to compete with the evident wealth and splendor of the sultans fostered a trans-imperial material culture comprising, among much else, tapestries, medals, portraits, and costume (Brotton and Jardine 2005). On some occasions it was not only their wares but artists themselves who accompanied embassies (Campbell and Chong (eds.) 2005; Roberts 2016).

Historical focus on the pacific aims of these diplomatic objects is hardly uncontroversial. In the first place, the presumed unity of Christendom (at least in the face of Ottoman threat) long lead scholars to characterize such overtures as "treacherous" and "unholy." To be sure, these characterizations find significant reinforcement in period polemic leveled against Christian princes who sought friendly relations with their Muslim peers. Yet would-be peacemakers (and simply the self-interested) had a host of strategies at their disposal for defusing these charges. Most significantly, as the increasingly dubious fiction of unity lost its purchase on European rulers, strategic engagement with the "infidel" was sometimes less charged than exchanges across Christian confessional lines. Elizabethan hostility toward Catholic princes fostered (and at times was seen to justify) productive exchanges between the queen and both the Safavids and Ottomans. In 1599, Elizabeth dispatched an embassy to Constantinople bringing, among other goods, a coach for the sultana and an elaborate clockwork organ, along with its maker Thomas Dallam (Jardine 2004). Both played upon the status of new technologies as expected tokens exchanged between rulers. The organ, however, is most significant in this discussion. As with books of music, instruments too were seen as appropriately pacific gifts, trading on harmony's unification of concord and discord. Elizabeth's gift of music helped to secure and commemorate over two decades of favorable relations between her government and that of Murad III.

Islamic conceptions of dividing the world—and their consequent justifications for hostilities—have also been cited with some frequency as impediments to peaceful interchange. One need only consult any standard treatment of the Mediterranean political and confessional environment to encounter the Ottoman adoption of the longstanding schema of the dar ül-İslam (domain of Islam) and dar ül-harb (domain of war) (Kafadar 1996; Goffman 2002). In principle, these boundaries mitigated against lasting peace with Christians, since only temporary (and theoretically abnormal) truces were recognized between these realms. In practice, pacific coexistence on the borderlands sometimes extended for generations, while strife within the Islamic lands meant that war between Muslim rulers was routine (Brummett 2015: 79–80). The Ottoman invasion and conquest of the Mamluk Sultanate (1516–17) effectively exposed one such rift, since even the modest justification of apostasy usually issued to justify Ottoman hostility to Shia rivals could not be applied to these Sunni former allies (Brummett 1994).

For example, the Mamluk sultan Sayf ad-Din Inal sent an embassy on November 22, 1453 to congratulate Ottoman sultan Mehmed II on his conquest of Constantinople. His envoys bore a host of precious gifts comprising gold-embroidered silk, various textiles of Alexandrian origin, and dozens of ceremonial weapons. Gifts like these helped to vouch-safe the uneasy alliance between these allies and rivals, while enforcing a long-standing hierarchy through a display of splendor and power (Muhanna 2010; Behrens-Abouseif 2014). Later giving among the Ottomans, Mughals, and Safavids, too had pacifying intentions which were not openly avowed since they were officially unnecessary within the Dar al-Islam (Komaroff (ed.) 2011). Conversely, gifts flowed into and issued from the so-called Domain of War, in the face of official censure. As Jessica Keating has shown, technologically novel clock-work automata from the Hapsburg lands made their way as far east as the Mughal capital of emperor Jahangir (1569–1647) (Keating 2015; and Keating 2018). Such "re-gifting" spread the material culture of peacemaking far beyond its intended milieu. The history of peace and its material culture were complex and variegated in an early modern world that was hardly as neatly divided as juridical and theological precepts supposed.

Making and maintaining peace produced a rich material culture, but it also fostered a pictorial tradition representing diplomacy and its agents. High profile embassies and negotiations—like the Dutch Trade embassy to Isfahan (1651-2)—found themselves as the subjects of visual commemoration. In a monumental canvas by Jan Weenix, the Dutch envoy Johannes Cunaeus and his entourage appear on horseback against the backdrop of a seascape and port town, probably the port city of Bandar Abbas. The painter's setting is a surprisingly generic one, obscuring the subject of the canvas for many later viewers. Rather, it is the material culture of diplomacy that dominates Weenix's account of this mission to rekindle economic cooperation between the VOC and the Safavids. Cunaeus, seated upon a gray horse, dons a splendid golden cloak. In addition to providing the painter with an opportunity to show off his virtuoso depiction of reflective textile surfaces, Erland de Groot has demonstrated that this detail is a reference to a ceremonial robe, or *khilat*, given to the envoy by the governor of Bandar Abbas, an important way station on the journey (de Groot 2009). Undoubtedly, this token represented a cherished souvenir for Cunaeus. Like the candelabrum commissioned by

FIGURE 5.5: Jan Baptist Weenix, *The Dutch Ambassador on his Way to Isfahan*, oil on canvas (1653–9), Amsterdam, Rijksmuseum. Courtesy of the Rijksmuseum.

Carlo de'Medici and the Signoria, Weenix's painting serves as a reminder that not only states but individuals had a vested interest in the representation of treaties, diplomacy, and peace.

Images of diplomacy and of the precious material culture it generated came increasingly to inform broader European pictorial traditions, especially those of the Netherlands and Flanders which placed exceptional value on descriptive naturalism. Rubens' compelling drawing in black and red chalk of a man in Korean garb was based upon a costume he had seen in Antwerp. Almost certainly, the artist had observed the robe and hat worn by a Jesuit but acquired at the Chinese court, where Korean diplomats were a regular feature, visiting several times each year. While the drawing itself likely had little circulation beyond the master's workshop and immediate circle, the distinctively clothed figure found himself reimagined and integrated into the crowd flocking around the saint in Goa in the artist's *Miracles of Saint Francis Xavier* for the Jesuits of Antwerp (1617) (Schrader (ed.) 2013). Here, the discrete details of early modern diplomatic culture are re-conceived as signifiers of the universality of the Catholic faith, diverse components of an ideal (and obviously fictive) harmony generated by the efforts of the Jesuit missions.

PEACE EMBODIED

Allegory was a fundamental medieval and early modern means not only of representing the world, but of making sense of and navigating that world (Baskins and Rosenthal (eds.) 2007). Basic divisions, whether conceptual like that between Ecclesia and Synagoga, or spatial, such as those of the continents, took human form whether on the walls of churches and palaces or within the pages of manuscripts and printed books. It would, in short, be hard to overstate the prevalence of allegory. Peace, like so many other intangible concepts, often depended on this mode to take visual form. From the beginning of our period, peace was most frequently and recognizably personified not in a single figure but through the appeal and influence of the goddess of love, Venus on her bellicose consort Mars. Indeed, by the later fifteenth century, the union of these Roman deities presented itself as a favorite theme for artists and their patrons. Representative of this paradigm is Andrea Mantegna's *Mars and Venus* (1497) for Isabella d'Este's studiolo at Mantua where the god and goddess hold court atop Mount Parnassus. At least initially the adulterous pair were understood as complimentary forces whose union did not represent a utopian (or apocalyptic) absence of war, nor even necessarily a cessation of hostility, but the balance of Venusian concord and Martian discord. In Mantegna's vision that harmony is amplified by the music of Apollo, who sits at the extreme lower left playing a harp. As in Fra Angelico's heavenly garden, this harmony produces dance, embodied in the graceful and fluid rhythm of the Muses (Campbell 2004: 120–1).

Mars and Venus likewise served to emphasize peace as an alternative to the ravages of warfare in a period of increasingly undeniable hostility and overt sectarian and political strife. One such allegorizing response is *The Return from War* of Rubens and Jan Brueghel the elder (Woolett and van Suchtelen (eds.) 2006). Still arrayed in his battle gear, the god of war is transfixed by his amorous partner's gaze as the nude Venus gently lifts the helmet from his head. Putti tug at the laces of Mars' sandals and scabbard and scurry away with his shield, hoping to add these to the piles of discarded arms and armor that fill the cavernous forge that serves as the scene's backdrop. While this traditional motif provided viewers with an optimistic vision of conflict's end, it nonetheless presented such pacific ends as achievable only following the violence of warfare. The uneasy relationship

FIGURE 5.6: Peter Paul Rubens and Jan Brueghel the Elder, *The Return from War: Mars Disarmed by Venus,* oil on panel (*c.* 1610–12), Los Angeles, Getty Museum. Courtesy of the Getty Museum.

between the exercise of martial power and its supposed peaceful results were only too well understood by Rubens who was himself a diplomat and artist. He famously declared "I have never worked for war . . . but have always procured, to the extent that I could, peace everywhere" (Heinen 2004: 197).

Allegory, both literary and pictorial, sought to claim peace and prosperity as effects fostered by the reign of monarchs and princes, often through reference to Ovidian notions of a golden age. This program was adopted by Ferdinando II, for example, in Pietro da Cortona's magnificent frescoes for the Stanza della Stufa of Palazzo Pitti (Contini and Solinas 2010). Nor were these allusions limited to the traditional Greco-Roman deities and their myths. Early modern allegory was flexible enough to embrace novel inventions—like the emblems of Alciati—and often combined mythic and literary narratives with improvisation. When Rubens was called upon to provide massive ceiling canvases for the Banqueting Hall at London's Whitehall Palace between 1630 and 1636, the diplomat painter combined classical myth with allegorical invention to memorialize the reign of his patron Charles I and to cement the pacific achievements of his dynasty. At the southern end of the hall, and designed to frame Charles during state occasions, the monarch's father James I appears enthroned. To his right, Mars and Minerva jostle to counsel the king. At his left, figures of peace and plenty embrace one another, reminding guests below that the prudent exercise of military power was a precondition of such prosperity (Martin 2011: 139-47; Rosenthal 2006).

FIGURE 5.7: Agnolo Bronzino, *Portrait of Cosimo I as Orpheus*, oil on panel (1537–9), Philadelphia, Philadelphia Museum of Art. Courtesy of Philadelphia Museum of Art.

In some cases, the powerful employed allegories not just as attributes, but as integral components of their own identities. One novel example is provided by a portrait of Florentine Duke Cosimo I de' Medici painted by Agnolo Bronzino around the year of the duke's marriage to Eleonora of Toledo (1539). In this panel, today in Philadelphia, the duke appears in the heroic guise of Orpheus (Simon 1985; Baskins 1994; Strehlke 2004; Faliciani and Natali (eds.) 2010; Gàldy 2013: 35–8). Cosimo sits with his muscular back—based on that of the Belvedere fragment—turned three-quarters toward the picture plane as he cranes his neck to look back at the viewer. He holds a lyre in his hand as its soothing strings calm the beast Cerberus, whose canine heads emerge from the darkness of the middle ground. Bronzino's masterpiece is striking in its originality; the intimate encounter with the duke's uncharacteristically nude and athletic body and the casual interruption suggested by his reciprocal gaze are particularly arresting given Cosimo's usual preference for portraiture in armor (Pilliod 2001; Van Veen 2006). The clearly erotic appeal of the panel has suggested that it too might belong in the epithalamic genre, serving as a gift for the bride, though such a reading ignores the near ubiquity of Orpheus as an object of specifically male, same-sex desire in Renaissance Florence (Cox-Rearick 1993: 23–53).[3]

Orpheus surely ranks among the most polysemous of figures carried forward from the classical world. He appeared variously as musician, pining and grieving lover, magician, and was among the first to stand in for Jesus within early Christian art. Yet whatever other associations Bronzino and his patron might have intended, the portrait plays upon the resonance of Orpheus as peace-maker; a role the young duke was eager to step into, having assumed power over an unruly and deeply divided citizenry following the assassination of his putatively tyrannical predecessor Alessandro (Strehlke (ed.) 2004). The taming of Cerberus, necessary for the futile attempt to rescue Eurydice, is also a reminder of the legendarily soothing effect of the hero's music-making on nature as a whole, his power in Alessandro Striggio's lyric (1607) to "hold the beasts spellbound with song" (Carter 2002). Likewise, the lyre itself was so closely connected with peacemaking that it appeared as an emblem in the ancient *Hieroglyphica* of the so-called Horapollo (Langedijk 1976: 47). The duke employed this image of Orpheus as harmonious bringer of peace elsewhere too; a menagerie of carved stone animals within the grotto at the Medici Villa of Castello was intended as a kind of pacified audience for the Orphic figure of the duke (Lausen-Higgins 2012).

Such grandiose language never completely lost its appeal, especially among the powerful. Yet if rulers like Cosimo and Charles—and artists like Bronzino and Rubens—clothed (or rather unclothed) peace in allegory, a more pragmatic mode was elsewhere taking hold. Detailed and emphatically naturalistic commemorations of peace came to intersect with traditions of representing diplomacy, like that of Weenix's *Embassy* (see figure 5.5). Perhaps the clearest indication of these changing winds is ter Borch's painting commemorating the treaty of Münster's ratification (see figure 5.1) (Kettering 1998; Israel 1997).[4] Following almost three years of negotiations that brought representatives from the entirety of both Catholic and Protestant Europe, the treaty was extraordinarily wide-ranging in its impact, ending a century of inter-state violence and laying the ground work for lasting coexistence (Bussmann and Schilling (eds.) 1999). Such an occasion was, of course, ideally suited to allegorical flights of fancy. Indeed, painters including Jacob Jordaens tried their hand at precisely that (Vander Auwera and Schaudies (eds.) 2013).[5] In contrast, ter Borch provided an earthbound, even prosaic record of the events.

Arrayed across the painting's surface are some seventy dignitaries packed into the cramped *ratskammer* of Münster's town hall for the formal ratification on May 15, 1648. Foremost among these are the Spanish and Netherlandish delegates who cluster around the central table, upon which copies of the agreement are displayed. Drawing on Dutch traditions of group portraiture, and including himself as a witness at the extreme left, ter Borch's painting seems, at first glance, to provide a record of this landmark event which matter-of-factly evacuates the mythic and theological underpinnings of previous pacific imagery. Made both as a commemorative monument and as a model for the commercially successful engraving of the subject by Jonas Suyderhoef (1649), this is a peace accomplished by earthly means to achieve earthly ends. Yet, as Alison Kettering suggests, ter Borch's peace is hardly less profound. On the contrary, through application of his consummate observational faculties, by drawing on the full power of Dutch art's veristic impulses, and by working on the mimetically responsive support of copper, the painter produced an unexpected and unprecedented document of "individual men bonded in idealized solidarity" (Kettering 1998: 46). The conviction that lasting peace might be achieved by human hands—literally here raised in the gesture of oath-taking—provides an apparently unspectacular, but hardly less remarkable, bookend for this study.

CHAPTER SIX

Peace Movements

DIEGO PIRILLO

In 1605, having returned home from his grand tour on the continent, the English gentleman Edwin Sandys published in London *A relation on the state of religion*, an overview of religious practices in Western Europe. The text enjoyed a wide circulation, reaching different corners of the Republic of Letters, from Italy to Switzerland and the Netherlands. It was translated into Italian, French, and Dutch, and was read by, among others, Paolo Sarpi and Hugo Grotius. By assessing "the state of religion," Sandys brought to light the thin line that on several matters separated Anglicans and Catholics, and pondered whether a reunion between England and Rome was still possible (Prosperi 2015). On the one hand, Sandys reflected upon the religious policy of James I who, having succeeded Elizabeth I to the English throne in 1603, had developed an ambitious ecumenical plan situating religious reconciliation at the heart of his domestic and foreign policy, best expressed by his motto, *beati pacifici* (blessed are the peacemakers) (Patterson 1997). On the other hand, Sandys bore direct witness to the fact that in continental Europe, despite the violence of the religious wars, irenic ideals were still alive in various countries:

> A kind of men there is whom a man shall meet withal in all Countries, not many in number, but sundry of them of singular Learning and Piety . . . [who] have entred into a meditation, whether it were not possible, that by the travel and meditation of some calmer minds, that at this day usually write, or deal on either side, these flames of controversies might be extinguished or asslaked, and some tolerable peace re-established in the Church againe. The earnestness of their vertuous desires to see it so, hath bred in them an opinion of possibility, that it might be wrought, considering first that besides infinitie other points not controversed, there is an agreement in the general foundation of Religion.
>
> —Sandys, *Relation*, 1673: 207–8

This famous passage of Sandys's *Relation* is a fundamental point of departure for the investigation of the peace movements that existed in Renaissance and early modern Europe. As Sandys pointed out, even in the seventeenth century the division of Christendom after the Reformation was not perceived by many as permanent, and irenical plans were still being considered in the effort to end the confessional strife and bring peace back to the continent. Despite the fact that Sandys was skeptical of the success of these peace plans, his *Relation* suggests a need to reconsider the history of sixteenth-century Europe and to focus not on its disunity and the outbreak of religious violence, but rather on the several attempts to restore peace and unity—even if these in the end

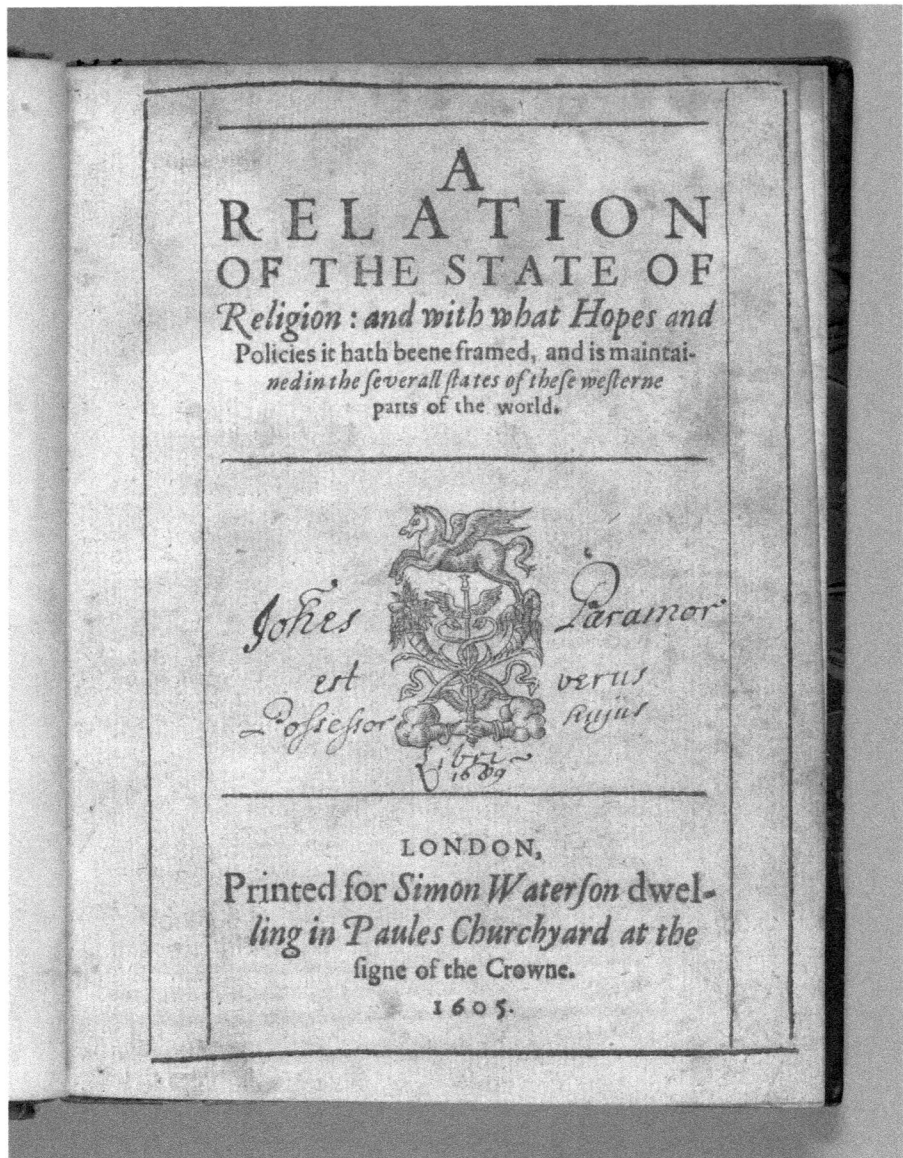

FIGURE 6.1: Edwin Sandys, *A Relation of the State of Religion*, London: Simon Waterson (1605): title page. Courtesy of the Bancroft Library, University of California, Berkeley.

remained "hopes which never materialised" (Yates 1988: 199). To be sure, early modern conciliation and irenicism have remained until recently a problematic area of research, one often bound up with the study of religious toleration (Louthan and Zachman 2004: 2). And yet, while the sixteenth and seventeenth centuries coincided with the eruption of the wars of religion, they also saw the rise of several pacifist sects and movements, from the Anabaptists to the Quakers.

FIGURE 6.2: Daniel Mytens, *King James I of England and VI of Scotland* (1621), oil on canvas, London, National Portrait Gallery.

In examining the different currents of Renaissance irenicism, this chapter will focus on three distinct peace movements that in the sixteenth century proposed different strategies to solve the confessional strife erupting with the Reformation. The first section of the chapter is dedicated to the *spirituali*, who in sixteenth-century Italy developed an ambitious plan of Church reform that, while accepting some elements of Protestant theology, did so without breaking off from the papacy. The irenical hopes of the *spirituali* will be reconstructed through the perspective of one of their most prominent members, the apostolic protonotary Pietro Carnesecchi (1508–67). In particular, this section will investigate the hopes for religious reconciliation raised by the council of Trent (1545–63), in the decades when the borders between confessional Churches were still fluid and the reunification of Christendom seemed within reach.

The second section is dedicated to the "Italian heretics," those Italian radical reformers who in the sixteenth century fled Counter-Reformation Italy, only to find themselves in conflict with the new orthodoxies no less than with the old. This emerges clearly in the itinerary of the Florentine heretic Francesco Pucci (1543–97), whose millenarian ideas led him to believe that, despite the failure of Trent, a new universal council would soon solve the religious disputes and create the conditions for peace among all faiths.

Finally, the third section concentrates on the rise of Erastianism, a movement inspired by the Swiss scholar Thomas Erastus (1524–83), who held that only the strengthening of secular powers could keep the religious strife under control. The rise of Erastianism will be considered through the writings of the prominent lawyer Alberico Gentili (1552–1608), an Italian Protestant exile in England, where he was regius professor of civil law at Oxford. It was there that he composed his masterpiece, the *De iure belli*, a fundamental work in the history of international law. Although their main preoccupation was always confessional Europe, all three movements discussed in the chapter regarded their actions as extending beyond European borders. Indeed, the peace plans they envisioned were never limited to Western Christendom, but also included non-Christian faiths, starting with Judaism and Islam, and even in some cases those religions that the Europeans were encountering in America and Asia in the age of the "first globalization."

IRENIC HOPES AT THE COUNCIL OF TRENT

On January 13, 1547, during its sixth session, the Council of Trent (1545–63) approved the decree on justification, which condemned Lutheran theology's assertion that man can be saved by faith alone. The council thereby contributed to the construction of clearer boundaries between orthodoxies. Indeed, according to its first historian, the Servite friar Paolo Sarpi (who famously labelled Trent the "Iliade of our age"), the decree, instead of reuniting the church, "established the Schisme, and made the parties so obstinate, that the discords are become irreconcilable" (Sarpi, *The historie of the Council of Trent,* 1620: 1).

And yet, such condemnations of Luther's doctrine of justification at Trent should not obscure the fact that in the sixteenth century the council was perceived by many not as the reckoning between Rome and Luther, but rather as a "great moment of hope" (Prosperi 2000: 74; Cantimori 1959, and 1960 (1992)). The call for the council with which Luther had reacted to his excommunication had echoed throughout Europe, where the memory of the councils of the fifteenth century, from Constance to Basel, nourished "the conciliarist tradition" (Oakley 2003). The hope that the council, as the supreme authority of the Church and thus superior to the pope, could bring peace back to Christianity after the divisions of the Reformation was not extinguished after the decree on justification, and not even after the end of the council itself. This is confirmed by the millenaristic expectations that the council provoked in sixteenth-century Italy, where many became convinced that the theological controversies were destined to end, thereby leaving space for the reconciliation of the Church and the unification of the world as "one flock" under "one shepherd" (*unum ovile et unus pastor*) (Jn 10:16).

The irenic hopes raised by the council animated the activities of the *spirituali*, a movement in sixteenth-century Italy that read and appropriated not only the texts by Martin Luther, Philip Melanchthon, and John Calvin, but above all those of the Spanish mystic Juan de Valdés (1500–41), who during his years in exile in Naples exerted a large influence first on the local aristocracy and later also on other groups of Italian society across the social spectrum (Firpo 2015: 135). Finding themselves incompatible with old and new orthodoxies alike, the *spirituali* "both absorbed and transcended the Protestant experience," accepting some Protestant doctrines, starting with the justification by faith

FIGURE 6.3: Paolo Sarpi, *Historiae Concili Tridentini libri octo*, Dordrecht: Paulus Vink (1658): frontispiece. Courtesy of the Bancroft Library, University of California, Berkeley.

alone, but never breaking away from Rome, and always holding on firmly to the idea of the unity of the church (Firpo 2015: 135). By the 1540s, the *spirituali*'s plan for Church reform had been presented in the *Beneficio di Cristo*, published in Venice in 1543 and then circulated in Trent (Firpo 1998: 119–45, Prosperi 2000: 72–101). Most importantly, until the mid-sixteenth century, the *spirituali* enjoyed the support of Charles V, who, before his abdication in 1556, was the real force behind the council. The Holy Roman Emperor—who in his instructions to Philip II prohibited the toleration of any heresy in his kingdom—was in fact the political point of reference for the leaders of the *spirituali*. These included cardinals Reginald Pole and Giovanni Morone, who in the 1550s began to face the first inquisitorial investigations (Firpo 2001).

The apostolic protonotary Pietro Carnesecchi had played a leading role in those events, maintaining close ties with both Valdés and Pole beginning in the 1530s, and becoming a prominent member of the circles of the *spirituali* in Naples, Viterbo, Florence, and Venice. In his lengthy inquisitorial trial, which began in 1546, reopened in 1557, and finally concluded with his execution in 1567, Carnesecchi explained that he had learned about the doctrine of justification by faith alone "in part through conversation with Valdés and in part through the reading of heretical books", but added that he accepted it only because he was convinced that "not only was it rooted in Holy Scripture but moreover corroborated and accepted by all the most important doctors of the church" (Firpo and Marcatto (eds.) 1998–2000 (cited hereafter as PC) II: 567). As Carnesecchi argued, until the council expressed itself on the matter, the doctrine of justification by faith alone was not considered heretical, and the clash between Rome and Luther seemed reconcilable (PC, II, 2: 568). The election of Paul IV in May 1555 had already placed the beliefs of the *spirituali* and their plan for religious reform under attack, as the new pope, departing from the conviction that only a "spiritual war" against the heretics could reform the Church, reinforced the Roman Inquisition (Prosperi 2009: 117–34). Among his most illustrious victims was Reginald Pole, "the poor cardinal from England," who died in London leading Mary Tudor's Catholic restoration while at the same time standing accused of heresy by the Roman Inquisition. Carnesecchi commented that Pole had died "a Lutheran in the opinion of Rome, and a papist in Germany" (PC, II, 2: 492).

In his bewildered state after Pole's death in 1558, Carnesecchi considered leaving Italy and following the example of those who had escaped to Protestant Europe to live according to their conscience. The debate over the legitimacy of flight had begun in 1542 in the wake of the escapes of Bernardino Ochino and Pietro Martire Vermigli, and it had continued over the following years as John Calvin published his writings against the Nicodemites, who, like the Pharisee Nicodemus in the Gospel of John, visited Christ secretly by night, conforming externally and hiding their true faith under the veil of simulation (Fragnito 1972 (2011)). Despite his close ties with the Italian Protestant community of Geneva, Carnesecchi ultimately decided to stay in Italy, a decision he made for several reasons. On the one hand, fleeing Italy would have meant recognizing the accusations of heresy launched by the inquisitors, thereby placing his patrons in difficulty. On the other hand, Carnesecchi's decision was also grounded in the millenaristic hope that the council would reunite the Church. Writing to Giulia Gonzaga, on October 7, 1559, Carnesecchi argued that, instead of fleeing to Protestant Europe, it was better to stay in Italy and wait for the end of the religious strife. As Carnesecchi explained to Gonzaga, the recent news that in Constantinople two Ottomans had converted to Christianity and preached "freely against the law of Muhammad," led him to believe that an angelic pope would soon arrive, and with him the conversion of the Muslims and the Jews, and the reunification of the whole world under one faith:

> When it pleases God to unite all of us as one flock under one shepherd, and it looks as if the time is growing near when He will do so, as many Jews have been enlightened, but they have not yet chosen to be baptized, because they prefer to wait until the controversies they see concerning the faith among us Christians have reached an end. Now we must wait to see what God will do, applying ourselves to praying to His Divine Majesty that he give us a pastor who is capable of gathering and uniting the poor lost sheep, of bringing in those who are still outside into the good pastures of salvation, and holding back those who have gone outside.
>
> —PC, II, 2: 715

Grounded in medieval apocalypticism, the myth of the angelic pope survived well into sixteenth-century Italy, when millenarian hopes often grew in the interregnum between the death of one pope and the election of the next (Prosperi 2001). In the last months of 1559, in the long conclave that followed the death of Paul IV in August of that year, Carnesecchi put his hopes in cardinal Giovanni Morone, who, after the death of Pole, had become the leader of the *spirituali*. In 1559, however, the conclave elected to the papacy cardinal Giovanni Angelo Medici (Pius IV) and not Morone, as Carnesecchi had hoped. The new pope was, however, well disposed toward Carnesecchi and in June 1561 absolved him. This outcome also depended on the protection Carnesecchi still enjoyed from his old patron, Cosimo de' Medici, to whom he immediately sent a copy of the sentence (PC, I: xcv). And yet, this was only a brief parenthesis. The death of Giulia Gonzaga in April 1566 put her rich correspondence with Carnesecchi in the hands of the inquisitors, who reopened the trial on the basis of new evidence. Neither Morone nor Cosimo de'Medici could protect Carnesecchi from the accusations of the Inquisition. In June 1566 he was sent to Rome, tried and executed the following year.

Carnesecchi's trial has been rightly considered "one of the most important—perhaps the richest and most stimulating—sources" for the study of the religious crisis of sixteenth-century Italy (Firpo 2005: 449). Indeed, his execution coincided with a crucial turning point in the history of early modern Italy and marked the last act of the "Roman Inquisition's grip on power" in the highest ranks of the church (Firpo 2014). On the other hand, Carnesecchi's trial constitutes an invaluable source for reconstructing not only what actually happened—the rise of the Inquisition and the Counter-Reformation—but also the hopes and expectations that the council raised in Italy in the mid-sixteenth century, when the boundaries between confessions were not yet clear cut and an agreement between Rome and the Protestant reformers seemed within reach.

IRENIC HOPES AFTER THE COUNCIL

The end of the Council of Trent in 1563 and the repression of religious dissent brought forth by the Inquisition did not completely dash the religious hopes embraced by Carnesecchi and the *spirituali*. Indeed, millenaristic expectations toward the reunification of Christianity survived in the circles of the radical reformers, who, unlike Carnesecchi, decided to flee Tridentine Italy and migrate to Protestant Europe. Often, however, they did not integrate with the new Protestant orthodoxies, continuing instead to believe that the religious strife could end and the unity of the church be preserved. In this respect the case of the reformer Francesco Pucci (1543–97) is emblematic, as his entire intellectual trajectory is marked by the expectation of a new general council able to reform Christianity and end the confessional controversy (Barnavi and Eliav-Feldon 1988; Carta 1999; Caravale 2015; Biagioni 2017). Indeed, Pucci has been considered "one of the last manifestations of the visionary and prophetic current which had a significant presence in Italian culture" until the end of the sixteenth century, while his belief in a possible peace between Rome and Protestant Europe indirectly recalled the hopes of the *spirituali* (Prosperi 2000: 371; Caravale 2015, 15).

Pucci grew up in a wealthy family in sixteenth-century Florence, where for some time Duke Cosimo I de'Medici's clash with the Papacy granted a certain degree of tolerance to the philo-Protestant circles (Firpo 1997). This Florentine education is crucial to understanding the nature of Pucci's religious views. As Pucci explained in a 1592 letter addressed to Pope Clement VIII, from his youth his interest in religious affairs led him to study not only the Bible but also "the writings of Savonarola . . ., the *Divine Comedy* of Dante, the most spiritual works of Petrarch," moved by his "desire to see Christianity reconciled, and suffering to see it in decline in Europe" (Francesco Pucci to Clement VIII, Amsterdam, August 5, 1592: Pucci 1955, I: 142). Dante, along with Girolamo Savonarola and Francesco Petrarca, deeply shaped Pucci's religious views. Indeed, Pucci referred to Dante in one of his first writings, the *Informatione della religione christiana*, published in London in 1579, in which he denounced the temporal claims of the Roman Church by citing the celebrated verses of *Purgatorio* 16 on the confusion between secular and spiritual power (Pucci, *Informatione* 1580 (1579), A1v; Biagioni 2011; Pirillo 2010, 57–75).

Along with his Florentine education, Pucci's religious views were marked by the experience of the St. Bartholomew's Day massacre, which he witnessed in Paris in 1572. This event led him to abandon the Catholic Church and to dedicate the rest of his life to convincing the European elite that the time had come to reunite Christianity thereby putting an end to the age of the wars of religion.

According to Pucci, a general council was the means by which Christianity would be reconciled. However, it had to be a free and universal council, unlike the Tridentine one

FIGURE 6.4: Francesco Pucci, *Informatione della religione christiana*. London: John Wolfe, 1580 (Florence, 1579): title page. Courtesy of the Zentralbibliothek Zurich.

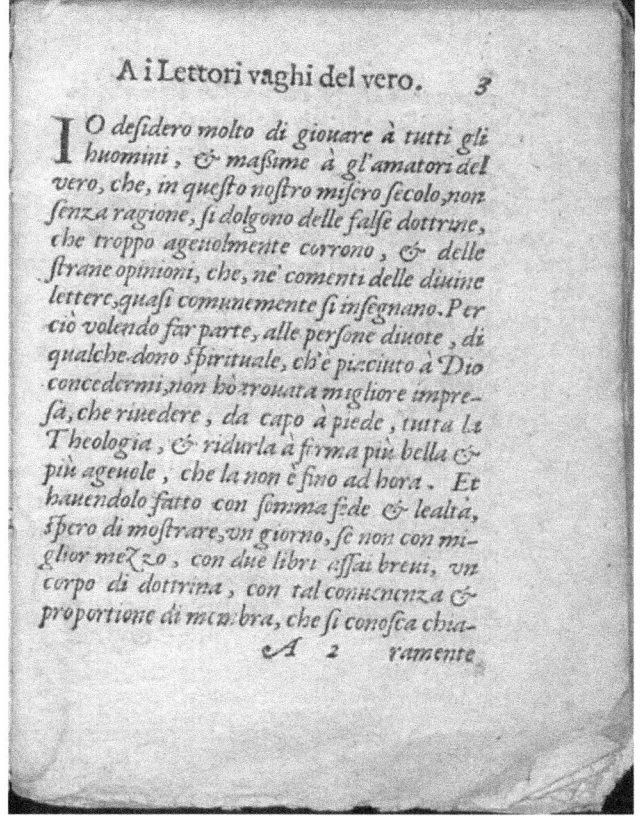

FIGURE 6.5: Francesco Pucci, *Informatione della religione christiana*. London: John Wolfe, 1580 (Florence, 1579): p. 2. Courtesy of the Zentralbibliothek Zurich.

that, according to Pucci, had not fulfilled the hopes that it had kindled because it was "general only in name, but in reality never sufficiently fair, free or spiritual" (Baldini 1999: 218). The future council would bring the church back to its origins, when the apostles themselves, despite holding the highest authority, used to defend the public good and make a decision only after having consulted the faithful (Pucci, *Informatione*, 1580 [1579]: 120–1). In the *Informatione della religione christiana*, Pucci outlined his conciliar project in precisely these strong republican tones, echoing Savonarola and Machiavelli on the virtues of the "multitude":

> And it is with such a majority and order of decision that one should reform the church, because there is no doubt that the judgment of the multitude is more correct and less corruptible than that of the few, when speaking of divine things and of the common good, and that it professes devotion and religion.
>
> —Pucci, *Informatione*, 1580 [1579]: 120–1

For Pucci, the council was not simply a way to heal the fractures that had arisen in Europe with the Protestant Reformation, but also a way to unify the world as "one flock" under "one shepherd" (*unum ovile et unus pastor*). While the focus was always confessional

Europe, the Florentine heretic regarded his peace plans as extending to the rest of the world too, from China to Ethiopia to South America. The religious peace Pucci dreamed of included not only Christians but also Jews and Muslims, "descendants of the holy father Abraham . . . and in agreement with we Christians in the profession of recognizing only one God," but also the Chinese, who "exceed we Christians greatly in their morality and political government," "the great empire of Ethiopia," and finally the American Indians, who inhabited "the unknown lands that are being discovered daily" (Baldini 1999: 185). Pucci's prophetic design was nourished on the one hand by the news of the new geographical horizons, and on the other by the shifting balance of power in Europe, where in the early 1590s an end to the religious wars seemed to be in sight. In fact, the political arm of this prophetic design was meant to be the king of France, Henry IV. In a letter sent in August 1591 to cardinal Paolo Camillo Sfondrati, Pucci described Henry IV as "a great king who has ardently turned his soul to religion and to the holy council," arguing that "it appears, beyond any doubt, that God intends to use him as His instrument in the forthcoming renewal of our age . . . in which an agreement will be reached between the circumcised and the baptized, in one flock and under one pastor" (Baldini 1999: 166).

What characterized Pucci's peace plans was an original mixture of utopianism and realism, of irenic prophetism and Machiavellian disenchantment. Indeed, in his most famous work, the *Forma d'una republica catolica*, drafted in London in 1581, Pucci outlined in every detail the structure of a secret society, 'a state within the state', whose members would have devoted their efforts to reform Christianity and achieve a universal peace among all faiths (Pucci, *Forma*, 1581 (1957)). The secret society was open to Christians of any church, as long as they were laymen who believed in an essential nucleus of doctrine. This was constituted by the Apostle's Creed, the Ten Commandments, the Pater Noster and in works of charity, which, according to Pucci were "accepted by all of Christianity, by the Greeks, by the Latins, and as much to the papists as to the Protestants, by the Armenians, the Syrians, the Ethiopians, the Indians and by every other type of Christian of which we are aware" (Pucci, *Forma*, 1957: 267) (Cantimori 1992: 380). Dispersed among different states, the members of the secret society were divided into different colleges and communicated with each other through epistolary correspondence in ciphers (Pucci, *Forma*, 1957: 275). Periodically, members of each college would meet in general diets, to be held either in a state whose prince was well disposed toward the society or in large centers of commerce, such as Frankfurt, Lyon, or Paris, where the members could avoid suspicion by disguising themselves as merchants (Pucci, *Forma*, 1957: 282–3). The idea of holding secret meetings of delegates in friendly territories suggests some similarities between the secret society envisioned by Pucci and the forms of organization used by the Italian Anabaptists, whose council secretly gathered in Venice in 1550 (Cantimori 1992: 385). There are, however, some important differences. Unlike the Anabaptists, Pucci did not deny the members of the secret society the right to participate in politics or to reject any form of oath requested by the authorities.

According to Pucci, the future council would have thus ended theological disputes and created religious peace among all the faiths. The problem, however, was deciding what to do in the meantime—in the interval between the present moment of confessional strife and the future fulfillment of the prophecy. Until that day should come, Pucci suggested hiding one's true religious beliefs under the veil of dissimulation and conforming externally to local laws. Thus, in Pucci it is possible to note the reemergence of the same connection between Nicodemism and conciliar hopes previously observed in the letters between Carnesecchi and Giulia Gonzaga. In the *Forma*, Pucci argued that it was necessary that the members of the secret society "behave very wisely and discreetly with the princes and magistrates of the places where they live, and that they understand under what circumstances must they adhere to our senate and people, and under what circumstances must they revere and honor the ordinary princes and magistrates" (Pucci, *Forma*, 1957: 270).

The secret society imagined by Pucci never became a reality. Disillusionment with Protestant orthodoxies led him to return to Catholicism and move back to Italy, where he was tried and executed on July 5, 1597. It is certain, however, that Pucci was not simply an isolated visionary, and his irenic ideals had a significant echo in early modern Europe. The most remarkable testimony is undoubtedly that of the Italian philosopher Tommaso Campanella, who after Pucci's execution wrote a sonnet remembering the discussions the two had had in the prison of the Roman Holy Office (Ernst 2005; Caravale 2011: 217–22). Like Pucci, Campanella also condemned the division of Europe into confessional Churches and opposed the new orthodoxies with "an ecumenical religion, indifferent to rites and ceremonies," founded on the theology of the universal salvation (Prosperi 2000: 380).

WAR, PEACE AND THE LAW OF NATIONS

While the cases of the *spirituali* and the Italian heretics indicate that hopes to restore peace and to unify the entire world under the same religion were still alive in the late sixteenth century, the same period also coincided with a split within Renaissance irenicism and with a growing division between the two currents that Guillaume H.M. Posthumus Meyjes labeled *irénisme utopique* and *irénisme étatique* (Meyjes 1997). The first current included those reformers who supported a spiritual and anti-institutional conception of Christianity and whose beliefs were grounded in a millenarian expectation of the unification of the world under "one flock and one shepherd." The second current refers instead to those reformers who, in the wake of the Swiss scholar Thomas Erastus, claimed the superiority of the State over the Church in ecclesiastical matters in the belief that only a strong secular government would be able to allow different faiths to coexist peacefully (Gunnoe, Jr. 2011). In the following pages the rise of Erastianism and the division between *irénisme utopique* and *irénisme étatique* will be examined through the works of the prominent Italian lawyer Alberico Gentili, regius professor of civil law at Oxford between 1587 and 1608 and author of the *De iure belli*, a summa of the entire humanist tradition on war and peace (Tuck 1999: 16; Panizza 1981; Kingsbury and Straumann (eds.) 2010; Minnucci 2016). Moving away from the millenaristic ideas of the *spirituali* and the Italian heretics, Gentili embraced a staunch Erastianism, for which the end of the religious wars could be reached only by reinforcing secular authorities. In the *De iure belli*, Gentili proposed a disenchanted vision of international politics in which a pre-emptive strike was always legitimate to defend the balance of power against an enemy that was poised to establish a universal monarchy.

Gentili was born in San Ginesio in the Papal States in 1552 and studied civil law at the University of Perugia. In 1579 his Protestant beliefs forced him to leave Italy and to resettle in England (Lavenia 2016). As he had briefly joined the Italian Protestant Church in London in 1580, torn at that moment between the radical and moderate wings, Gentili was presumably able to meet Francesco Pucci (Boersma and Jelsma (eds.) 1997: 170). Though specific references to Pucci are absent from Gentili's works, it would have been difficult for him to ignore the Florentine heretic, who in May 1581 convinced the ministers of the Italian Protestant Church to listen to his proposals and to open a public theological debate (Boersma and Jelsma (eds.) 1997: 59). Moreover, in the Italian community in London, conciliar hopes were widespread and were reinforced at the end of the century by the growing power of Henry of Navarre, the future King Henry IV of France. This is confirmed by the *Aviso piacevole dato alla bella Italia*, an Italian pamphlet, whose title page attributes the text to the French scholar François Perrot, the former secretary of the French ambassador Arnaud du Ferrier, but which was in fact published in 1586 in London in John Wolfe's print shop and edited by one of his many Italian collaborators (Balsamo 1998). Conceived as a rebuttal to Sixtus V's excommunication of Henry of Navarre, the *Aviso piacevole* included a long anthology of anticlerical passages taken from Dante, Boccaccio and Petrarch, and was intended to demonstrate that "the papal seat (that is, Rome) is the true Babylon" (*Aviso piacevole* 1586, 11r). In defending Henry of Navarre the *Aviso piacevole* also accused the pope of heresy, declaring that the French sovereign would soon prove this fact "in a free council, gathered legitimately, to which, if the pope does not participate and submit . . ., [the king] will hold him to be the Antichrist and will wage perpetual war against him" (*Aviso piacevole* 1586, 1r).

While there are no explicit references to Pucci in Gentili's works, his engagement with the ideas of the Italian reformers is clear in the *De papatu Romano Antichristo*, presumably composed in the early 1580s and later revised, but never printed. (Panizza 1981: 19–40; Lavenia 2009; Quaglioni and Minnucci 2014). Here Gentili cited many of the most prominent figures of the Italian Reformation, from Bernardino Ochino to Peter Martyr Vermigli, Giacomo Aconcio to Pier Paolo Vergerio. On the one hand, Gentili inserted himself into the Italian debate on the Antichrist, which Ochino, in the wake of Martin Luther, had identified as the papacy (Rotondò 1991; Felici 2007). On the other hand, Gentili also made reference to the discussions around the Council of Trent that had raised expectations among the Italian reformers. Gentili did not, however, share the conciliar hopes widespread in sixteenth-century Italy. Following Vergerio, he dismissed Trent as a failed opportunity, in which nothing was seriously discussed because the council was always under the control of Rome (*De Papatu*, 15r). According to Gentili, however, the degeneration of the papacy went back not to the Council of Trent but rather to the donation of Constantine, whose forgery had been demonstrated by many authors, such as Lorenzo Valla, Niccolò Cusano and, more recently, Francesco Guicciardini. Through the donation of Constantine the bishop of Rome claimed a universal authority over the Church and the secular kingdoms, abandoning the model of the primitive Church, whose jurisdiction was purely spiritual (*De Papatu*, 7r–v). No reconciliation was possible with the papacy, and those who—like Carnesecchi and Pucci—believed that the reunification of the Church was still within reach risked becoming Rome's ally. In the *De Papatu*, Gentili made that clear by attacking the radical wing of the Reformation and blaming "the Anabaptists, the Libertines, the Schwenckfeldians, the Servetians, the Antitrinitarians" for the internal divisions in the Protestant camp (*De Papatu*, f. 84r).

It was also by criticizing the Radical Reformation that Gentili developed the ideas found in his most important works, such as the *De iure belli*, published for the first time in London in 1589 and later revised in an expanded edition in 1598 (Gentili 1589; Gentili 1598). In contrast to the millenarian and spiritualistic beliefs widespread among the Italian heretics, Gentili embraced a strict Erastianism, beginning with the conviction that an end to the war of religions could come only through the reinforcement of secular authorities. Like Erastus, Gentili in several of his works opposed both the Catholic theory of papal power in international affairs and the Calvinist presbyterian model of Church organization—taken up in England by the Puritans—arguing that the civil magistrate was the ultimate authority in both secular and religious affairs (Gentili 1587; Gentili 1605).

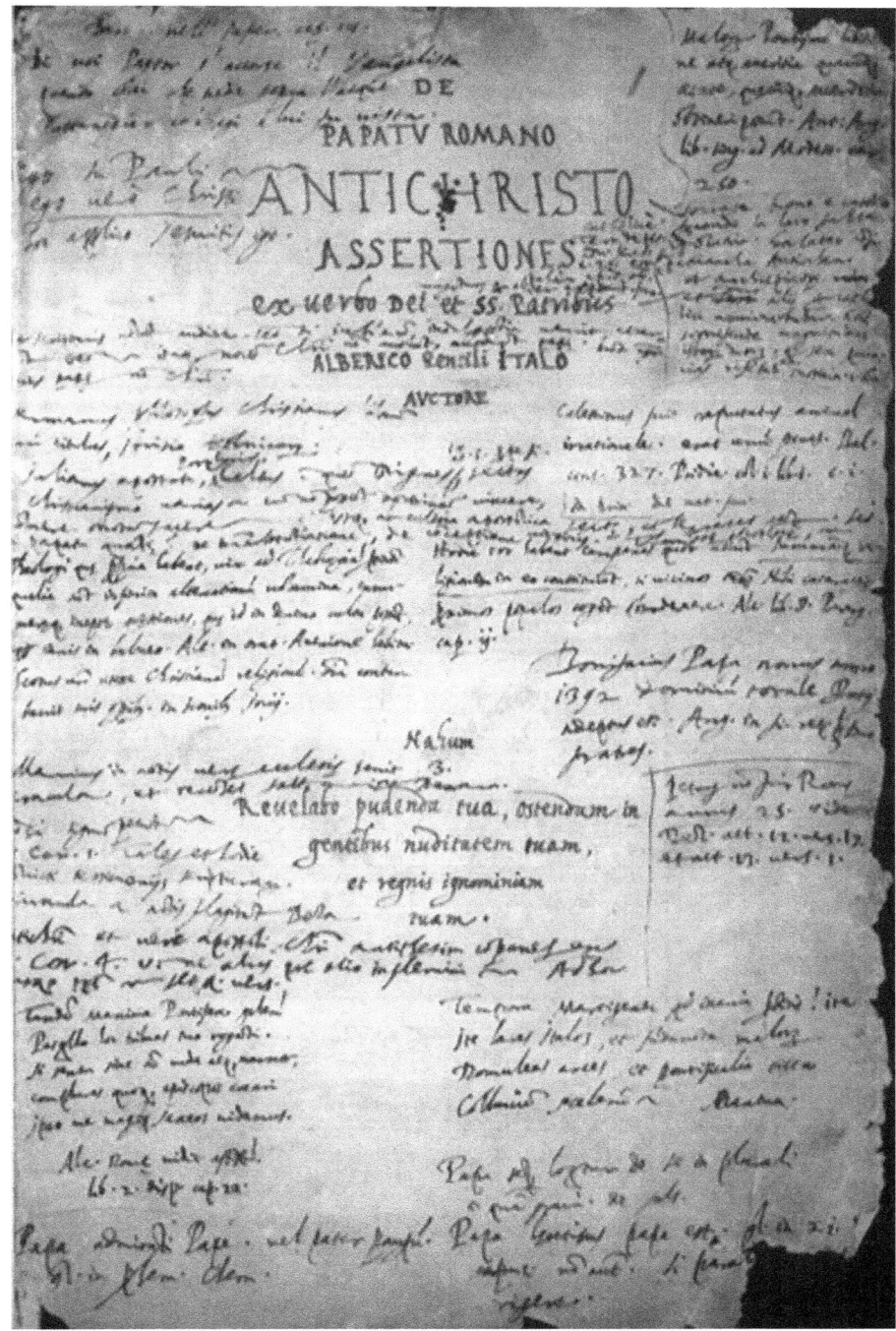

FIGURE 6.6: Alberico Gentili, *De papatu Romano Antichristo Assertiones (ex verbo Dei et SS. Patribus)* ms. D'Orville 607, title page, Bodleian Library, Oxford. Courtesy of the Bodleian Library.

The only legitimate change of religion must be decided by the prince and implemented progressively, as had happened in Germany with Luther and in England with Henry VIII (Gentili 1612: 562–3). In the same years, these Erastian ideas also circulated among Italian reformers close to Gentili. It was not a coincidence that Thomas Erastus' *Explicatio gravissimae quaestionis utrum excommunicatio. . .mandato nitatur divino, an excogitata sit ab hominibus* was published in London in 1589 by the Italian reformer Giacomo Castelvetro, who in the same year paid to produce and market Gentili's *De iure belli* (Maclean 2009: 291–338).

Indeed, in the first chapters of the *De iure belli* Gentili's distance from the irenic expectations of the Italian heretics already appears clearly. According to Gentili, war was a constitutive element of international politics, a necessary force for solving the disputes between sovereigns, who by definition did not have any authority above them (Gentili, *De iure belli*, 1612: 22–3; Gentili 1933, II: 15). Only the sovereign therefore had the right to wage war, which Gentili defined as "a just and public contest of arms" (*bellum est publicorum armorum iusta contentio*), clarifying that war "is not a broil, a fight, the hostility of individuals" (Gentili, *De iure belli*, 1612: 17–8). The *De iure belli* examined war according to the Aristotelian doctrine of the four causes. Having singled out the prince as war's efficient cause, Gentili moved on to a discussion of its material cause, treating the reasons for waging war. In this section the *De iure belli* denounced the use of religion as a pretext for the justification of violence, blaming the fact that "each man declares his own war a holy one . . . there is no abominable crime which is not shielded under the name of piety" (Gentili, *De iure belli*, 1612: 63–4; Gentili 1933: 40). Writing at the end of a century marked by the eruption of religious strife at every level, Gentili argued that religious difference was not the real cause of violence. Instead of harming the stability of the state, religious tolerance represented a useful tool to reinforce the authority of the prince and prevent civil unrest. Agreeing with Jean Bodin, Gentili declared that "violence should not be employed against subjects who have embraced another religion than that of their ruler" (Gentili, *De iure belli*, 1612: 71; Gentili 1933: 44).

Having discussed in the second book the formal cause of war—the rules that must be respected even in a conflict concerning weapons, truces, rights of prisoners and victims—Gentili dedicated the last book of the *De iure belli* to the final cause, discussing the conclusion of war and the establishment of peace. In the wake of Augustine, peace is defined as "ordered concord" (*concordia ordinata*: Gentili, *De iure belli*, 1612: 472). In principle, Gentili declared, peace should be perpetual, "since it is the nature of peace to be permanent"; citing Cicero, he argued that "peace does not consist in laying aside the arms, but in casting aside all fear of arms. Therefore, we must strive for the establishment of a perpetual and assured peace" (Gentili, *De iure belli*, 1612: 577; Gentili 1933: 361). For this reason, the *De iure belli* argued that peace treaties should always be sanctioned by oaths, since these are "the strongest and most powerful of pledges," as they "bind men most firmly and sacredly." At the same time, Gentili recognized that justice and politics are often in conflict. Oaths are often disrespected as princes make their decisions on the basis of expediency (*utilitas*) rather than morality (*honestas*) (Gentili, *De iure belli*, 1612: 583; Gentili 1933: 357).

In confessional Europe, the violence of the ongoing religious strife constituted another obstacle to attaining a perpetual peace. In the third book of the *De iure belli*, Gentili asked whether it was right to establish a treaty with peoples of different faiths. As has been pointed out, the answer given in the text highlights Gentili's strong commitment to biblical Protestantism and undermines the traditional image of Gentili as a secular and humanist lawyer (Malcolm 2010). Indeed, citing the Italian reformer Peter Martyr Vermigli, "the most learned theologian of our age'," Gentili declared that "it is never right to make a military alliance with infidels," and on this basis condemned Francis I's coalition with the Ottoman empire to fight Charles V (Gentili, *De iure belli*, 1612: 659–60). Oaths taken with infidels and heretics did not have any value, a conviction Gentili further underlined by citing Francesco Guicciardini on the behavior of the papacy, noting that "it was regarded as characteristic of pontiffs not to keep their promises" (Gentili, *De iure belli*, 1612: 622; Gentili 1933: 403).

Having put aside any hope of religious reconciliation in a Europe by then divided into confessional churches, Gentili saw the only possible peace as based on the defense of the balance of power, thereby preventing any single state from becoming too powerful. For this reason, the *De iure belli* suggested following the example of Lorenzo de' Medici, whom Gentili described as a "wise man, friend of peace, and father of peace." In late sixteenth-century England, in the wake of the Spanish Armada, Gentili considered Spain a danger to Europe's equilibrium. A coalition of small states would make it possible to preserve the balance of power, undermining Spain's attempt to establish a *monarchia universalis*:

> This . . . was the constant care of Lorenzo de' Medici . . . that the balance of power should be maintained among the princes of Italy. This he believed would give peace to Italy, as indeed it did so long as he lived and preserved that condition of affairs . . . Is not this even to-day our problem, that one man may not have the supreme power and that all Europe may not submit to the domination of a single man? Unless there is something which can resist Spain, Europe will surely fall.
>
> —Gentili, *De iure belli*, 1612: 104–5; Gentili 1933: 65

The balance of power had to be preserved by any means in order to prevent Europe from falling under one dominion. This reasoning demanded not only defending against preexisting hostilities but also preventing conflicts that might develop in the future. Preemptive attack was thus a legitimate self-defense: "It is lawful to anticipate a wrong. It is lawful for me to attack a man who is making ready to attack me . . . One ought to provide not only against an offence which is being committed, but also against one which may be possibly be committed" (Gentili, *De iure belli*, 1612, 98; Gentili 1933: 62) (Hoekstra 2012).

CONCLUSION

In the *Relation on the state of religion*, Edwin Sandys indicated that, despite the division into confessional churches and the outbreak of the religious wars, there still existed peace movements in seventeenth-century Europe that directed their efforts to reestablish "some tolerable peace . . . in the Church againe" (Sandys, *Relation*, 1605, par. 48). Departing from Sandys's *Relation*, this chapter has brought to light three different Renaissance peace movements that emerged in the sixteenth century when the long struggle for the council kindled irenic expectations that Trent would reconcile Christianity and fulfill the biblical prophecy unifying the world as "one flock" under "one shepherd" (Cantimori 1959; Prosperi 2009). The conciliar hopes might be just one of the many myths and misunderstandings that accompanied the council during its history and reception (O'Malley 2013). And yet, such expectations had a large echo in the sixteenth-century, even among church elites, as is confirmed by the case of the *spirituali*, who, for a moment, found the direct support of the Holy Roman Emperor Charles V (Firpo 2001). After the end of the council of Trent, the millenarian expectations that a new universal council would end the conflict between confessions, and at last recreate a unified Christendom did not wane but continued to nourish the thought of the Italian heretics. Pucci's decision to move back to Italy and his effort to win Rome's favor were not simply part of a tragic misunderstanding, but reveal the deep roots of conciliar hopes at the end of the sixteenth century. For this reason, Pucci should be regarded not as an isolated utopian thinker but as one of the last representatives of the lively current of sixteenth-century prophetism, which found new strength in the age of the council (Prosperi 2000: 365–74).

Finally, the case of Gentili brings to light the rise of Erastianism and the opposition between two different currents of sixteenth-century irenicism—between *irénisme utopique* and *irénisme étatique* (Meyjes 1997). To the Italian heretics' millenaristic expectations and spiritual interpretation of Christianity, Gentili opposed an Erastian conception of the relationship between Church and State—a conception in which only a strong secular government would be able to impose itself on the different parties and thus allow different faiths to coexist peacefully. According to Gentili and the supporters of the *irénisme étatique*, the example to follow was England, where the monarchy guided religious change with the aim of avoiding extremes, while building the ideal Christian commonwealth, in which the prince was also pastor. Thus, the waning of the millenarian expectations kindled by Trent left space for a disenchanted vision of the international order, a vision in which peace could not be guaranteed if not through the armies of the European princes.

CHAPTER SEVEN

Peace, Security, and Deterrence

REBECCA BOONE

The progress made during the Renaissance era in the fields of arts and sciences was not accompanied by a similar progress in the establishment of lasting peace. As a general rule, war existed as the status quo in many places throughout the world from 1450–1650. Nevertheless, a variety of efforts, both diplomatic and military, aimed at the limitation of violence, or "negative peace." This essay looks at peace efforts in Europe and the wider world, focusing on a few global areas that experienced similar aspects of war, peace, and state formation such as Japan and France, the Spanish and Ottoman Empires, and Italy and the Low Countries. In all cases, the success of the peace efforts depended on the motives of those in power. This essay looks at a variety of motivations—strategic, bureaucratic, and economic—that led to increasing levels of peace and stability by the middle of the seventeenth century.

A number of factors led to the proliferation of war in the early modern world. Conditions conducive to conflict dominated when an aristocracy defined itself by its military function. Although feudal conditions declined in the early modern era, the hereditary nobility often retained traditional militarism as part of its identity. Historians have struggled to find an exact definition of feudalism, but it remains a useful concept in describing a society where land was exchanged for military service. In this situation, land ownership divided and subdivided, and disputes among militarized land holders proliferated, especially when a weak central government could not prevent the outbreak of violence. The elites in these societies felt honor bound to serve as loyal vassals to more powerful lords who in turn fought to protect attacks on their land or reputation. For the sake of simplicity, one might take the examples of France and Japan as feudal states through most of the era. This essay will look at the peace efforts of Hideyoshi of Japan and Henry IV of France to establish peace within this feudal dynamic.

A second factor leading to endemic warfare was the revival of the imperial idea from antiquity that inclined monarchs toward conquest. The destructive energy of the imperial ideology intensified as it merged with a religious mandate to crusade and spread the word of God. Originating in the early Middle Ages, the rivalry between the Iberians and the Muslims entered an even more destructive phase in the sixteenth century as religious justifications for war assumed a more sophisticated approach derived from the study of antiquity. Charles V and Suleiman the Magnificent epitomize this ideology. Both claimed that their empire-building was essentially one of "pacification" despite the carnage that their conquest caused. Nevertheless, as these empires consolidated their territorial gains, subsequent rulers increasingly focused on governing the lands they held rather than acquiring new domains. This new emphasis on management of territories ushered in a greater emphasis on peace and stability.

Finally, this essay looks at attitudes toward trade that predisposed societies to war in the early part of this era, but gradually enticed a number of regions toward peace by the seventeenth century. The nature of trade shifted in a number of ways, from a peaceful endeavor in the ancient world to an aggressive practice that originated out of the religious rivalry between the Iberians and Muslims. Despite the rise of predatory trade, however, some regions sought to limit war for the sake of increased profits. This segment looks at the rise of Portuguese trade in Africa, the rise of merchant diplomacy in Renaissance Italy, and the development of commercial justification for peace in England and the Dutch Republic.

FRANCE AND JAPAN: FROM INTERNAL CHAOS TO PACIFICATION

Throughout the sixteenth century, the kingdom of France and empire of Japan experienced eras of destructive civil wars followed by eras of internal peace beginning in the seventeenth century. In both situations, an aristocracy that embraced warrior values adopted the norms of court society in a centralized state.

In its long-term movement toward state formation in the early modern era, the kingdom of France experienced a number of conflicts. The early efforts at political centralization were resisted by the feudal nobility in the War of the Public Good in 1465, in which Louis XI defeated a powerful rival, the duke of Burgundy. In 1494, the kingdom was powerful and united enough to engage in a series of foreign wars under the young king, Charles VIII, who began the era of the Italian Wars, 1494–1559. These were wars fought between the Valois and Habsburg dynasties, in which the Valois claimed to be a bulwark against the hegemonic claims of the Holy Roman Empire, ruled by the Habsburgs. During these years, the kingdom of France enjoyed a certain amount of domestic peace until the wars of religion between Protestants and Catholics divided the kingdom from 1567–98. At this point, Henry IV pacified the kingdom and laid the foundations for increasing stability (Collins 2002: 181, 188–9; Knecht 2001: 34–67; Holt 1995).

Throughout these military engagements, the medieval perspective that regarded war as inevitable prevailed. Defending one's honor and reputation required armed conflict. Even during the religious wars, nobles often fought to defend themselves against slights to their honor as they sought to champion their faith. Experiencing the dangers of personal combat and leading troops into battle were expected of nobles and kings throughout the era (Neuschel 1989: 65; Dewald 1996: 108–9; Schalk 1986). Especially during the Italian Wars, treaties and defensive alliances largely aimed at ending conflicts only long enough to regain a position of advantage for the next confrontation. Although kings increasingly hired jurists to argue points of law, they mainly served to justify territorial claims that led to even more outbreaks of war. Nothing seemed to warrant greater consideration than the honor and reputation of the prince.

Several transformations in warfare and society served to make conflict in France much more widespread and destructive. Clearly, the entry of handheld firearms in the form of arquebuses caused unprecedented devastation. However, the rise of infantry, especially in the form of the pike phalanx, may have had an even greater role in the transformation of warfare. The rediscovery of antiquity brought with it new military strategies for amassing

FIGURE 7.1: *Henry IV as Mars*, attributed to Jacob Brunel (*c*. 1605), Musée National du chateau de Pau. Wikimedia Commons.

and directing enormous armies. Technologies of fortification grew more sophisticated. These changes brought more people into the fight—peasants to serve as infantry and scholars to serve as experts, advisors, diplomats, and spies (Boone 2007: 107–12). During the French Wars of Religion, people from all walks of life served in armies, although both Protestants and Catholics looked to members of the nobility to lead them. The extreme violence of the religious wars themselves were largely a result of another, important innovation during these years—the printing press.

Because the scope of the Religious Wars went beyond motives of honor and reputation to include ideological convictions, intervals of peace did not last very long. Both sides considered the enemy in league with Satan and unworthy of existence. The queen regent, Catherine de' Medici and her sons, Charles IX and Henry III, sought peace on many occasions, but neither religious faction could agree on a settlement. From the treaty of Cateau-Cambrésis that ended the Italian Wars in in 1559 to Catherine's death in 1589 there were ten peace agreements: the edicts of Toleration (1562), Amboise (1563), Longjumeau (1568), and St. Germain (1570), followed by the peace of La Rochelle (1573), Monsieur (1576), Bergerac (1577), Fleix (1580), and finally the edict of Union (1588). Peace did not come to France until the heir to the throne, Henry IV, converted from Protestantism to Catholicism (the majority religion in France) and conquered his enemies, the ultra-Catholic league and Spain, as well as put down a number of peasant revolts by 1598 (Holt 1995: xi–xiii, 162–3).

Despite sporadic warfare that lasted until 1629, Henry IV set France on a course toward peace. He and his Bourbon descendants reduced the prevalence of war by converting noble warriors into courtiers. With the help of his main advisor, the Duke of Sully, Henry drew the aristocracy to Paris as a capital city. The requirements of social control at court pacified the most unruly element of medieval society. From the fifteenth century, the French government had been in the process of establishing legal and administrative systems to centralize the state at the expense of noble power. After the wars of religion, the nobility embraced this administrative structure. Encouraged by financial rewards, appeals to national identity, and the extraordinary charisma of Henry of Navarre, the aristocracy came to a consensus about the need for a more rigid social order (Major 1994: 93–6; Salmon 1979: 14–20).

The movement from feudal violence to the consolidation of state power also defined early modern Japan. From 1467 to 1582, Japan experienced an era of turbulence, the *Sengoku jidai*, characterized by a weak central government and endless rivalries between regional *daimyo* (lords) and *samurai* (vassals). The chaos and brutality of these wars intensified after 1543, when shipwrecked Portuguese merchants landed on a southern island and brought with them the technology of hand-held firearms. Within six months, the Japanese had manufactured hundreds of arquebuses. Ruthless and cruel, Oda Nobunaga was the first warlord to arm large peasant armies in an effort to establish hegemony in Japan. His talented and charismatic general, Hideyoshi, succeeded after Nobunaga's assassination in uniting all of the provinces of the Japanese empire under his military command in 1582. Although Toyotomi Hideyoshi pacified the state, he quickly engaged the warlords and samurai in a fight for Korea (1592–8), considered by him a stepping stone to his intended conquest of China and India (Berry 1982: 208).

Hideyoshi had risen from a peasant background into the samurai nobility, but his regime solidified a social hierarchy that would make this kind of mobility impossible. He disarmed the peasantry and tied them to the land. His successor, Ieysu Tokugawa, completed the unification process by establishing a capital in east Edo (modern Tokyo) and enticing the aristocracy to adopt a courtly lifestyle there. Unlike Nobunaga and Hideyoshi, Tokugawa made peace and stability a priority. Accepting the title of Shogun, he created the Tokugawa Shogunate that provided Japan with peace until 1868.

The pacification of Japan mirrored that of France in many significant ways. In both, subjects were willing to tolerate peace after decades of destruction. In France, the excessive violence of the religious wars and the Catholic League's reign of terror in the city of Paris caused many to embrace peace. In Japan, Nobunaga's countless atrocities against religious institutions and rivals created a sense of fear that made Hideyoshi's appeals to peace acceptable to warlords and peasants alike. In both cases, Henry IV and Hideyoshi stressed that loyalty to them was loyalty to the nation and the public good. Rigid social stratification and court spectacle, and a flourishing of literature and entertainment accompanied the pacification of these states. As in France, warriors became courtiers (Berry 1982: 82–7; Naohiro 1991: 40–78).

FIGURE 7.2: *Toyotomi Hideyoshi*. Wikimedia Commons.

THE SPANISH AND OTTOMAN EMPIRES: CONQUEST TO BUREAUCRATIC STATE

Although the rulers of France and Japan used the language of imperialism, they ultimately discarded world domination as a practical goal of foreign policy. In contrast, the Spanish and Ottoman empires of the sixteenth-century boldly strove for global hegemony. These composite states included a variety of peoples, languages, and customs within their jurisdictions. Although not entirely free from internal conflict, these empires mobilized their resources to send armies beyond their borders. Both states conquered in the name of peace and the rule of law, the classic justifications of imperialism.

The Spanish Empire grew out of two dynastic traditions which fused in the figure of Charles V. As Charles I of Spain, he inherited Castile and Aragon from his maternal grandparents, Ferdinand and Isabella in 1516. Three years later, he claimed the title of Holy Roman Emperor, largely due to his status as the heir to the Habsburg domains, as the grandson of Maximilian I. After 1519, the Spanish court served as a fountain of imperial ideology which merged a variety of separate strands into one powerful justification for empire. A great deal of biblical prophecy from the era of the *Reconquista* claimed that a Spanish king would defeat the Moors in Spain and then carry the fight across North Africa and liberate the Holy Land from the infidels. Uniting the world under the Christian religion, the Spanish king would usher in the Millennium, a thousand years of peace on earth before the coming of the kingdom of God. Christopher Columbus, who himself wrote a book of prophecies, saw himself as a prophet spreading Christianity throughout the world in order to prepare for the coming of the kingdom of God on earth. While it is true that similar prophecies said similar things about French kings or the papacy, the Spanish, perhaps because of the experience of the *Reconquista*, seemed poised to extend the prophetic tradition into the global arena (Reeves 1969: 358–74; Boone 2014).

The Ottoman Empire also emerged from a crusading tradition. Having inherited an ideological division of the world into two realms, the *dârülislâm* (house of Islam) and the *dârülharb* (house of war), the Turks sought to extend the frontiers of Islam by *gâza* (holy war). From the middle of the thirteenth century, Osman and his holy warriors had made successful raids into the Byzantine Empire in Anatolia, and by the sixteenth century, Osman's descendants ruled over an empire that stretched from the Danube to the Euphrates (Inalcik 1988: 5–7). Like the Spanish, the Ottomans justified expansion as a crusade for their faith, the ultimate end of which was world domination.

In the sixteenth century, the religious claims to empire drew strength from classical influences. The revival of antiquity influenced both empires. Suleiman the Magnificent was said to have been influenced by the model of Alexander the Great, while Charles V used the imagery of Augustus Caesar. Imperial officials asserted that uniting the world under one government was both necessary and possible. The classical argument for empire was the establishment of peace by the cessation of wars caused by political fragmentation. The Ottoman empire adopted many administrative structures from pre-Islamic empires in the Middle East. These were viewed as more conducive to peace than the feudal landscape that dominated the region in the thirteenth and fourteenth centuries (Inalcik 1988: 13). As in antiquity, empire claimed justification by providing the benefits of legal protection to its subjects. Ottoman historians have traditionally revered Suleiman as "The Lawmaker," because he provided uniform law codes for the many provinces of the empire, which contained a great variety of religions, languages, and customs. Aiming

FIGURE 7.3: *Charles V Enthroned Among his Enemies*, British Library Add. 33733, f. 5, London. Courtesy of Europeana Collections.

for peace within his lands, he followed the principle of religious toleration and allowed different ethnic groups to rule themselves at the local level. As in the Persian and Byzantine empires, the Ottomans claimed that their sultan had been charged by God to administer justice to his subjects (Kunt and Woodhead (eds.) 1995).

Spanish officials portrayed themselves the heirs to the tradition of Roman law. As a revived Roman imperium, they justified their rule by bringing good administration and law to their subjects (Pagden 1995). After expanding their empire into the Americas, Spanish jurists revived the arguments of Thomas Aquinas concerning what constituted a just war. Francisco de Vitoria, writing in the 1530's was the first to ask by what right were the *indios* subjected to Spanish rule (Matsumori 2011, 30). Viewing the indigenous people of the Americas as fully human, Vitoria suggested that the *jus gentium* (law of peoples) had endowed them with natural rights. They could not be conquered without just cause (Draper 1992: 187). The theorists of the School of Salamanca, where Vitoria lectured, are considered the first advocates of international law, a system of international relations that would aim for peace among nations.

By the end of the sixteenth century, the Ottoman and Spanish empires experienced an era of retrenchment and consolidation. Both had concluded phases of conquest and had begun to focus on administration of conquered territories. Indicative of this shift was the ending of the practice of sending Ottoman princes to the provinces for training in war. After the 1570s, the imperial princes were raised in the palace, which was increasingly dominated by palace officials rather than military commanders (Pierce 1993: x, 21). In the Spanish empire in the Americas, the era of the Conquistadors gave way to a colonial society concerned with bureaucratization and Christianization (Matsumori 2011: 32;

FIGURE 7.4: *Suleiman the Magnificent After the Capture of Buda* (1529), sixteenth century, Topkapı Palace Museum, Istanbul. Wikimedia Commons.

Anghie 2004). Wars continued throughout the early modern era, but by the seventeenth century, the destructive force of territorial conquest subsided in these lands.

GLOBAL TRADE AND WAR

As the phenomenon of state consolidation ultimately encouraged more peaceful conflict resolution by the seventeenth century, the rise of global trade created both opportunities for aggression and for cooperation between states. From the earliest times in human history, trade had been associated with peace. The Silk Road had only operated when war had ceased within the lands along its trail. Peace and commerce were the dual promises of empire in terms of benefits provided to subjects. However, attitudes toward trade changed during the years of the *Reconquista*, when Christians and Muslims fought for control of the Iberian Peninsula. Out of this rivalry emerged a new approach to trade as an alternative form of warfare (Curtain 1984: 136–40). Trade taken away from rivals depleted their resources for war, as money was considered the "sinews of war."

By the fifteenth century, Portuguese rulers such as Prince Henry the Navigator, began to see the quest for more trade as part of a crusade against the infidels. Although the Venetians may have been the first to arm ships with artillery in the fourteenth century, the Portuguese introduced more destructive gun boats to their fleets in the Indian Ocean. The heavily armed ships were better able to commit acts of piracy against Muslim shipping, seize and control ports and islands, and break trade monopolies from Africa to India and beyond (Parry 1963: 133–41).

The Spanish soon followed suit, and the rivalry that began in the Mediterranean eventually extended to encompass the entire globe. The linking of trade with war continued as the Spanish and Portuguese conquered and settled the Americas. Throughout the sixteenth century, as rulers began to see trade and the extraction of resources as a means to engage in greater military expeditions, the carnage of war proliferated. The kings of Spain used war to extract gold and silver from the New World almost exclusively for the purpose of conquest in Europe. At first, this meant establishing hegemony in Italy as the cornerstone to a revival of the Holy Roman Empire as the dominant power in Europe (Boone 2014: 44). After the rise of Protestantism as a political force in German regions and in England, and in the religious wars in France, the gold went to fight for Catholic unity on the continent. Therefore, between the fourteenth and seventeenth centuries, there is no way to detach the motives of enrichment from motives stemming from religion in the Spanish practice of global trade. Nor is there any way to untangle trade from motivations stemming from feudal obligations to maintain one's honor and reputation, or from imperial ideology. Essentially, no ruler in the sixteenth century was at a loss for justifications for warfare, and that situation made the work of peace very difficult. Everyone agreed on principle that Christians should not kill each other, but also assumed that wars with non-Christians, in the form of a crusade, were an essential part of the natural order (Lesaffer 2004: 29–30).

A NEW LANGUAGE OF DIPLOMACY

An important movement toward peace occurred when independent states entered into voluntary agreements in order to establish a balance of power among them. In many cases, the desire to profit from commerce free from disadvantages of military conflict motivated governments to seek peace. This movement rested on important theoretical concepts and practices, most importantly, the development of the abstract state as a political entity separate from the personal power of a ruler. As state institutions and diplomatic practices developed, the state became increasingly independent. By the sixteenth century, the concept of sovereignty would allow independent states to make more lasting peace agreements. It is useful to think of this development as lasting 200 years, from the peace of Lodi to the treaty of Westphalia (Lesaffer 2004: 10–11).

By the middle of the fourteenth century, several Italian cities adopted more sophisticated means of administering their governments. The cities needed stronger institutions to deal with a number of issues, including territorial expansion, endemic warfare with rival cities, and factional conflict that developed into crises of legitimacy within the city-states. At this time, the cities had access to a variety of new political tools borrowed from many sources including papal government, Roman law, and ancient history. As the number of government offices proliferated, a new vocabulary of politics emerged that increasingly allowed the cities to settle differences through communication rather than military conflict (Lazzarini 2015: 5–6, 105).

The practice of diplomacy lay at the heart of this transition. By the fifteenth century, the powerful cities of Italy, including Milan, Venice, and Florence used diplomats among other agents as a means of information gathering, negotiation, and representation (Lazzarini 2015: 33). In the middle of the last century, Garrett Mattingly described the importance of the institution of the resident, or permanently stationed, ambassador, which became standard in Italy in the decades after the peace of Lodi, 1454 (Mattingly 1964 (1955): 71–7). Before this agreement, states had sent diplomats bilaterally to negotiate or make alliances. In the several decades before Lodi, the five main powers, Milan, Venice, Florence, Papacy, and Naples, had engaged in ever-shifting alliances and nearly continuous warfare. Each major power aimed to expand its territories and absorb nearby communes. By 1454, however, fear of foreign invasion from France or the Ottoman Empire (which had conquered Constantinople in 1453) enticed them to seek a general settlement that would lead to a general peace. The Most Holy League, as it was called, was a defensive alliance intended to last twenty-five years. Although it did not eliminate all conflict, it successfully maintained the balance of power in Italy until 1494. Mattingly argued that the institutions of the resident ambassador and the voluntary association of independent states eventually spread to the European monarchies north of the Alps in the following century (Mattingly 1964 (1955): 105).

More recently, Isabella Lazzarini has provided a comprehensive overview of the development of diplomacy from 1350–1520. During these years, the massive influx of information collected by diplomats and other government agents led to a new way of looking at politics. The information required the analysis of specialists who had refined and elaborated the language of politics to include more abstract concepts and sophisticated reasoning. In essence, diplomacy led to a reality-based consensus among a large circle of political actors in Italy (Lazzarini 2015: 264).

The Republics of Venice and Florence provide useful examples of states whose citizens understood the state as an abstract concept. The Most Serene Republic was able to instill loyalty not to a person or family, but to the republic itself. Writing around 1490, Ermolao Barbaro, in his work on the duties of the ambassador, stated, "The purpose of the ambassador is to do, say, advise, and think those things which they judge might possibly pertain to the best condition and maintenance and amplification of their city ... In brief, he must serve not himself but his *patria*" (King 1986: 203). An aristocratic state ruled by a closed group of noble, but commercial families, Venetians prided themselves on their lack of civic discord and their vast commercial empire. In the fifteenth century, Venice had expanded its territories well into the mainland of Italy. However, by the sixteenth century it had ceased to grow and consolidated its domains. When a large part of Italy succumbed to Spanish domination, Venice survived largely through complicated diplomatic maneuvers pitting major European powers against each other. As it approached the seventeenth century, Venetians realized that to remain free, they would have to embrace peace (Tenenti 1973: 36).

A new way of looking at the state as an abstract entity simultaneously emerged in Florence. For nearly half a century, since the publication of Hans Baron's *Crisis of the Early Italian Renaissance*, historians have debated whether the political values that emerged in the fifteenth century might be described as "civic humanism," an ethos that stressed self-government and virtuous sacrifice of personal interests for the common good as the foundation of liberty (Baron 1966: 205–6). Critics of this view point to Florence's own imperialism as it sought to destroy the liberty of its rivals, especially Pisa. By the 1470s, at least, the republic had effectively ceded control to one family, the Medici, making it essentially a monarchy in all but name. Nevertheless, the republic of Florence stood as an exception to normal politics in early modern Europe in terms of how its citizens thought and wrote about politics (Grafton 2002: 164–5; Skinner 1978, 83).

Florentine thinkers, in particular Niccolò Machiavelli and Francesco Guicciardini, emerged in the early sixteenth century as key figures in the discourse of political realism. Inspired by the historians of antiquity, these political realists attempted to describe the truth about political reality, basing their conclusions on the historical record and contemporary experience. These writers avoided mythology and religion in their description of why people behaved the way they did in political communities. Of course, they, like ancient models such as Thucydides, were not immune to the influence of tragic drama in their writings. Nevertheless, these lawyers and diplomats used a political language developed in the fifteenth century, which treated facts and intelligence as fundamental to constructing reality.

Basing observations on reason and experience, Florentine political thinkers understood the political landscape as divided into a variety of states. Furthermore, within each state, a plurality of factions jockeyed for power. This vision of political reality contrasted sharply with ideology of political unity that dominated in the medieval world. Whereas political writers in monarchical regimes mirrored the unified perspective of the single ruler, the Florentine perspective expressed the multivalent nature of the Italian city states, which more closely resembled the political reality of Europe as a whole.

These two visions, unity and plurality, emerged as ideologies in medieval Italy from a longstanding rivalry between the Ghibelline and Guelf factions. Whereas the Ghibelline support of the Holy Roman Emperor led the faction to support the principle of political unity, the Guelf support of France and the papacy against the empire led to the acceptance of political plurality. Both looked to Roman law to support their positions. The postglossators, Baldus and Bartolus, had argued that unity of the empire (under the jurisdiction of the Holy Roman Empire) withstood the internal divisions that had arisen after the fall of Rome. Thus, a religious and political unity still existed in Christendom (Headley 1992: 261). On the other hand, Bartolus argued that even though the empire still commanded authority over the other powers in Europe *de jure*, the emperor had to realize that independent states existed *de facto*. By the sixteenth century, rulers in France and other major kingdoms were recognized as *superiorem non recognoscentes* (not recognizing any superior) (Lesaffer 2004: 14). In the real world, independent states competed against each other without any recognition of a superior temporal power.

The implementation of a reality-based language of politics combined with the recognition of divided power was a pre-requisite to a system of international relations among states. At base, this new way of describing political reality encouraged states to recognize the right of others to exist as free and independent states. The development of another concept, state sovereignty, in the late sixteenth century would eventually allow these states to enter into voluntary associations for the express purpose of promoting a general peace.

THE DEVELOPMENT OF SOVEREIGNTY

By the early sixteenth century, the language of political realism that developed in the Italian states moved to monarchies north of the Alps, and this movement transformed the language of European politics considerably. The reality-based way of thinking about politics that emerged from the Italian republics proved extremely useful and effective. The nature of war, with massive armies, fortifications, and firearms had become extremely complicated, and collecting and allocating resources for war as well as complex diplomatic negotiations required experts (Mallett 1974: 259; Parker 1998: 156; Soll 1995). Not surprisingly, the trans-Alpine courts often employed Italians, or those trained in Italy, as advisors, diplomats, jurists, and propagandists. For example, Claude de Seyssel, a Savoyard jurist from Turin, advised Louis XII of France from 1498–1515 during the Italian Wars. He wrote the first treatise on the French constitution, the *Monarchy of France*, in 1515. Although his primary aim was to offer advice on how to strengthen the monarchy for its maintenance and growth, his work provided a description of the French state as an institution rather than a personal domain of the king.

Nevertheless, a more sophisticated appreciation of the machinery of the state apparatus and political maneuvering did not (at least in the short term) diminish of the personal power of the ruler. Indeed, sometimes the political expertise and humanist education of Italian advisors was put to use to exalt the authority and prestige of a king or emperor. Interestingly, Seyssel's student from his time as a law professor at the University of Turin, Mercurino di Gattinara, found employment in Spain as the Grand Chancellor of Charles V. There he used his juridical expertise and humanist background to champion a new ideology for the Spanish empire. The sophisticated approach to politics developed in the Renaissance enabled advisors such as Gattinara to transform a composite monarchy based on law and representative institutions into a world monarchy under a semi-divine savior-emperor (Boone 2014: 1–10).

Throughout the sixteenth century, a political language that originally applied to a republic ruled by justice and reason had transformed into a predatory tool of domination. This language, sometimes referred to as "Reason of State" had no other aim than the preservation and enlargement of the state without reference to justice or religion (Viroli 1992: 2; Soll 1995: 25). Adhesion to Roman, feudal, and canon law as common juridical systems broke down (Lesaffer 2004: 11).

Interpreting the works of ancient Greece and Rome as well as Machiavelli and Guicciardini, government officials in the north began to transform legislative monarchies, in which monarchs focused on making the law, to administrative monarchies, in which the government went beyond providing justice and protection and became a part of everyday life for its subjects (Collins 1995: 3). As government officials used the latest administrative tools to maintain and expand their state, they fell away from the fiction of a politically unified Christendom under imperial authority.

At the same time, the Reformation destroyed the reality of Catholic unity. After 1550, about half of Christian princes no longer recognized the spiritual leadership of the pope, and appeals for a common peace among Christian princes in order to sustain a united front against the Turks disappeared (Collins 1995: 33–4). The medieval system of international relations based on a common Catholic identity had disintegrated, and this created a power vacuum in Europe at the end of the sixteenth century. Without the pope as a guarantor of treaty obligations, there was little to provide weight to diplomatic negotiations. The abstract concept of sovereignty would provide a new foundation for diplomacy between political powers.

The articulation of state sovereignty was the work of Jean Bodin. Writing during the French Wars of Religion, he developed the theory of sovereignty as a rebuttal to Huguenot theorists who had questioned the legitimacy of the Catholic French monarchy after the St. Bartholomew's Day massacre. In contrast to the resistance theorists, he defined sovereign power as the ability to make law and described it as absolute, perpetual, and indivisible. According to his *Six Books of the Republic* of 1576, sovereignty was located in the ruler in monarchies, although in aristocracies and democracies, it would be located in a group or the entire body of citizens. He denied subjects the right to rebel, but he did believe that the sovereign was answerable to God. The sovereign also needed a magistracy for counsel and to administer the kingdom effectively. This abstract concept of sovereignty would allow European powers to recognize each other as sovereign states, which resulted in a greater ability for states to enforce diplomatic negotiations and agreements (Knecht 2001: 390–400; Salmon 2004: 447–50).

GLOBAL TRADE AND PEACE

While the states of Europe slowly began to adopt a new language of diplomacy and state sovereignty, the increasing profitability of global trade enticed many of them to seek more lasting peace agreements. During the era of discovery and conquest, European rulers engaged in predatory and aggressive trade practices in an effort to boost their honor and reputation as well as spread religious faith. By the seventeenth century, the rulers of a number of European states began to consider the profitability of peaceful cooperation. The states most interested in making peace agreements tended to be those with powerful merchant interests.

The relationship between several European states and the Ottoman Empire illustrates how many rulers directed policy toward trade rather than military conquest or religious conversion. Although both Christians and Muslims acknowledged that a permanent state of war existed between the two faiths, both sides found support for temporary peace agreements in the Quran and medieval canon law. Venice had signed treaties of "peace and friendship" with the Ottoman sultan as early as 1446. In the next century, as Charles V's empire surrounded and threatened France, the kingdom sought an alliance with the Ottomans. Beginning in 1535, the sultan and the king signed a series of "capitulations" which established free navigation, travel, and trade to their subjects among other rights and privileges. Similar capitulations were concluded with England after 1580 and the Netherlands after 1612 (Ziegler 2004: 340–4). The Habsburg monarchy had only established temporary truces until the peace of Zsitvatorok in 1606 between Rudolph II and Sultan Ahmet I. The desire of Venice, France, England, and the Netherlands to cultivate peaceful relations with the Ottomans expressed a new understanding of self-interest based on commerce rather than religious ideology. With these agreements, rulers moved toward an understanding of peace as more beneficial than war to themselves and their subjects. Monarchs such as Elizabeth I of England appreciated the income that customs duties brought to the crown. Ruling over an administrative state, she needed money to staff the numerous offices held by the nobility and gentry. Increasingly, patronage took the form of commercial licenses and monopolies. In this way, global trade helped the queen ensure the loyalty of the aristocracy to the court (Guy (ed.) 1995: 5).

Not surprisingly, the states most involved with global trade were more likely to support agreements establishing peace among states. As the merchant republics of Venice and Florence sought a balance of power between states in the peace of Lodi in the fifteenth century, the Dutch Republic championed cooperative agreements between states in the seventeenth century. The seventeen provinces of the Low Countries had been a banking and commercial hub in the late middle ages. Independent until the house of Burgundy established rule over many of them, they were united by Charles V in 1543. Under the Spanish empire, the port in Antwerp became one of the wealthiest cities in Europe (Pirenne 1963: 201–9). However, the religious dissent and the heavy-handed rule of Philip II resulted in a rebellion against Spanish authority. In 1579, seven provinces declared independence as the Dutch republic in the Union of Utrecht. When the Spanish brutally besieged Antwerp and reoccupied it with troops, Dutch merchants and foreign traders took their interests, capital, and enterprising outlook to the port of Amsterdam. Here the Dutch emerged as leaders in global trade thanks to the development of ships which greatly reduced the costs of shipping. The unusual attitudes of the Dutch to religious pluralism, unfettered immigration, and innovative financial services enabled

FIGURE 7.5: Hendrik Cornelizs Vroom, *Battle Between Dutch and Spanish Ships on the Harleem Mermeer (The Dutch Revolt)* (1626), Rijksmuseum, Amsterdam. Courtesy of Europeana Collections.

a state of perhaps one and a half million citizens to establish a world empire in the seventeenth century (Haley 1972: 9–20).

At the center of this expansion was the Dutch East India Company. Formed in 1602, the VOC, as it was known, was a joint-stock company with a federal management structure. It was granted a monopoly from the Dutch Republic to trade in Asia for unlimited profits. In return, the state demanded a modest tax dividend. Its flexibility, military force, and more relaxed approach to conversion allowed the Dutch to wrestle lucrative Asian markets from the Portuguese (Brook 2008: 15–6). Soon, other European countries established similar enterprises. Their novelty stemmed from the fact that these institutions had a corporate identity independent of the people who governed them, unlike the family firms that had been the economic norm before the seventeenth century. With an institutional structure able to amass a permanent stock of capital, these joint-stock companies greatly expanded Europe's participation in the global economy (de Vries 1989: 131–3).

The new approach to trade pioneered by the Dutch was accompanied by new theoretical structures with which to discuss war and peace. Hugo Grotius (1583–1645) is most famous for his magisterial treatise, *De Iure Belli ac Pacis* (*The Law of War and Peace*) published in 1625. Having served as a magistrate, historiographer, and diplomat, Grotius had written a treatise commissioned by the VOC, defending the company's right to plunder a Portuguese ship. In *De Iure Belli*, he described the possibility of an international society comprising voluntary member states which acted for the common good. Although previous theorists had also described a *ius gentium* or law of nations, Grotius went further to provide a thorough discussion of rights. This earned him the honorary title of father of International Relations (Kingsbury and Roberts 1992: 15–6).

Richard Tuck has described Grotius's concept of sovereignty as revolutionary. After decades in which theorists developed the concept of sovereignty to apply to the state, Tuck suggested that Grotius transferred that idea of sovereignty to the individual, thereby proposing a theory of individual rights. Significantly, in terms of the individual, the state, or the voluntary agreements between them, Grotius followed ancient Roman and Italian humanist theorists in emphasizing the motive of self-preservation and self-interest of the state in seeking mutual cooperation (Tuck 1999: 85–90).

Despite economic motivations toward peace, war still remained as a constant state of existence in many parts of Europe. Most notably, Eastern Europe endured the devastating Thirty Years War (1618–48), caused and sustained in large part by confessional politics and the crumbling of imperial Habsburg power (Parker 1987: 219–26). Out of this chaos a new international order emerged based on mutual agreements made by sovereign states, exemplified by the treaty that ended the war, the peace of Westphalia (1648).

Much debate surrounds the significance of the peace of Westphalia, but it did mark a definitive end to any claims to imperial or religious unity within Europe (Lesaffer 2004: 43). It did not bring lasting peace to the continent, nor did it provide legal constructs that helped to prevent the prolonged chaos and war that characterized the previous century (Duchhardt 2004: 47). In addition, the following 150 years would see an endless parade of colonial wars and atrocities committed against non-Europeans. In the end, however, Europeans residing on the continent experienced much less political turmoil than they had between 1450 and 1650.

For much of the world, the two centuries after 1450 witnessed an unusual amount of violence and upheaval. The proliferation of guns and printing brought more people into war with each other than in previous eras. With every new innovation in technology, administration, and knowledge acquisition, it seemed as though the destructive forces of those seeking power grew exponentially. At the same time, these very forces increased the amount of hatred and enmity felt among groups at all social levels. However, by the middle of the seventeenth century, several states in Europe, Asia, and the Americas returned to stability.

By 1650, all elements of the sovereign states had motivations to exchange disruption for stability and war for peace. The force and energy of the common people had been exhausted by constant warfare and economic crisis. Depleted in strength, they rarely raised violent protests against an increasingly rigid social system that kept them at the bottom of society. A greatly strengthened aristocracy found non-violent ways to assert dominance through social distinction in some states such as France and Japan. In others, such as England and the Dutch Republic, the aristocracy occupied itself by searching for economic opportunities presented by global trade. The rulers of Europe, by and large, settled into a peaceful state of coexistence with their rivals. Confronted with an increasingly complex political and economic reality, they found their dreams of imperial glory and world domination greatly diminished. At least, that is, temporarily.

CHAPTER EIGHT

Peace as Integration

KAZUHISA TAKEDA

INTRODUCTION

The world is composed of a vast diversity of peoples with myriad cultures and customs. On the one hand, that diversity has been the source of serious carnage and destruction. At the same time, however, throughout history, mankind has also demonstrated a strong desire for peace. In fact, it is hardly an exaggeration to say that every human desires peace. In this sense, peace is a universal concept that transcends space-time. There exists a diversity of means of achieving peace. Mankind has consistently sought peace throughout history, but it has consistently proven difficult to realize.

Integration is one of the key concepts designed to promote peace in our world. This noun derives from the verb, to integrate, which refers to the process by which "two things become closely linked or form part of a whole idea or system." (Collins Cobuild Advanced Learner's English Dictionary 2003). The United Nations (UN), an intergovernmental organization founded after the Second World War to promote international peace, represents one attempt to integrate two or more constituent groups—in this case nations—to create universal rules and principles for the purpose of realizing peace (Bjurner and Wallensteen (eds.) 2015).

What form did the integrative principle of peacemaking take in the late-middle and early-modern ages? This chapter examines that question from a global perspective through a series of case studies. It is worth noting at the outset that, for Europeans in the period, politics and religion were intimately interlinked and the expansion of political hegemony thereby implied the expansion of Christianity as well. The concept of integration was closely linked to governance, and the problem of governance was inseparable from religion. To contextualize this link historically, our discussion will begin with the famous narrative poem, *Divine Comedy*, by Dante Alighieri (1265–1321).

PAX ROMANA AND *PAX CHRISTI*

On Good Friday of the year 1300, Dante happened to meet the ancient Roman poet Virgil (70–19 BC) in the dark forest. Guided by Virgil, Dante traveled widely through Inferno, Purgatory, and Paradise. The following is a passage from *Purgatorio*, Canto III, 73–6. The term "you" indicates Virgil and "I" corresponds to Dante.

> "O you elect who ended well your lives,"
> Virgil began, "I ask you, in name
> of that same peace I know awaits you all,"

—Alighieri, *Purgatory*, III, 73–6, 1985: 31

According to Dante, everyone so eagerly awaited Virgil because he would bring long-awaited "peace."

Dante was famously devoted to Virgil, and a number of different quotations from Virgil's various works are found in the *Divine Comedy*. Virgil is doubtless one of the most prominent poets in the history of Latin literature.

In the *Divine Comedy*, Virgil appears associated with peace, but how was that association defined? A clue is contained in another short passage from Virgil's famous unfinished masterpiece, the *Aeneid*, one of the great Latin epic poems of antiquity.

> remember, Roman, it is for you to rule the nations with your power,
> (that will be your skill) to crown peace with law,
> to spare the conquered, and subdue the proud.
>
> —Vergil, *Aeneid*, VI: 851–3; Kline 2002

Virgil exhorted Romans to use their power to rule nations. According to Virgil, the Romans were able to establish peace through legislation, to pity the vanquished, and to defeat the conceited. In other words, he advocated the expansion of Rome's political and military power in order to establish global empire. The violent repression of insurgents was acceptable in the name of peace.

Virgil lived in the period of the late Roman republic (147–30 BC), a time of serious political disorder. He admired the great political skill of the first Roman emperor, Augustus (63 BC–AD 14), who laid the foundations for the future *pax Romana* (Levi 1998). Virgil reserved his greatest praise for Augustus' political and military power since, as he saw it, skillful rule by those means brought peace. As a consequence, he saw authoritative rule as acceptable in certain cases.

The *Divine Comedy* reveals Dante's positive view of Roman expansion in Europe through military force, and he derived this view from Aristotelian political thought. Another of Dante's works, *De Monarchia*, makes clear his ardent admiration for Aristotle. The following passage is from Book II, Chapter VII of the same work:

> As the human race, then, has an end, and this end is a means necessary to the universal end of nature, it follows that nature must have the means in view. [. . .] And as nature cannot attain through one man an end necessitating a multiplicity of actions and a multitude of men in action, nature must produce many men ordained for diverse activities. To this, beside the higher influence, the virtues and properties of the lower sphere contribute much. Hence we find individual men and whole nations born apt for government, and others for subjection and service, according to the statement of the Philosopher [Aristotle] in his writing concerning *Politics*; as he says, it is not only expedient that the latter should be governed, but it is just, although they be coerced thereto.
>
> —Alighieri, *De Monarchia*, 1904: 101–2

The title of Chapter VII is "The Roman people were ordained for empire by nature." Dante considered the expansion of the Roman Empire as historically predetermined, and viewed the clear distinction between ruler and ruled as "just." We can trace this classical dichotomy back to Aristotle. In a famous passage from Book I, Part II of *Politics*, Aristotle wrote:

> We shall, I think, in this as in the other subjects, get the best view of the matter if we look at the natural growth of things from the beginning. The first point is that those

which are incapable of existing without each other must be united as a pair. [...] Equally essential is the combination of the natural ruler and ruled, for the purpose of preservation. For the element that can use its intelligence to look ahead is by nature ruler and by nature master, while that which has the bodily strength to do the actual work is by nature a slave, one of those who are ruled. Thus there is a common interest uniting master and slave.

—Aristotle, *The Politics*, 1981: 56–7

Dante obviously agreed with Aristotle's thesis of the existence of two separate species of human beings, including "natural rulers" or "natural masters" on the one hand, and "natural slaves" on the other, which should be separated in order to promote the "common interest."

Dante wrote *De Monarchia* during a period of intense political dispute between the Holy Roman Emperor and the Pope. Dante's main objective in this work was to defend the autonomy of Florence from the intervention of Pope Boniface VIII (1230–1303). In this context, Dante looked to the Roman Empire as an ideal representation of secular authority. The title of each of the three Books of *De Monarchia* reflects Dante's use of Rome as a model:

Book I: Whether temporal monarchy is necessary for the wellbeing of the world
Book II: Whether the Roman people rightfully appropriated the office of monarchy
Book III: Whether the authority of the Roman monarch derives from God immediately or from some vicar of God

Dante uses "vicar of God" in Book III as a synonym for "Vicar of Christ," which referred to the Pope. The main question framing this book is whether the secular authority of the Roman Empire was offered as a divine gift from God or was bestowed by the supreme pontiff. Apart from the final conclusion, the most noticeable aspect of *De Monarchia* is that Dante's discussion took for granted the fact that the Roman Empire's secular authority was closely linked to the divine authority of Christianity. In other words, Dante approved of and applauded the simultaneous expansion of the Roman *imperium* and Christianity. The mutual constitutive relationship between *pax Romana* and *pax Christi* persisted after the issuing of the edict of Milan in 313, which legalized Christianity, and after the official approbation of Christianity as the state religion by Theodosius I (347–395) in 392. This marked a historical turning point as many persecuted Christians emerged from the shadows and began building magnificent churches. The political leaders of the Empire gradually became Christian, and Christianity spread across all social classes (Westbury-Jones 1971).

PAX ET TREUGA DEI

The initiative of the Catholic Church to create a peaceful social order

According to Takashi Shogimen, the late thirteenth century saw a boom in the authorship of treatises whose main themes were power, peace, and integration (Shogimen 2013: 101–2). The rediscovery of the *Corpus Aristotelicum*, and its application to Christian doctrine, was key to the birth of Christian political thought in medieval Europe. Dante shared a common pious belief in the Christian religion. As noted, the representative secular authority of the Roman Empire was linked to the supreme religious authority of the Catholic Church. This partnership produced the most powerful political and religious entity in medieval Europe and fascinated a number of feudal lords for its ideal collaboration. The Carolingian empire of the early Middle Ages (800–888), led by the Frankish king Charlemagne (748–814) and his supporter, Pope Leo III (750?–816), represents a prime example of this collaborative model.

The intervention of the Catholic Church in its effort to realize peace and integration in medieval Europe became known as the *pax et treuga Dei* (Peace and Truce of God). This was a medieval political movement supported by the Catholic Church. Its main purpose was to rein in the unjust violence between feudal lords. Charlemagne's death caused political and territorial upheaval in his former kingdom and gave rise to a number of private wars. In 989, the synod of Charroux took place in central France. Its resolution was to condemn those who disturb peace as "anathema" and to exclude them "from the holy church of God" (Head and Landes (eds.) 1992: 327–8). This implied the enforcement of religious sanctions and the increased definition of lawful activity in order to create a more peaceful social order. The movement expanded broadly throughout much of the rest of France and Flanders.

It is especially fascinating to note that, in the process of this movement's expansion, Aymon, the archbishop of Bourges, in central France, convened a special council in the first half of the eleventh century whose aim was to require not only horsemen, but all males more than fifteen years of age to take up arms against violators of peace (Duby 1980: 185–6). This justification of the use of armed force was closely related to that in the pope's speech from the late eleventh century, which called Christians to arms to wage the First Crusade (1096–9).

The Christian soldier (Miles Christi)

The Catholic Church's first attempt to achieve peace after the collapse of the Western Roman Empire was to impose religious sanctions through the general assemblies of various ecclesiastical synods. In addition, in the High Middle Ages, holy military expeditions outside Christendom were considered to contribute to establishing a peaceful social order within Europe.

Pope Urban II (1042–99) famously expressed this second idea in an emotional speech before the council of Clermont in 1095. In it, he encouraged the audience join the first sacred expedition (Crusade) to Jerusalem. This was the first official papal declaration calling for the integration of the Holy Sepulchre, then under Islamic rule, into Christendom (McNeal and Thatcher (eds.) 1905: 513–7). The purpose of this speech was to unite various types of immoral, barbarous persons behind the sacred mission of reconquering Jerusalem, which was expected to bring peace to Europe as well. This mission also implied the integration of the Holy Land within Christendom.

Even before launching the First Crusade, the papacy had organized a number of military expeditions. In 1053, for instance, Leo IX (1002–54) formed a holy militia to defend the Papal States, and as commander, he led his soldiers against the Normans in southern Italy. Alexander II (?–1073) intervened in a number of political disputes across Europe, and bestowed his allies with *vexillum sancti Petri* (St. Peter's standard) as a papal guarantee endorsing their war as holy. Popes awarded that standard to various leaders across Europe: Erlembald (?–1075), the political and military leader of the Patarian movement in Milan; Roger I (1031–1101), the conqueror of Sicily; the French-Spanish allied forces (crusade of Barbastro) in northeastern Spain (1064); and William I (1028–

FIGURE 8.1: *The Death of Harold*, La tapisserie de Bayeux, Musée de Bayeux (France). Wikimedia Commons.

87) in the Norman conquest of England (1066). Regarding the Norman conquest in particular, the Bayeux Tapestry contains a historical representation of the future William I with the standard in his left hand, identifying the Battle of Hastings in 1066 as a holy war. In another example, Pope Gregory VII mobilized the so-called *Milites sancti Petri*, an army of feudal lords against Henry VI (1050–1106), Holy Roman Emperor (Brown 1988; Jinno 2013: 44–5).

Papal military expeditions were also directed against other religious groups within Europe, labeled "heretics." In his letter to the archbishop of Arles in the south of France in November 1209, Pope Innocent III (1161–1216) referred to the *negotium pacis et fidei* (the business of peace and faith) (Power 2013: 1077–80). The same motto appears frequently in the document against Catharism. The business of peace and faith also appears frequently in the vast edited volume, *Patrologia Latina* (*The Latin Patrology*), published by Jacques-Paul Migne (1800–75), concerning the Albigensian crusade (1209–29), a military campaign organized by Innocent III to eradicate Catharism from southern France (Migne (ed.) 1986–8).

As the papal letters show, in the military campaign against Catharism, heresy was considered a violation of peace. Heretical doctrine was regarded as a destabilizing element in a peaceful society, and many feudal lords collaborated in suppressing the Cathars. Decree 27 of the Third Lateran Council (1179) (Fujisaki 2015: 171–80) and Decree 3 of the Fourth Lateran Council (1215) (Fujisaki, (ed.), 2015: 94–6) officially justified the use of armed force against heretics.

PAX HISPANICA

Making a Global Christian Republic

The idea of realizing peace through the integration of human beings into homogeneous political and religious regimes took shape in antiquity and gathered pace in medieval times. That process accelerated in the early modern period, spreading deeply and widely. Michel Foucault delivered a lecture on this topic at the *Collège de France* in 1978–9.

According to Foucault, the art of government was a hot topic, and was increasingly debated in Europe from the middle of the sixteenth century through the end of the eighteenth. He argued that the debate over government in early modern Europe revolved around four central concepts: (1) the government of oneself, (2) the government of souls and lives, (3) the government of children, and (4) the government of the state by the prince (Foucault 1979: 5).

As is well known, the early modern era served as the precursor to the modern era, but what exactly does the term "modern" mean? One of the characteristics typical of the modern period is the increase in theories and practices aimed at more tightly integrating the state and society (Schilling 1992: 209). This concept of integration spread widely across Europe, permeating a variety of discussions around politics, economics, and culture. Even more importantly, it was in the early modern period that the idea of integration began expanding on a global scale. Spain was a major proponent of this idea. After Christopher Columbus' "discovery" in 1492, Spain initiated a global process of colonial expansion, culminating in the *pax Hispanica*, of the late sixteenth and early seventeenth century. It was in reference to this period that future historians would eventually reflect back on Spain as "the empire on which the sun never set."

Soon after the surprising news of "discovery" reached the Iberian peninsula, Spanish Monarchy began dispatching expeditions of conquest and exploration accompanied by Christian missionaries. This resulted from the agreement between the monarchy and Pope Alexander VI (1431–1503) that all newly "discovered" lands would become possessions of Spain on the condition that the Spanish Christianize the native peoples of those lands. It was also due to the fact the Spanish monarchs were themselves deeply pious Christians. The fact that the capitulation of the last Muslim polity in Granada and the "discovery" of America both occurred in 1492 cultivated a sense that Spain was predestined for global monarchy and that the Christian faith would spread globally in the process of Spain's political expansion (Kamen 2005).

While integrating much of this newly "discovered" world into its ever expanding empire, the Spanish monarchy continued to prosecute heretics in the Iberian peninsula as well. Although intermittent military conflicts between Christian and Muslim armies persisted throughout the nearly 800-year process known as *Reconquista* (718–1492), it is also true that Iberia's Christian, Muslim, and Jewish communities lived in peaceful coexistence for much of that period (Menocal 2002). The year 1492, however, marked a major turning point in relations between these three groups. The Spanish monarchy began implementing a range of policies persecuting Muslims, Jews, and other groups labeled heretical. The main groups targeted were the *Mudéjares*, Muslims living peacefully in parts of Iberia under Spanish rule; the *Moriscos*, former Muslims who voluntarily or forcefully had converted to Christianity; *Conversos*, former Jews who accepted the faith of Christ; and *Marranos*, meaning literally "filthy as pigs," also former Jews who remained in the Iberian peninsula and converted to Christianity, but who continued to practice their faith in secret. In 1492, the Spanish monarchy forced all Jews either to be baptized and become true Christians, or to leave the Iberia peninsula for good within four months. The policy provoked a massive Jewish diaspora of some 150,000 to 200,000 people (Beinart 2002). Then, over a century later, in 1609 King Philip III issued his famous decree expelling the *Moriscos* (García-Arenal and Wiegers (eds.) 2014).

The *encomienda* was one the central means by which the Spanish aimed to convert Native Americans to Christianity, and it had its origin in the *Reconquista* of the Iberian peninsula. In that process, the crown awarded *encomiendas* to individuals who assisted in the conquest of territory from Muslim rule. In the process of conquering the New World, the Spanish crown awarded grants of Native Americans to *encomenderos*, the recipients of *encomiendas*, who were permitted to collect tribute from indigenous peoples and utilize them as labor. In exchange, the *encomendero* was required to instruct those indigenous peoples in the Spanish language and Christian faith. Although the institution was intended to advance the public good through consolidating Spanish control over newly conquered areas, it was often exploited for private ends. Fray Nicolás de Ovando (1460–1511), the Spanish governor of Hispaniola from 1502 to 1509 and a knight in the Order of Alcántara, first instituted the *encomienda* on the island in 1505. In reality, however, the goal of Christianizing natives under *encomienda* served mainly as a pretext for what became a harshly exploitative institution. In fact, although protecting Amerindians in *encomienda*, many *encomenderos* held them as slaves (Simpson 1966).

The legal and philosophical bases of *encomienda* in the Americas, and the justification of the exploitative treatment of Amerindians can be traced back to ancient Europe. Aristotelian theory insisted that barbarians were inferior to human beings and similar to animals. Identifying Amerindians as barbarians, many Spaniards emphasized the dramatic differences between the traditional customs and culture of Native Americans and Europeans. Spaniards cited the cannibalism, human sacrifice, and mysterious rituals practiced by many natives as evidence of their barbarism. Moreover, the Spanish justified their natural right to sovereignty over the newly "discovered" world on the pretext that the natives lacked legitimate laws, rulers, and political structures (Hanke 1970).

Spaniards based their justifications of Amerindian slavery not only on Aristotelian but also on Ciceronian and Augustinian thought. Ciceronian texts were the only ancient Roman political literature circulating in Western Christendom after the fall of the Western Roman Empire. The systematic translation of classical texts from ancient Greece began in the middle of the twelfth century. Aristotle's *Politics* was finally translated into Latin in the thirteenth century (R. Carlyle and A. Carlyle 1928). Prior to this, European intellectuals drew on treatises such as Cicero's *De invention* and *De officiis* in developing theories of social formation and political integration based on Stoicism, and of natural philosophy based on the Christian doctrine of original sin (Cicero, *De officiis*, I. 11–12; Cicero, *De inventione*, I. 2–3). According to this theory, moral corruption and original sin caused humans to commit injustices. At the same time, however, the theory insisted that despite these flaws, humans were by nature inclined to seek an ideal republic. To gain awareness of their own true nature, humans required persuasion by reason and eloquence. In other words, the theory viewed humans as possessing a natural desire to seek an ideal republic, but recognized that it could not be realized naturally. To realize this goal, some groups had to persuade other groups through reason and without violence (Nederman 1988: 6–10).

Augustine of Hippo (354–430) dreamed of creating a republic with an ideal form of government. His theological doctrine concerning the origin of political authority and its nature was influential until the thirteenth century although humans were naturally innocent before the depravity, they had become hostile, steeped in vice, driven by emotion and ambition. In this sense, government by force was indispensable to control humans' desires and correct their immorality (Markus 1988: 197–230).

Amerindian practices such as cannibalism and human sacrifice represented nothing more than vice in the eyes of Europeans. People who lacked morality were naturally prone to conflict. The introduction of political institutions was necessary in order to establish and maintain peace and justice in the world. In other words, forceful political power had the capacity to improve and correct the lives of the immoral. Although Cicero stressed the importance of reason and eloquence by persuasion, Augustin concluded that it was impossible for humans to overcome their natural proclivity to sin and vice. Several early modern Spanish authors drew on these arguments to justify the colonization and domination of the Americas as a means of eradicating the vices of Amerindians.

Many Iberian intellectuals endorsed and justified Spanish colonization of the New World. One of the most prominent was Juan López de Palacios Rubios (1450–1524), a jurist, member of the Council of Castile, faculty member of the universities of Salamanca and Valladolid, and the author of the *Requerimento*, a declaration read aloud to Amerindians explaining the bases of Spain's right to take possession of their lands. This was nothing more than an attempt to provide legal cover for the forceful colonization of the Americas (Williams Jr 1992: 88–93).

Interestingly, however, the Spanish crown simultaneously displayed two contradictory attitudes toward Amerindians: the desire to seize and colonize their land, and profound regret regarding their enslavement. In fact, the Spanish crown issued a number of royal decrees prohibiting excessive abuse and exploitation of Amerindians and providing them charitable protection based on the principles of Christianity (Konetzke, (ed.), 1953: v. I, nn. 5, 19, 32, 39, 44, 46, 47, 48). In 1550-1551 the crown organized the Valladolid debate between Juan Ginés de Sepúlveda (1494–1573), a Renaissance humanist and proponent of Amerindian slavery, and the Dominican friar Bartolomé de las Casas (1484–1566), also known as the "Protector of the Indians," who advocated on behalf of Amerindians throughout Spain's American empire. This debate demonstrated the great concern of the Spanish monarchy for the "human rights" of Amerindians. The debate centered on the rights and treatment of colonized peoples (Losada 1971).

Citing the Latin phrase, *compelle intrare*, from the Gospel of Luke in the New Testament, Sepúlveda explained the legitimacy of waging war against Amerindians, who were inferior by nature (Sepúlveda 1997: 92). Las Casas, meanwhile, greatly influenced by the *Summa Theologica* of Thomas Aquinas (*c.* 1225–74), argued in response that rulers were compelled to govern in the interest of the *bonum commune* and to strive to establish civilized harmony among their subjects (Valdivia Giménez 2010: 98). In other words, Las Casas imagined a colonization process that was more benevolent toward Amerindians, less exploitative, and less coercive in integrating them into the Spanish colonial regime (Hanke 1965).

The University of Salamanca was the center of debates regarding the legality and morality of Spain's colonization of "the Indies." There were a number of specialists on the "Affairs of the Indies" at Salamanca with a diversity of opinions, but the most influential was without doubt, the Dominican Francisco de Vitoria (*c.* 1483–1546), known today as one of the founders of international law. According to Natsuko Matsumori, the modern political order began to take shape at precisely the moment that the so-called School of Salamanca was flourishing (Matsumori 2012).

In medieval Christian thought, the non-Christian world was defined as "barbarous," as a "disturbed area" lacking the laws of war to regulate military action. Christendom, in contrast, was considered a world governed by the rule of law and justice. The German jurist and political theorist, Carl Schmitt (1888–1985) argued that, based on "global linear thinking," this dichotomous view of the world distinguished between what he referred to as "lines of amity" and that which lay "beyond the line" (Schmitt 2006: 86–100). The following argument from the Russian medievalist historian A.J. Gurevich (1924–2006) is also worth noting:

> The religious conception of space in the Middle Ages also finds expression in the division of the world into the Christian world on the one hand and the non-Christian world, the world of the infidel on the other. [. . .] Christianity represented a major advance on earlier conceptions of man, which had been restricted to the tribe (among the barbarians), a chosen people (the Jews) or a single and unique political formation (the Romans). [. . .] Only in so far as it was graced by the Christian faith and subjected to the church could the world be described as a cultured well-ordered world in which God's blessings could proliferate. Beyond the limits of this Christian world, space lost its positive qualities [. . .]
>
> —Gurevich 1985: 75

The School of Salamanca, however, first conceptualized a legal, moral, and political worldview that included not only those peoples within the "lines of amity," but also those beyond them, incorporating a range of non-European societies with a diversity of cultures and customs. In other words, the School of Salamanca's most innovative proposal was to establish a new republic, which integrated "barbarians," who were traditionally considered incapable of forming part of the same political order as Christians (Matsumori 2014: 53).

European theories distinguishing Christendom from the Pagan world with all its evils can be traced back to the writings of the Italian jurist, Gratian (c. 1100–c.1150?), the canonist, Hostientsis (c. 1200–71), and Pope Innocent IV (1195–1254). Drawing on their arguments, many generations of later European writers denied infidels' rights to property ownership and territorial jurisdiction (Matsumori 2009: chs. 2 and 4).

In the sixteenth century, many Europeans viewed the Amerindians from this perspective. Palacios Rubios, mentioned above, and the Dominican friar, Matias de Paz (c. 1468–1524), argued that ecclesiastical authorities could declare Amerindians' rights as invalid given their status as infidels. Another Dominican, Bernardo de Mesa (1470–1524), and the jurist, Gregorio López (1496–1560), based their theories on the inhumanity of Amerindians and the barbarity of their customs in a similar attempt to strip the natives of their rights (Matsumori 2005: 106–7, 122–3). It was in these circumstances that, in 1537, forty-five years after the "discovery" of the New World, Pope Paul III (1468–1549) issued the bull *Veritas Ispa*, which enjoined Europeans to respect the freedom and property rights of Native Americans (García (ed.) 1974: 517–8, *Traducción de las letras apostólicas o bula "Veritas Ispa"* [. . .], Roma, 9 de junio de 1537"). This bull was the fruit of a letter to the Pope from the Franciscan, Julián Garcés (1452–1542), who lived and worked in New Spain and highly praised the talents and virtues of the Amerindians there. (García (ed.) 1974: 507–16, *Traducción de la carta que el Ilmo. y Rmo. Sr. D. Fr. Julián Garcés, [. . .] escribió a la Santidad de Paulo III*, 1537).

Vitoria, one of the most prominent scholars of the School of Salamanca, wrote that, although immature, people labeled "barbarians" nonetheless possessed reason, polities, and property rights, and that no one could invalidate those rights. Vitoria's astonishing argument that Amerindians possessed innate rights and reason eventually became emblematic of the Salamanca school more broadly (Matsumori 2014: 57).

Modern scholars have divided the academic production of the Salamanca School into two periods, the first covering 1526 to 1575, and the second, 1576 to 1615. In the first period, Dominican friars were the main contributors, and they based their theories on the presence of advanced indigenous empires in the New World. Vitoria, for instance, placed great emphasis on the cities, rulers, laws, commerce, and religion of both the Aztec and

Inca empires. Although they were quite distinct from those found in Europe, the existence of the two vast Amerindian empires was obvious, and their political power and systems of government were undeniable. Vitoria also noted various commonalities between Europeans and Amerindians. As soon as Spaniards arrived in the New World, many compared the Amerindians to European peasants. Based on these debates, Vitoria concluded that Native Americans were human beings, but that they were only partially rational (Parry and Keith (eds.) 1984: 290–323).

Vitoria's conclusion that Amerindians were capable of self-government in certain cases represented the antithesis of the theory advocating Spain's absolute right to conquest and sovereignty in the New World. In a letter to the abbot of the Dominican monastery, where Vitoria lived, king Charles V (1500–58) expressed his clear displeasure at Vitoria's conclusion, deriding it as "pernicious and scandalous" (Vitoria, 1967: 152–3, *Carta de Carlos V al Prior de San Esteban de Salamanca, Madrid, 10 de noviembre de 1539*).

In the second period (1576–1615) of the Salamanca School, members of the Society of Jesus emerged as the most influential contributors to debates concerning the "Affairs of the Indies." In the first period, Dominicans had insisted on the civility of Amerindians by citing the examples of the Aztec and Inca empires. Other Amerindian groups, however, continued to be viewed as primitive and naïve, leading to their identification as disordered barbarians. Many Spaniards justified the forceful conquest, subjugation, and enslavement of Amerindians on this basis. Jesuits at the University of Salamanca, however, in particular Luis de Molina (1535–1600), argued that all communities of people, including infidels, possessed some level political power and organization, even if they could not be defined as possessing "states." This argument represented, essentially, an expansion of that initially advanced by Vitoria (Molina 1614: I, 370, in Matsumori 2014: 61).

The Jesuits even expressed doubt about Europeans' supposed superiority over Amerindians. Some members of the Society in southern Italy argued that many Europeans, especially those living in rural areas, could be described as barbarous, uncivilized heathen lacking stable social and political organization (Selwyn 2004: 95–6). The French Jesuits argued that villagers in Brittany were as "poor, abandoned, and ignorant" as the indigenous peoples of the New France (Deslandres 1999: 261). Although these arguments remained premised on the inferiority of Amerindians, they were remarkable in questioning the categorical superiority of Europeans. All of these authors based their comparisons of Europeans and Amerindians on Christian behavioral norms in evaluating degrees of civility. The ultimate aim was to determine whether a given group was capable of and qualified for membership in the ideal Christian republic.

Although collectively these debates continued to represent an imposition of European law, justice, and ethics on non-Europeans, the School of Salamanca nonetheless succeeded in establishing an innovative theory that sought to integrate "barbarians" into the Christian republic, in which a type of *jus gentium* would serve to maintain peaceful order. It was a significant attempt to advance beyond the bounds of the medieval European worldview, and seek peace and order not only within the "lines of amity," but also beyond them.

Many missionaries that sailed the Atlantic shared this utopian dream of building a new Christian republic composed of a variety of peoples from a range of cultural and historical backgrounds. In the following section, we will examine two examples of Christian republics that flourished in Spanish America.

Two Cases of Christian Republics in Spanish America: Mexico and Paraguay

The extraordinary news of Columbus' "discovery" inspired both conquerors and Christian missionaries to set sail for the New World. Missionaries hoped to realize a magnificent dream in this newly "discovered" land: to recreate the primitive Christian community that had once existed in ancient Europe. Throughout the Middle Ages, which lasted roughly a thousand years, Europeans developed various types of charitable and philanthropic beliefs and institutions, all rooted in Christianity. In time, however, secularization and politicization became a serious problem in Christendom. The East–West Schism (1054) and the Western Schism (1378–1417), for instance, were two of the most notable events in the ecclesiastical history of medieval Europe. As these disputes persisted into the sixteenth century, several clergymen, especially monks in the mendicant orders, dreamt of a rebirth of the ideal brotherhood. The monks saw the Amerindians of the New World as essential partners in recreating the primitive church. To this end, missionaries established new, settled communities of Amerindians, instructed them in Christian doctrine, custom, and culture, and thereby contributed to realizing the soft integration of Amerindians into the Spanish Empire (Phelan 1970: Part I).

One of the most notable of these enterprises was that established by the Franciscans in New Spain, in present-day Mexico. In 1523, three Flemish priests, Juan de Testo, Juan de Ahora, and Pedro de Gante, arrived at Veracruz on the Gulf of Mexico. Gante was the most famous of the three since he went on to become a well-known composer of Christian doctrine in the indigenous language, Nahuatl, and founded the School of San José of the Natives, the first Amerindian school in the New World (Torre Villar 1974). In June 1524, the famous "Apostles of Mexico," a delegation of twelve Franciscans, arrived in Mexico City (Ricard 1966). According to the Franciscan historian, Gerónimo de Mendieta (1525–1604), the Minister General, Francisco de Quiñones (*c.* 1480–1540), dispatched those twelve colleagues with instructions, in which he drew metaphorical comparisons between them and the Twelve Apostles of the Holy Bible (Mendieta 1971a: 199–206, and chs. 9–10).

The Franciscans' principal activity in New Spain was the humanistic education of the children of the indigenous nobility. The Basque Franciscan, Juan de Zumárraga (1468–1548), established the educational policy in both the above-mentioned School of San José of the Natives, as well as in the College of Santa Cruz of Santiago Tlatelolco (Plassmann, et al. 1949). The curriculum of both indigenous schools was the same as that of contemporary institutions in Europe, and was equally rigorous. We know from the extant book catalogues of the College of Tlatelolco that the elite Amerindians who attended that institution were highly educated ("Códice de Tlatelolco," 1971: 255–7, 259–61, 267–8). One of the keys to the success of Franciscan initiatives in education was existence in Mexico of a traditional, pre-European system of education, called *Calmecac*, for the sons of the Aztec nobility (Calnek 1988: 169–77). In an instance typical of connected history (Subrahmanyam 2011), the Franciscans succeeded in introducing a new European curriculum upon the basis of an indigenous educational tradition, which predated Spanish conquest.

The most significant outcome of Franciscan education was to transform the Amerindian elite into faithful subjects of the Spanish empire through literacy training (Restall, Sousa, and Terraciano, (eds.) 2005: 11–20, esp. I, 2). By transforming traditional hieroglyphic characters into alphabetic writing, and instructing Amerindians in European forms of literacy, the Franciscans contributed to the "educational conquest" of Amerindians by integrating many of them into the colonial regime (Lewis 1903).

FIGURE 8.2: College of Santa Cruz of Santiago Tlatelolco (Mexico). Wikimedia Commons.

In addition to the Franciscans' initiatives in education, we should not forget to mention another magnificent humanistic projects in New Spain. In 1532, Vasco de Quiroga (c. 1470–1565), the first bishop of Michoacán, in western Mexico, founded Santa Fe de México in Álvaro Obregón, one of the sixteen municipalities within Mexico's present-day capital city. The next year, he founded Santa Fe de la Laguna, by Lake Pátzcuaro, in what is today the state of Michoacán. Quiroga designated each of these newly established Amerindian villages as a "Hospital" (Verástique 2000).

We know from the notes Quiroga left in his copy of Thomas More's (1478–1535), *Utopia*, that he greatly admired that book (Warren 1963: 22). *Utopia* is a fictional work, but it well reflected More's political philosophy. First published in Latin in 1516, the book tells the story of a legendary island society and describes in detail its unique political, economic, and cultural characteristics. Disillusioned by the many political disputes and divisions within Christendom, in *Utopia*, More emphasized the ideal of monastic life, which functioned as a model for how humans might live peacefully (Davis 1981: 58).

Quiroga aimed to realize More's dream in his Hospitals. There were a number of striking commonalities between the descriptions contained in *Utopia* and the rule of government of the Hospital of Santa Fe. In both, land was held in common, men and women devoted six hours per day to collective works, agricultural crops were distributed equally among inhabitants, and residents chose administrative officials by general election (Quiroga, *Reglas y ordenanzas para el gobierno de los Hospitales de Santa Fe de México y de Michoacán*, in Spencer 1970: 241–69).

While viewing Europeans as corrupted by vice and other evils, Quiroga saw Amerindians, in contrast, as innocent children. The creation of communal life among Amerindians represented a return to primitive Christianity among them, and a transfer of millenarianism from the Old World to the New (Cohn 1970; Phelan 1970).

The process by which Quiroga and the Franciscans submitted Amerindians to Christian life and religion was referred to as *reducción*. This became a fundamental policy of Spanish colonialism. In its verb form, *reducir* meant to relocate Amerindians into new settlements according to ideal designs of Spanish urban planning. In these spaces, Spaniards instructed Amerindians in *policía* (civility), which consisted of Spanish religion, language, customs, lifestyle, and culture (Rosas Lauro, and Saito (eds.) 2017).

We can divide *reducciones* into two types. The first included settlements administered by Spanish civil authorities. The best example of this is the general resettlement of approximately 1.4 million Andean people into roughly 840 towns under the authority of the viceroy of Peru, Francisco de Toledo (1515–82) in 1569 (Mumford 2012: 190). The second type includes the Utopian towns missionaries built in other parts of Spanish America. The thirty *reducciones* the Jesuits founded in Paraguay (1609–1767) are the most famously successful examples of this second type. Their history was dramatically portrayed in the 1986 film, *The Mission* (Sarreal 2014).

The Spanish resettlement policy reflected an important contradiction. Spaniards forcibly obliged Amerindians to abandon their traditional culture and customs, and to learn and adopt the ways of Spanish Christian civilization. Although the School of Salamanca advanced a theory aimed at incorporating infidels into Christendom, the

FIGURE 8.3: Location of thirty *Reducciones* in the first half of the eighteenth century. Wikimedia Commons.

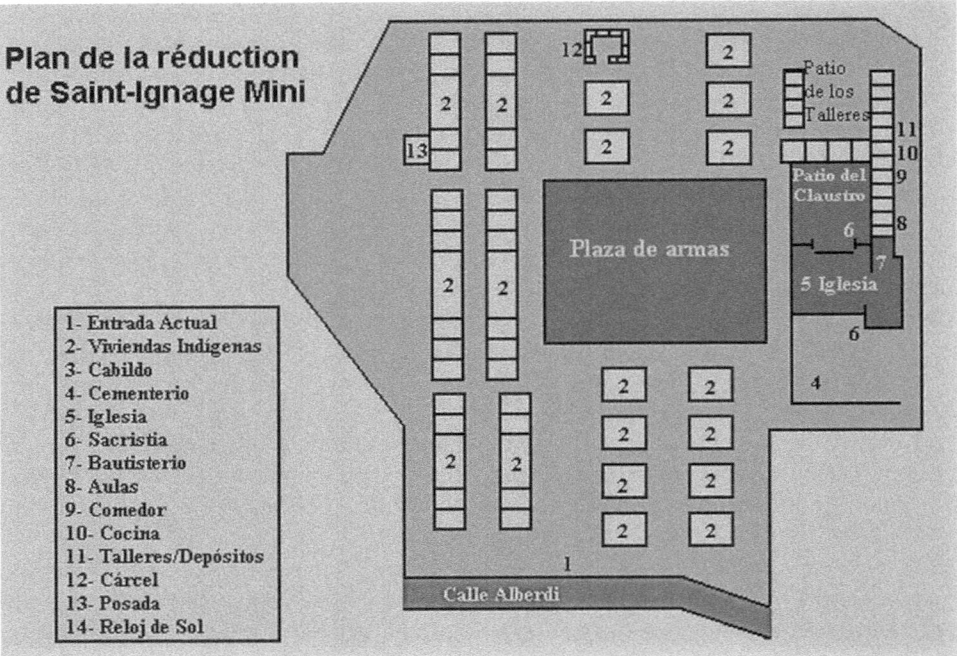

FIGURE 8.4: Typical plan of a Jesuit Mission, San Ignacio Miní (Argentina). Wikimedia Commons.

FIGURE 8.5: Jesuit-Guaraní Mission of La Santisima Trinidad (Paraguay). Wikimedia Commons.

proponents of the theory held that Amerindians had to be educated under the guidance and protection of "superior human beings." Their theory also justified Spaniards' use of armed force in cases where Amerindians refused that education. This opinion was common among the scholars of both the first and second Salamantine periods,[1] as well as among many missionaries and civil officials of the Spanish American colonial administration (Pereña 1984: 326, 328–37). In these circumstances, Amerindians often attempted to flee, both as individuals and in large collectives, and migrate to other regions in order to escape. The Amerindians who continued to live in relocated towns, however, gradually developed new identities through their experience in European Christian life.

A more concrete attempt to create an Indian Christian republic was to establish municipal councils, known in Spanish as *cabildos*, in each *reducción*. *Cabildos* were political councils originally founded in medieval Spain, and their members were chosen by both appointment and election. Council members were normally landowners and the heads of influential families (Gerli, et al. (eds.) 2003: 28–32).

Almost immediately upon arriving in the New World, Spaniards began establishing *cabildos* as the local political unit. Interestingly, Spanish colonial officials encouraged the introduction of *cabildos* in indigenous *reducciones* as well, and their members were chosen through periodic elections (Morínigo 1946).

The fact that missionaries held the final approval over those elections meant that indigenous municipalities were not truly autonomous. The Paraguayan Jesuit, José Cardiel (1704–82), described this in detail in the second half of the eighteenth century (Cardiel 1913). Importantly, however, in Paraguay, after the expulsion of the Jesuits by the Spanish crown in 1767–8, members of Amerindian *cabildos* began to take legal action against local colonial authorities. Regardless of the result of such action, the legal appeals advanced by Amerindian *cabildo* members were grounded in the general juridical customs and frameworks of early modern Iberia (Ganson 2003). This represented an example not only of the indigenization of a European institution, but also the peaceful integration of Amerindians into the Spanish colonial regime.

CONCLUSION

This chapter has focused on the various attempts of world empires and the Catholic Church to create forms of political and religious government by integrating diverse nations and believers in the name of peace (*pax*). Interestingly, the dream of establishing integrative forms of government was subsequently manifest through the attempts of Great Britain and the United States to achieve global political and religious hegemony. The spirit of *pax Romana* was clearly present during the subsequent periods of *pax Britannica* and *pax Americana* (Parchami 2009: 209), and the empires of Great Britain and the United States also represented the Christian empires of the modern age (Carey 2013; Conroy-Krutz 2015).

In the late-middle ages and the early-modern period, the desire to spread a peaceful social order through political and religious power began spreading beyond Europe. In the Ming (1368–1644) and the Qing (1644–1912) dynasties of China, for example, the state gained an increasingly powerful influence over the legal, commercial, and social structures throughout the vast regions on China's periphery. The multifaceted imperialistic tendencies of both dynasties also contributed to further integrating Chinese culture and religion (Crossley, Siu, and Sutton (eds.) 2006). We see another example of this in South America, even before the Spanish conquest. The Incas aimed to integrate a diversity of nations with myriad customs and cultures into a singular empire united in its worship of a common deity, the sun God. The French economist, Louis Baudin (1887–1964), defined the Inca polity as "socialist" (Baudin (1928) 1961). Baudin also became interested in the history of the Jesuit *reducciones* in Paraguay, and published a short monograph in which he labeled their polity a "socialist theocracy" (Baudin 1962). Although seemingly anachronistic, these examples from beyond Europe provide supplementary reading material for a better understanding of how different nations in the Renaissance (1450–1650) sought to mobilize integrative forms of government as a means of achieving political and religious peace.

NOTES

Chapter 1

1. Constantinople falls in 1453. In 1529 Vienna is under siege, and Suleiman II the Magnificent allies himself with Francis I of France in 1535. Cyprus is conquered in 1570.
2. Columbus accomplishes his voyage in 1492. The zones of influence are established with the *Raya* in 1493, while the slave trade officially begins in 1517, with the first *asiento*. Tenochtitlàn is destroyed by Cortez in 1521, and Peru is conquered by Pizarro in 1535.
3. Luther's theses are posted at Wittenberg in 1517 and the diet of Worms takes place in 1521. The Augustan confession is proclaimed in 1530, while the Catholics are excluded from political life in England with the first (1534) and second (1559) Supremacy Act. Calvin publishes the *Institutio religionis christianae* in 1536, and the Augusta's peace is signed in 1555.
4. The Peasants' War is fought in 1524–5, and Münster's Kingdom of God falls in 1535. Michele Servetus is condemned in 1555, while a large diaspora of Italian heretics radiates in Europe from the 1540s on, with Bernardino Ochino, Jacopo Aconcio, Celio Secondo Curione, Lelio and Fausto Socini among others.
5. This is testified by the support of Charles V's chancellor, Jean le Sauvage, who promotes Erasmus's pacifist effort in support of the treaty of Cambrai in 1529.
6. Not, however, with arms, which are the emperor's to command.
7. This is masterfully represented by Giorgio Martini's fresco in the Basilica inferiore of San Francesco in Assisi.
8. The final text is published in Latin in 1637.
9. *The Prince* is only published in 1532.
10. I.e. not below, above, or outside the State, for which war and confrontation are the natural and unavoidable condition, e.g. at international level.

Chapter 5

1. It can also be difficult to say with certainty whether some niello plaques were produced as paxes, since such objects were used for a variety of decorative purposes and have often since been disassembled. Speculation, beginning in the sixteenth century also linked niello paxes to the origins of engraved plates for prints, and some confusion remains about the relationship between the two arts.
2. Further, the graphic complexities of musical notation made music printing a continued challenge throughout early modernity. Manuscripts were generally preferred for their clarity and remained popular as late as the nineteenth century among musicians, composers, and patrons.
3. I am grateful to Patricia Simons for her observations on same-sex viewing and Bronzino's portraits of Cosimo.
4. Though in the collection of the National Gallery, London the painting is on long-term loan to the Rijksmuseum.
5. Oslo, National Gallery of Norway.

Chapter 8

1. For the representative opinion of first period of the School of Salamanca, see Vitoria, *Relectio de Indis* 1967, 30–1, 97. Regarding a typical assessment from second period of the School of Salamanca, see Suárez, "A Work on the Three Theological Virtues: Faith, Hope and Charity, divided into Three Treatises to Correspond with the Number of the Virtues Themselves," in Williams, et al. (eds.) 1944: 739–95. Particularly see Disputation xviii on the means which may be used for the conversion and coercion of unbelievers who are not apostates.

BIBLIOGRAPHY

AA.VV. (1961–2), *La paix*. Bruxelles: Editions de la librairie encyclopedique.
Abulafia, David (2008), *The Discovery of Mankind: Atlantic Encounters in the Age of Columbus*. New Haven-London: Yale University Press.
Adams, Robert P. (1962), *The Better Part of Valor: More, Erasmus, Colet and Vives on Humanism, War, and Peace, 1496–1535*. Seattle: University of Washington Press.
Adolf, Anthony (2009), *Peace: A World History*. Cambridge: Polity.
Alciati, Andrea (1996), *Emblematica*, (Lyons, 1550), trans. Betty I. Knott. Aldershot: Scholar Press.
Alciati, Andrea (2004), *A Book of Emblems: The Emblematum Liber in Latin and English*, trans. by John Moffat. Jefferson NC: Mcfarland.
Alighieri, Dante (1904), *De monarchia*, trans. by Aurelia Henry. Boston: Houghton, Mifflin.
Alighieri, Dante (1985), *Purgatory*, (*Divine Comedy*, vol. 2), trans. by Mark Musa. New York: Penguin Books.
Alighieri, Dante (1998), *Dante's Monarchia*, trans. with a commentary by Richard Kay. Toronto: Pontifical Institute of Medieval Studies.
Allen, Paul C. (2000), *Philip III and the Pax Hispanica, 1598–1621: The Failure of Grand Strategy*. New Haven, CT: Yale University Press.
Alpers, Svetlana (1983), *The Art of Describing: Dutch Art in the Seventeenth Century*. Chicago: University of Chicago.
Anghie, Antony (2004), *Imperialism, Sovereignty and the Making of International Law*. Cambridge: Cambridge University Press.
Anonymous (2003), *Collins Cobuild Advanced Learner's English Dictionary*, 4th ed. Glasgow: Harper Collins.
Antunes, Cátia, Leor Halevi and Francesca Trivellato eds. (2014), *Religion and Trade. Cross-Cultural Exchanges in World History 1000–1900*. Oxford, Oxford University Press.
Aquinas, Thomas (1964–81), *Summa theologiae*. London: Blackfriars edition.
Ariosto (1910), *The Orlando furioso of Ludovico Ariosto*, trans. by William Stewart Rose 2 vols. London: G. Bell.
Aristophanes (1998), *Aristophanes*, ed. and trans. by Jeffrey Henderson. Cambridge MA: Harvard University Press.
Aristotle (1981), *The Politics*, trans. by Thomas A. Sinclair. New York: Penguin Books.
Augustine (1957–72), *The City of God Against the Pagans*, ed. and English trans. by George E. McCracken et al. Harvard MA: Harvard University Press.
Augustine (1993), *The City of God (De Civitate Dei)*, trans. by Marcus Dods. New York: The Modern Library.
Augustine (2000–5), *Letters*. Hyde Park, NY: New City Press.
Augustine (2004) *De Doctrina Christiana*, ed. by Roger P.H. Green. Oxford Scholarship Online: April 2004 (DOI:10.1093/0198263341.001.0001).
Aviso piacevole dato alla bella Italia da un nobile giovane Francese, sopra la mentita data dal Serenissimo Re di Navarra a Papa Sisto V (1586). Munich: Giovanni Swartz [London: John Wolfe].

Baccelli, Luca (2016), *Bartolomé de Las Casas. La conquista senza fondamento*. Milan: Feltrinelli.
Bailey, Meryl (2008) "Salvatrix Mundi: Representing Queen Elizabeth as a Christ Type." *Studies in Iconography* 29: 176–215.
Bainton, Roland H. (1960), *Christian Attitudes Toward War and Peace: A Historical Survey and Critical Re-evaluation*. New York: Abingdon Press.
Bajczy, Istvan, (1997), "Tolerantia: A Medieval Concept," *Journal of the History of Ideas*, 58 (3): 365–84.
Baker, Nicholas S. and Brian J.Maxson, eds. (2015), *After Civic Humanism: Learning and Politics in Renaissance Italy*. Toronto: Toronto University Press
Baldi, Barbara (2006), *Pio II e le trasformazioni dell'Europa Cristiana*. Milan: Unicopli.
Baldini, Artemio E. (1999), "Tre inediti di Francesco Pucci al Cardinal Nepote e a Gregorio XIV alla vigilia del suo 'rientro a Roma'," *Rinascimento* 39: 157–224.
Balsamo, Jean (1998), "Dante, l'*Aviso piacevole* et Henri de Navarre," *Italique* 1: 79–94.
Barnavi, Elie and Miriam Eliav-Feldon, (1988), *Le périple de Francesco Pucci. Utopie, hérésie et vérité religieuse dans la Renaissance tardive*. Paris: Hachette.
Baron, Hans (1966), *The Crisis of the Early Italian Renaissance. Civic Humanism and Republican Liberty in an Age of Classicism and Tyranny*. Princeton: Princeton University Press.
Bascour, Hildebrand and Raymond Klibansky, (1956), "Praefatio editorum", in Nicolai de Cusa, *De pace fidei*, vii–liii.
Baskins, Cristelle (1994), "Gender Trouble in Italian Renaissance Art History," *Studies in Iconography*, 16: 1–36.
Baskins, Cristelle and Lisa Rosenthal, eds. (2007), *Early Modern Visual Allegory*. Burlington: Ashgate.
Baskins, Cristelle et al. (2008), *The Triumph of Marriage*. Boston: Isabella Stewart Gardner Museum.
Baudin, Louis [1928] (1961), *A Socialist Empire: The Incas of Peru*, trans. by Katherine Woods. Princeton: D. Van Nostrand.
Baudin, Louis (1962), *L'État jésuite du Paraguay: une théocratie socialists*. Paris: Génin.
Baumgärtel, Bettina (2002), "Is the King Genderless? The Staging of the Female Regent as Minerva Pacifera." in Annette Dixon, ed., *Women Who Ruled*, 97–110.
Behrens-Abouseif, Doris (2014), *Practising Diplomacy in the Mamluk Sultanate*. London and New York: I.B. Tauris.
Beinart, Haim (2002), *The Expulsion of the Jews from Spain*, trans. by Jeffrey M. Green. Oxford: Littman Library of Jewish Civilization.
Bellamy, Alex (2006), *Just Wars; From Cicero to Iraq*. Cambridge: Polity Press.
Belotti, Bartolo (1933), *La vita di Bartolomeo Colleoni*. Bergamo: Istituto italiano d'arti grafiche.
Bély, Lucien (2007), *L'art de la paix en Europe: naissance de la diplomatie moderne, XVIe–XVIIIe siècle*. Paris: Presses Universitaires de France.
Benoist, Élie (1693), *Histoire de l'Edit de Nantes contenant les choses les plus remarquables qui se sont passées en France avant et après sa publication [. . .]*, 3 vols. Delft: A. Beman.
Bentley, Jerry H., Sanjai Subrahmanyam, and Merry E. Wiesner-Hanks eds. (2015), *The Construction of a Global World, 1400–1800 CE*, vol. 6.1 of *The Cambridge World History*. Cambridge: Cambridge University Press.
Benvenuti, Anna (2006), "Draghi e confini. Rogazioni e litanie nelle consuetudini liturgiche," *Annali aretini*, 13: 49–63.

Bérenger, Jean (2002), *Tolérance ou paix de religion en Europe centrale (1415–1792)*. Paris: Champion.

Berlin, Isaiah ([1972] 2013), "The Originality of Machiavelli," in Henry Hardy and Roger Hausheer, eds., *The Proper Study of Mankind*. London: Vintage (original edition in *Studies on Machiavelli*, ed. by Myron P. Gilmore. Florence: Sansoni, 1972).

Berry, Mary Elizabeth (1982), *Hideyoshi*. Cambridge: Harvard University Press.

Biagioni, Mario (2011), *Francesco Pucci e l'*Informatione della religione christiana. Turin: Claudiana.

Biagioni, Mario (2017), *The Radical Reformation and the Making of Modern Europe. A Lasting Heritage*. Brill: Leiden.

Bisaha, Nancy (2004), "Pope Pius II and the Crusade," in Norman Housley, ed., *Crusading in the Fifteenth Century: Message and Impact*, 39–52. London: Palgrave Macmillan.

Bisaha, Nancy (2006), *Creating East and West: Renaissance Humanists and the Ottoman Turks*. Philadelphia: University of Pennsylvania.

Bjurner, Andres and Peter Wallensteen, eds. (2015), *Regional Organizations and Peacemaking: Challengers to the UN?* London: Routledge.

Black, Anthony (1998), "Popes and Councils", in Christopher Allmand, ed., *New Cambridge Medieval History*, vol. VII: *c*. 1415–1500, 65–86. Cambridge: Cambridge University Press.

Bloch, Ernst (1959) *Das Prinzip Hoffnung*, Frankfurt. a. M.: Suhrkampf Verlag; English trans. *The Principle of Hope*, trans. by Neville Plaice, Stephen Plaice, and Paul Night. Cambridge MA: MIT Press.

Bloch, Ernst (1968), *Atheismus in Christentum. Zur Religion des Exodus und des Reichs*, Frankfurt a. M.: Suhrkamp; English trans by J.T. Swann, *Atheism in Christianity: The Religion of the Exodus and the Kingdom*. New York: Harder and Harder, 1972.

Blockmans, Wim, André Holenstein, and Jon Mathieu, eds. (2009), *Empowering Interactions: Political Cultures and the Emergence of the State in Europe. 1300–1900*. Aldershot: Ashgate.

Bobbio, Norberto. (1983), "Pace," in Norberto Bobbio, Nicola Matteucci and Gianfranco Pasquino, eds., *Dizionario di politica*, 737–42. Turin: UTET.

Bodin, Jean (1962), *The Six Books of a Commonwealth*, ed. by Kenneth D. MacRae. Cambridge MA: Harvard University Press.

Boersma, Owe and Aike J. Jelsma, eds. (1997), *Unity in Multiformity. The Minutes of the Coetus of London, 1575 and the Concistory Minutes of the Italian Church of London 1570–1591*. London: Huguenot Society Publications.

Bondanella, Peter (1976), *Francesco Guicciardini*. Boston: Twayne Publishers.

Bonora, Elena (2011), *Roma 1564. La congiura contro il papa*. Rome-Bari: Laterza.

Boone, Rebecca Ard (2007), *War, Domination, and the Monarchy of France. Claude de Seyssel and the Language of Politics in the Renaissance*. Leiden: Brill.

Boone, Rebecca Ard (2014), *Mercurino di Gattinara and the Creation of the Spanish Empire*. London: Pickering and Chatto.

Borghesi, Francesco (2012), "For the Good of All. Notes on the Idea of Concordia during the late Middle Ages," *Italian Poetry Review*, 5: 215–44.

Brambilla, Elena (2006), *La giustizia intollerante. Inquisizione e tribunali confessionali in Europa (secoli IV–XVIII)*. Rome: Carocci.

Brock, Peter (1978), "A Polish Anabaptist Against War: The Question of Conscientious Objection in Marcin Czechowic's Christian Dialogues of 1575," *The Mennonite Quarterly Review*, 52: 279–93.

Brook, Timothy (2008), *Vermeer's Hat: The Seventeenth Century and the Dawn of the Global World*. New York: Bloomsbury Press.

Brook, Timothy (2010), *The Troubled Empire: China in the Yuan and Ming Dynasties*. Cambridge, MA: Belknap Press.
Brotton, Jerry (2002), *The Renaissance Bazaar: From the Silk Road to Michelangelo*. Oxford: Oxford University Press.
Brotton, Jerry and Lisa Jardine (2005), *Global Interests: Renaissance Art Between East and West*. London: Reaktion.
Brown, Shirley Ann (1988), *The Bayeux Tapestry: History and Bibliography*. Woodbridge: Boydell Press.
Brummett, Palmira (1994), *Ottoman Seapower and Levantine Diplomacy in the Age of Discovery*. Albany: State University of New York.
Brummett, Palmira (2015), *Mapping the Ottomans: Sovereignty, Territory, and Identity in the Early Modern Mediterranean*. Cambridge: Cambridge University Press.
Burke, Peter (1995), *The Fortunes of the Courtier: The European Reception of Castiglione's "Cortegiano."* Cambridge: Cambridge University Press.
Burkhardt, Albrecht ed. (2007), *Commerce, voyage et expérience religieuse XVIe–XVIIIe*. Rennes: Presse Universitaires de Rennes.
Bussman, Klaus and Heinz Schilling, eds. (1999), *1648, War and Peace in Europe*. Münster: Council of Europe.
Butterfield, Andrew (1996), "The Candelabrum by Andrea del Verrocchio," *Bulletin van het Rijksmuseum*, 44: 120–2.
Butterfield, Andrew (1997), *The Sculptures of Andrea del Verrocchio*. New Haven: Yale University.
Caferro, William (2011), *Contesting the Renaissance*. Chichester: Wiley-Blackwell.
Caferro, William ed. (2017), *The Routledge History of the Renaissance*. Abingdon: Routledge.
Cahn, Jean-Paul, Françoise Knopper and Anne-Marie Saint-Gil, eds. (2008), *De la guerre juste à la paix juste. Aspects confessionnels de la construction de la paix dans l'espace franco-allemand (XVIe–XXe siècle)*. Villeneuve d'Ascq: Presses Universitaires du Septentrion.
Cailes, Michael J. (2012), "Renaissance Ideas of Peace and War and the Humanist Challenge to the Scholastic Just War," Thesis for a Doctor of Philosophy in Politics, University of Exeter.
Calnek, Edward (1988), "The Calmecac and Telpochcalli in Pre-Conquest Tenochtitlan", in Jorge J. Klor de Alva, ed., *The Work of Bernardino de Sahagún: Pioneer Ethnographer of Sixteenth-Century Aztec Mexico*, 169–77. Albany: IMS.
Calvin, Joannis (1863–1900), *Ioannis Calvini Opera quae supersunt omnia*, Ediderit Guilielmus Baum, Edouard Cunitz, Eduard Reuss. Berolini: Brunsvigae.
Campanella, Tommaso (2008), *La città del sole*, Con traduzione, apparati critici, note a cura di Tonino Tornitore Torino: Aragno; English edition, Tommaso Campanella (1981) *The City of the Sun: A Poetical Dialogue* trans. by Daniel J. Donno. Berkeley-London: University of California Press.
Campbell, C. Jean (2008), *The Commonwealth of Nature*. University Park, PA: Pennsylvania State University.
Campbell, Caroline and Alan Chong, eds. (2005), *Bellini and the East*. New Haven: Yale University.
Campbell, Stephen J. (2004), *The Cabinet of Eros: Renaissance Mythological Painting and the Studiolo of Isabella d'Este*. New Haven: Yale University.
Cantimori, Delio (1959), "Nicodemismo" e speranze conciliari nel Cinquecento italiano," in *Studi di storia*. Turin: Einaudi, 518–39.
Cantimori, Delio (1960), *Prospettive di storia ereticale*, republished in Id., *Eretici italiani del Cinquecento*, 421–81.

Cantimori Delio (1992), *Eretici italiani del Cinquecento e altri scritti*, ed. by Adriano Prosperi. Turin: Einaudi.

Capizzi, Joseph (2015), *Politics, Justice, and War: Christian Governance and the Ethics of Warfare*. Oxford: Oxford University Press.

Caravale, Giorgio (2011), *Il profeta disarmato. L'eresia di Francesco Pucci nell'Europa del Cinquecento*. Bologna: Il Mulino.

Caravale, Giorgio (2015), *The Italian Reformation outside Italy. Francesco Pucci's Heresy in Sixteenth-Century Europe*. Brill: Leiden.

Cardiel, José (1913), "Breve Relación de las Misiones del Paraguay," in Pablo Hernández, *Organización social de las doctrinas guaraníes de la Compañía de Jesús*, vol. 2, 514–614. Barcelona: Gustavo Gili.

Carey, Hilary M. (2013), *God's Empire: Religion and Colonialism in the British World, c. 1801–1908*. Cambridge: Cambridge University Press.

Carlyle, Robert W. and Alexander J. Carlyle (1928), *A History of Mediæval Political Theory in the West*, vol. 5. Edinburgh and London: William Blackwood.

Carrió-Invernizzi, Diana (2014), "A New Diplomatic History and the Networks of Spanish Diplomacy in the Baroque Era," *International History Review* 36: 603–18.

Carta, Paolo (1999), *Nunziature ed eresia nel Cinquecento. Nuovi documenti sul processo e la condanna di Francesco Pucci 1592–1597*. Padua: Cedam.

Carter, Tim (2002), *Monteverdi's Musical Theatre*. New Haven: Yale University.

Casadei, Alberto (2007), "Guerra/Pace," in Remo Ceserani, Mario Domenichelli, Pino Fasano, eds., *Dizionario dei temi letterari*, 1072–84. Turin: UTET.

Cassirer, Ernst (1946), *The Myth of the State*. New Haven: Yale University Press.

Cassirer, Ernst (2002), *Individuum und Kosmos in der Philosophie der Renaissance*, in *Gesammelte Werke*. Hamburger Ausgabe, XIV. Hamburg: F. Meiner.

Castiglione, Baldesar (1967), *The Book of the Courtier*, trans. George Bull. London: Penguin.

Cavallo, Jo Ann (2004), *The Romance Epics of Boiardo, Ariosto, and Tasso: From Public Duty to Private Pleasure*. Toronto: University of Toronto.

Cellini, Benvenuto (1898), *The treatises of Benvenuto Cellini on goldsmithing and sculpture* (made into English from the Marcian codex by C.R. Ashbee). London: Edward Arnold.

Cesa, Marco (2014), *Machiavelli on International Relations*. Oxford: Oxford University Press.

Chen, Frederick Tse-shyang (1991), "The Confucian View of World Order," *Indiana International & Comparative Law Review*, 1 (1): 45–69.

Christin, Olivier (1997), *La paix de religion. L'autonomisation de la raison politique au XVIe siècle*. Paris: Seuil.

Christopher, Paul (1994), *The Ethics of War and Peace: An Introduction to Legal and Moral Issues*. Upper Saddle River, NJ: Pearson.

Coates, Anthony J. (1997), *The Ethics of War*. Manchester and New York: Manchester University Press.

Coates, Anthony J. (2006), "Culture, the Enemy and the Moral Restraint of War," in David Rodin and Richard Sorabji, eds., *The Ethics of War*, 208–21.

Cohl Ahl, Diane (2008), *Fra Angelico*. New York: Phaidon.

Cohn, Norman (1970), *The Pursuit of the Millennium: Revolutionary Millenarians and Mystical Anarchists of the Middle Ages*. New York: OUP.

Cole, Michael W. (2015), *Leonardo, Michelangelo, and the Art of the Figure*. New Haven: Yale University.

Collins, James B. (1995), *The State in Early Modern France*. Cambridge: Cambridge University Press.

Collins, James B. (2002), *From Tribes to Nation. The Making of France 500–1799*. Toronto: Wadsworth.

Conroy-Krutz, Emily (2015), *Christian Imperialism: Converting the World in the Early American Republic*. Ithaca: Cornell University Press.

Contini, Roberto and Francesco Solinas (2010), *Una gloria europea. Pietro da Cortona a Firenze (1637–1647)*. Milan: Silvana.

Copenhaver, Brian and Charles Schmitt (2002), *Renaissance Philosophy*. Oxford and New York: Oxford University Press.

Cortright, David (2008), *Peace. A History of Movements and Ideas*. Cambridge: Cambridge University Press.

Cox-Rearick, Janet (1993), *Bronzino's Chapel of Eleonora in the Palazzo Vecchio*. Los Angeles and Berkeley: University of California.

Cressy, David (1989), *Bonfires and Bells: National Memory and the Protestant Calendar in Elizabethan and Stuart England*. London: Weidenfeld and Nicolson.

Crossley, Pamela Kyle, Helen F. Siu, and Donald S. Sutton, eds. (2006), *Empire at the Margins: Culture, Ethnicity, and Frontier in Early Modern China*. Berkeley: University of California Press.

Crouzet, Denis (1990), *Les guerriers de Dieu. La violence au temps des troubles de religion, vers 1525–vers 1610*, 2 vols. Seyssel: Champ Vallon.

Croxton, Derek and Anuschka Tischer (2002), *The Peace of Westphalia: A Historical Dictionary*. Westport, CT: Greenwood Press.

Crucé, Éméric de (2004), *Le nouveau Cynée ou discours d'Etat*, introduction par Alain Fenet; édition du texte, index, mise en page et composition par Astrid Guillaume; notes par Astrid Guillaume et Michel Bouvier. Rennes: Presses Universitaires de Rennes.

Curtain, Philip D. (1984), *Cross Cultural Trade in World History*. Cambridge: Cambridge University Press.

Cusa, Nicolai de (1956), *De pace fidei cum epistula ad Ioannem de Segobia*, ediderunt, commentariisque, illustraverunt, Raymundus Klibansky et Hildebrandus Bascour. London: The Warburg Institute.

Czechoslovak Academy of Sciences, ed. (1964), *The Universal Peace organization of King George of Bohemia: A Fifteenth Century Plan For World Peace, 1462/1464*, edition of the document by Jiří Kejř. Prague: Publishing House of the Czechoslovak Academy of Sciences.

D'Elia, Anthony F. (2005), *The Renaissance of Marriage in Fifteenth-Century Italy*. Cambridge, MA: Harvard University.

Dale, Stephen F. (2010), *The Muslim Empires of the Ottomans, Safavids, and Mughals*. Cambridge: Cambridge University Press.

Davis, James C. (1981), *Utopia and the Ideal Society: A Study of English Utopian Writing 1516–1700*. Cambridge: Cambridge University Press.

de Girolami Cheney, Liana (1998), "Peace," in Helene E. Roberts, ed., *Encyclopedia of Comparative Iconography: Themes Depicted in Works of Art*, 701–6. Chicago and London: Fitzroy Dearborn.

de Groot, Erlend (2009), "The Dutch Embassy to Isfahan (Persia) in 1651–52, led by Johannes Cunaeus: A New Interpretation of Weenix's Monumental History Painting," *The Rijksmuseum Bulletin*, 57: 312–25.

de Vries, Jan (1989), *The Economy of Europe in an Age of Crisis, 1600–1750*. Cambridge: Cambridge University Press.

de Vries, Jan (2010), "The Limits of Globalization in the Early Modern World", *Economic History Review*, 63: 710–33.

Decker, John R. and Mitzi Kirkland-Ives, eds. (2015), *Death, Torture, and the Broken Body in European Art, 1300–1650*. Burlington, VT: Ashgate.

Descrizione delle feste fatte in Firenze per le reali nozze de serenissimi sposi Ferdinando II Gran Duca di Toscana e Vittoria Principessa d'Urbino (1637). Florence: Zanobi Pignoni.

Deslandres, Dominique (1999), "*Exemplo aeque ut verbo*: The French Jesuits' Missionary World", in John W. O'Malley et al., eds., *The Jesuits: Cultures, Sciences, and the Arts, 1540–1773*, 258–73. Toronto: University of Toronto Press.

Deutsche illustrierte Flugblätter des 16. und 17. Jahrhunderts (1980), Bände I–III, Teil 2. München: Kraus–Tübingen: M. Niemeyer.

Dewald, Jonathan (1996), *The European Nobility, 1400–1800*. Cambridge: Cambridge University Press.

Diefendorf, Barbara (1991), *Beneath the Cross: Catholics and Huguenots in Sixteenth-Century Paris*. Oxford: Oxford University Press, 1991.

Dixon, Annette (2002), "Women Who Ruled: Queens, Goddesses, Amazons 1500–1650: A Thematic Overview," in Annette Dixon, ed., *Women Who Ruled*, 119–78.

Dixon, Annette, ed. (2002), *Women Who Ruled: Queens, Goddesses, Amazons in Renaissance and Baroque Art*. London: Merrell.

Draper, Gerald I.A.D. (1992), "Grotius' Place in the Development of Legal Ideas about War," in Hedley Bull, Benedict Kingsbury, and Adam Roberts, eds., *Hugo Grotius and International Relations*, 177–208. Oxford: Clarendon Press.

Dubost, Jean-François (2009), *Marie de Médicis: la reine dévoilée*. Paris: Payot.

Duby, Georges (1974), "Histoire sociale et idéologies des sociétés," in Jacques Le Goff and Pierre Nora, eds., *Faire de l'histoire. Nouveaux problèmes*, 147–68. Paris: Gallimard.

Duby, Georges (1980), *The Three Orders: Feudal Society Imagined*, trans. by Arthur Goldhammer. Chicago: University of Chicago Press.

Duchhardt, Heinz (2004), "From Westphalia to the Revolutionary Era," in Randall Lesaffer, ed., *Peace Treaties and International Law*, 45–58.

Duffy, Eamon (1996), *The Stripping of the Altars*. New Haven: Yale University.

Duindam, Jeroen (2015), *Dynasties: A Global History of Power, 1300–1800*. Cambridge: Cambridge University Press.

Duindam, Jeroen, Tülay Artan, and Metin Kunt, eds. (2011), *Royal Courts in Dynastic States and Empires: A Global Perspective*. Leiden: Brill.

Dursteler, Eric (2006), *Venetians in Constantinople: Nation, Identity, and Coexistence in the Early Modern Mediterranean*. Baltimore, MD: Johns Hopkins University Press.

Elias, Norbert (1982), *The Civilizing Process. State Formation and Civilization*, trans. by Edmund Jephcott. Oxford: Blackwell.

Elliott, John H. (1992), "A Europe of Composite Monarchies," *Past and Present*, 137, 1992: 48–71.

Elliott, John H. and Lawrence W.B. Brockliss, eds. (1999), *The World of the Favourite*. New Haven, CT: Yale University Press.

Elshtain, Jean Bethke (1987), *Women and War*. New York, NY: Basic Books.

Erasmus, Desiderius (1917), *The Complaint of Peace*, trans. by Thomas Paynell. Chicago: Open Court (accessed on line Sept. 2016 http://oll.libertyfund.org/titles/87).

Erasmus, Desiderius (1977), *The Education of a Christian Prince, with the Panegyric for Archduke Philip of Austria*, ed. by Neil M. Cheshire, Michael J. Heath, and Lisa Jardine. Cambridge: Cambridge University Press.

Erasmus, Desiderius (1988), *Collected Works of Erasmus*. Toronto, Buffalo. London: University of Toronto Press.

Ernst, Germana (2005), "*Sicut amator insaniens*. Su Pucci e Campanella," in Lech Szczucki ed., *Faustus Socinus and His Heritage*, 91–112. Krakow: Polish Academy of Arts and Sciences.

Escuela de Salamanca (1988), *Carta magna de los indios: fuentes constitucionales, 1534–1609*. Madrid: CSIC.

Evans Pim, Joam (2010), "Peace Research: History," in Nigel J. Young, ed., *The Oxford International Encyclopedia of Peace*, III, 449–53.

Falciani Carlo and Antonio Natali, eds. (2010) *Bronzino: Painter and Poet at the Court of the Medici*. Florence: Mandragora.

Fantoni, Marcello (1999), "The Grand Duchy of Tuscany: The Courts of the Medici, 1532–1737," in John Adamson, ed., *The Princely Courts of Europe: Ritual, Politics and Culture Under the Ancien Régime, 1500–1750*, 255–73. London: Weidenfeld and Nicolson.

Felici, Lucia (2007), "Il papa diavolo: il problema dell'Anticristo nella pubblicistica europea del Cinquecento," in Florence Alazard and Frank La Brasca, eds., *La Papauté à la Renaissance*, 533–69. Paris: Champion.

Ferente, Serena (2007), "Guelphs! Factions, Liberty, and Sovereignty: Inquiries about the Quattrocento," *History of Political Thought*, 4: 571–98.

Fernández-Santamaria, José (1977), *The State, War and Peace. Spanish Political Thought in the Renaissance, 1516–1559*. Cambridge, Cambridge University Press.

Finden, Paula (1998), "Possessing the Past: The Material World of the Italian Renaissance," *American Historical Review*, 103: 83–114.

Findly, Ellison Banks (1993), *Nur Jahan: Empress of Mughal India*. Oxford: Oxford University Press.

Finley, Moses I. (1967), "Utopianism Ancient and Modern", in Kurt H. Wolfe and Barrington Moore, eds., *The Critical Spirit: Essays in Honour of Herbert Marcuse*, 3–20. Boston: Beacon Press.

Finnis, John (1996), "The Ethics of War and Peace in the Catholic Natural Law Tradition", in Terry Nardin, ed., *The Ethics of War*, 15–39.

Firpo, Luigi (1957), "Gli scritti di Francesco Pucci," *Memorie dell'Accademia delle scienze di Torino* 3 (4): 263–98.

Firpo, Luigi (1996), *Scritti sulla Riforma in Italia*. Naples: Prismi.

Firpo, Massimo (1997), *Gli affreschi di Pontormo a San Lorenzo. Eresia, politica e cultura nella Firenze di Cosimo I*. Turin: Einaudi.

Firpo, Massimo (1998), *Dal sacco di Roma all'Inquisizione. Studi su Juan de Valdés e la Riforma italiana*. Alessandria: Edizioni dell'Orso.

Firpo, Massimo (2001), "Politica imperiale e vita religiosa in Italia nell'età di Carlo V." *Studi storici* 2: 245–61.

Firpo, Massimo (2005), *Inquisizione romana e Controriforma. Studi sul cardinal Giovanni Morone (1509–1580) e il suo processo di eresia*. Brescia: Morcelliana.

Firpo, Massimo (2014), *La presa di potere dell'Inquisizione romana, 1550–1553*. Rome-Bari: Laterza.

Firpo, Massimo (2015), *Juan de Valdés and the Italian Reformation*. Farnham: Ashgate.

Firpo, Massimo and Dario Marcatto, eds. (1998–2000), *I processi inquisitoriali di Pietro Carnesecchi (1557–1567)*, 2 vols. Vatican City: Archivio Segreto Vaticano.

Fisch, Jörg (1984), *Die europäische Expansion und das Völkerrecht : Die Auseinandersetzungen um den Status der überseeichen Gebiete vom 15. Jahrhundert zur Gegenwart*. Stuttgart: Steiner.

Fletcher, Catherine and Jennifer Mara DeSilva (2010), "Italian Ambassadorial Networks in Early Modern Europe—An Introduction," *Journal of Early Modern History* 14: 505–12.

Foa, Jérémie (2011), "Peace commissioners at the beginning of the Wars of Religion. Toward an interactionist interpretation of the pacification process," in Thomas Max Safley, ed., *Handbook: Multiconfessionalism in the Early Modern World*, 239–64. Leyden: Brill.

Foa, Jérémie (2015), *Le tombeau de la paix. Une histoire des édits de pacification (1560–1572)*. Limoges: Presses universitaires de Limoges.

Forclaz, Bertrand, ed. (2013), *L'expérience de la différence religieuse dans l'Europe moderne (XVIe–XVIIIe siècles)*. Neuchâtel: Éd. Alphil-Presses universitaires suisses.

Foucault, Michel (1979), "Governmentality," *Ideology & Consciousness*, 6: 5–21.

Fournel, Jean-Louis and Jean-Claude Zancarini (2009), *La grammaire de la république. Langages de la politique chez Francesco Guicciardini*. Geneva: Droz.

Fournel, Jean-Louis and Jean-Claude Zancarini (2014), "Guerra e pace," in *Enciclopedia Machiavelliana*, I: 674–9. Rome: Istituto dell'Enciclopedia Italiana, Treccani.

Fragnito, Gigliola (1972), "Gli spirituali e la fuga di Bernardino Ochino," *Rivista storica italiana* 84: 777–813.

Fragnito, Gigliola (2011), *Cinquecento italiano. Religione, cultura e potere dal Rinascimento alla Controriforma*. Bologna: Il Mulino.

Fried, Michael (2010), *The Moment of Caravaggio*. Princeton: Princeton University.

Frijhoff, Willem (2002), *Embodied Belief: Ten Essays on Religious Culture in Dutch History*. Hilversum, The Netherlands: Verloren.

Fujisaki, Mamoru (2015), "Stratified Identities in the Medieval Catholic World: Discourse Analysis of Ecclesiastical Council during the 12–13th Centuries," *The Journal of Historical Studies*, 937: 171–80.

Fujisaki, Mamoru, ed. (2015), "Decrees of the Fourth Lateran Council (1215)," *Clio: A Journal of European Studies*, 9: 87–130.

Gáldy, Andrea M. (2013), "Identity and Likeness: Bronzino's Medici Portraits," in Andrea M. Gáldy, ed., *Agnolo Bronzino*, 36–8.

Gáldy, Andrea M., ed. (2013), *Agnolo Bronzino: Medici Court Artist in Context*. Newcastle upon Tyne: Cambridge Scholars Publishing.

Galtung, Johan (1990), "Violence and Peace," in Paul Smoker, Ruth Davies, and Barbara Munske, eds., *A Reader in Peace Studies*, 9–14. Oxford: Pergamon Press.

Gamberini, Andrea and Isabella Lazzarini, eds. (2012), *The Italian Renaissance State*. Cambridge: Cambridge University Press.

Ganson, Barbara (2003), *The Guaraní under Spanish Rule in the Río de la Plata*. Stanford: Stanford University Press.

García-Arenal, Mercedes and Gerard Wiegers, eds. (2014), *The Expulsion of the Moriscos from Spain: A Mediterranean Diaspora*, trans. by Consuelo López-Morillas and Martin Beagles. Leiden: Brill.

García, Genaro, ed. (1974), *La inquisición de México: autos de fe, tumultos y rebeliones en México, el clero durante la dominación española, Don Juan de Palafox y Mendoza*, 2 ed. México: Porrúa.

Gelder, Maartje van and Tijana Krstic (2015), "Introduction: Cross-Confessional Diplomacy and Diplomatic Intermediaries in the Early Modern Mediterranean," *Journal of Early Modern History* 19: 93–105.

Genet, Jean-Philippe (2011), "L'historien et les langages de la société politique," in Andrea Gamberini, Jean-Philippe Genet and Andrea Zorzi, eds., *The Languages of the Political Society. Western Europe, 14th–17th Centuries*, 17–38. Rome: Viella.

Genet, Jean-Philippe et al., eds. (1985–90), *Genèse de l'État moderne*, CNRS, Madrid, Rome, Paris.

Gentili, Alberico (1587), *Disputationum decas prima*. London: John Wolfe.
Gentili, Alberico (1589), *De iure belli commentationes tres*. London: John Wolfe.
Gentili, Alberico (1598), *De iure belli libri tres*. Hanau: Heirs of Wilhelm Antonius.
Gentili, Alberico (1605), *Regales disputationes tres*. Hanau: Wilhelm Antonius.
Gentili, Alberico (1612), *De iure belli libri tres*. Hanau: Heirs of Wilhelm Antonius.
Gentili, Alberico (1933), *De iure belli libri tres*, trans. by John C. Rolfe. Oxford: Clarendon Press.
Gerli, E. Michael, et al., eds. (2003), *Medieval Iberia: An Encyclopedia*. New York: Routledge.
Geuna, Marco (2012), "Old and New Justifications for War: Just Wars and Humanitarian Interventions," in Thomas Maissen and Fania Oz-Salzberger, eds., *The Liberal-Republican Quandary in Israel, Europe, and the United States. Early Modern Thought Meets Current Affairs*, 133–53. Boston: Academic Studies Press.
Gilbert, Creighton (2003), *How Fra Angelico and Signorelli Saw the End of the World*. University Park, PA: Pennsylvania State University.
Giorgini, Giovanni (2014), "Uomini," in *Enciclopedia Machiavelliana*, II: 632–6. Rome: Istituto dell'Enciclopedia Italiana, Treccani.
Gittings, John (2012), *The Glorious Art of Peace from the* Iliad *to Iraq*. Oxford: Oxford University Press.
Glover, Jonathan (1999), *Humanity: A Moral History of the Twentieth Century*. New Haven and London: Yale University Press.
Goffman, Daniel (2002), *The Ottoman Empire and Early Modern Europe*. Cambridge: Cambridge University.
Goffman, Daniel (2007), "Negotiating with the Renaissance State: The Ottoman Empire and the New Diplomacy," in Virginia H. Aksan and Daniel Goffman, eds., *The Early Modern Ottomans: Remapping the Empire*, 61–74. Cambridge: Cambridge University Press.
Gordimer, Nadine (2007), *Beethoven was One-Sixteenth Black*. New York, Penguin.
Grafton, Anthony (2002), "Humanism and Political Theory," in Zachary S. Schiffman, ed., *Humanism and the Renaissance*, 157–71. Boston: Houghton Mifflin Company.
Gratian (1879–91), *Corpus Iuris Canonici*, eds. Emil Friedberg, Emil Ludwig Richter. Leipzig: B. Tauchnitz.
Greer, Margaret R., Walter D. Mignolo, and Maureen Quilligan, eds. (2008), *Rereading the Black Legend: The Discourses of Religious and Racial Difference in the Renaissance Empires*. Chicago: University of Chicago.
Gregory, Sharon (2012), *Vasari and the Renaissance Print*. Burlington, VT: Ashgate.
Grotius, Hugo (2005), *The Right of War and Peace*, ed. and with an introduction by Richard Tuck. Indianapolis: Liberty Fund.
Guicciardini, Francesco (1969), *The History of Italy by Francesco Guicciardini*, trans., ed., with notes and an introduction by Sidney Alexander. New York-London: Macmillan.
Guidi, Andrea (2009), *Un Segretario militante. Politica, diplomazia e armi nel cancelliere Machiavelli*. Bologna: Il Mulino.
Guidi, Andrea (2017), "Les conclusions 'galliardes' du Secrétaire florentin: esprit de finesse, initiative et efficacité politique dans l'activité pratique de Machiavel," in *Essere uomini di "lettere": segretari e politica culturale nel Cinquecento*, 51–61, ed. by Antonio Geremicca e Hélène Miesse. Florence: Franco Cesati.
Gunnoe, Jr., Charles D. (2011), *Thomas Erastus and the Palatinate: A Renaissance Physician in the Second Reformation*. Leiden: Brill.
Gurevich, Aron J. (1985), *Categories of Medieval Culture*, trans. by G.L. Campbell. London: Routledge.

Guy, John, ed. (1995), *The Reign of Elizabeth I. Court and Culture in the Last Decade*. Cambridge: Cambridge University Press.

Habermas, Jürgen, *The Theory of Communicative Action*, Vol. II: *Lifeworld and System* (1984–7), trans. by Thomas McCarthy. Boston: Beacon.

Habermas, Jürgen (1990), *Moral Consciousness and Communicative Action*. Cambridge MA: Cambridge University Press.

Hale, John R. (1962), "War and Opinion: War and Public Opinion in the Fifteenth and Sixteenth Centuries Author(s)," *Past and Present*, 22: 18–35.

Hale, John R. (1971), "Sixteenth-century Explanations of War and Violence," *Past and Present*, 51: 3–26.

Hale, John R. (1998), *War and Society in Renaissance Europe 1450–1620*. Stroud: Sutton Publishing.

Haley, Kenneth H.D. (1972), *The Dutch in the Seventeenth Century*. London: Thames and Hudson.

Hampton, Timothy (2009), *Fictions of Embassy: Literature and Diplomacy in Early Modern Europe*. Ithaca, NY: Cornell University Press.

Hampton, Timothy, (2016), "The Slumber of War: Diplomacy, Tragedy, and the Aesthetics of the Truce in Early Modern Europe," in Nathalie Rivère de Carles, ed., *Early Modern Diplomacy, Theatre and Soft Power: The Making of Peace*, 27–45. London: Palgrave Macmillan.

Hanke, Lewis (1965), *The Spanish Struggle for Justice in the Conquest of America*. Boston: Little Brown.

Hanke, Lewis (1970), *Aristotle and the American Indians: A Study in Race Prejudice in the Modern World*. Bloomington: Indiana University Press.

Hankins, James ed. (2000), *Renaissance Civic Humanism: Reappraisal and Reflections*. Cambridge: Cambridge University Press.

Hanlon, Gregory (1993), *Confession and Community in Seventeenth-Century France: Catholic and Protestant Coexistence in Aquitaine*. Philadelphia: University of Pennsylvania Press.

Hanlon, Gregory (2016), *Italy 1636: Cemetery of Armies*. Oxford: Oxford University Press.

Harvey, Karen (2005), *The Kiss in History*. Manchester: Manchester University.

Hayden-Roy, Patrick M. (1994), *The Inner World and Outer World: A Biography of Sebastian Franck*. New York: P. Lang.

Head, Thomas and Richard Landes, eds. (1992), *The Peace of God: Social Violence and Religious Response in France Around the Year 1000*. Ithaca: Cornell University Press.

Headley, John (1992), "Rhetoric and Reality: Messianic, Humanist, and Civilian Themes in the Imperial Ethos of Gattinara," in Marjorie Reeves ed., *Prophetic Rome in the High Renaissance Period*, 241–70. Oxford: Clarendon Press.

Headley, John M. (2008), *The Europeanization of the World: On the Origins of Human Rights and Democracy*. Princeton: Princeton University Press.

Heath, Michael (1989), "Unholy Alliance: Valois and Ottomans," *Renaissance Studies* 3: 303–15.

Heinen, Ulrich (2004), "Rubens' Pictorial Diplomacy at War (1637/1638)," *Nederlands Kunsthistorisch Jaarboek*, 55: 196–225.

Helfferich, Tryntje (2013), *The Iron Princess: Amalia Elisabeth and the Thirty Years War*. Cambridge, MA: Harvard University Press.

Helmers, Helmer (2016) "Public Diplomacy in Early Modern Europe," *Media History* 22 (3/4): 401–20.

Hind, Arthur M. (1938), *Early Italian Engraving*. London: Bernard Quaritch.

Hobbes, Thomas (1998), *De Cive [On the Citizen]*, trans. and eds. by Richard Tuck and Michael Silverthorne. Cambridge: Cambridge University Press.
Hobbes, Thomas (2012), *Leviathan*, ed. by Noel Malcolm. Oxford: Clarendon Press.
Hoekstra, Kinch (2012), "Thucydides and the Bellicose Beginnings of Modern Political Theory," in Katherine Harloe and Neville Morley, eds., *Thucydides and the Modern World: Reception, Reinterpretation, and Influence from the Renaissance to the Present*, 22–54. Cambridge: Cambridge University Press.
Holt, Mack P. (1995), *The French Wars of Religion 1562–1629*. Cambridge: Cambridge University Press.
Hood, William (1993), *Fra Angelico at San Marco*. New Haven: Yale University.
Horodowich, Elizabeth (2017), "The Wider World: Foreigners, Travels, and Geography," in Monica Azzolini and Isabella Lazzarini, eds., *Italian Renaissance Diplomacy. A Sourcebook*, 190–213. Toronto: Pontifical Institute of Medieval Studies.
Horodowich, Elizabeth and Lia Markey, eds. (2017), *The New World in Early Modern Italy, 1492–1750*. New York: Cambridge University Press.
Hsia, Po-chia R. (1996), *Trent 1475: Stories of a Ritual Murder*. New Haven: Yale University.
Inalcik, Halil (1988), *The Ottoman Empire: The Classical Age 1300–1600*. London: Phoenix Press.
Israel, Jonathan (1997), *Conflicts of Empires*. London: Hambledon.
James, William (1910), "The Moral Equivalent of War." Available online: www.consitution.org/wj/meow.htm (accessed July 20, 2018).
Janssen, Wilhelm (2004²). "Friede", in Otto Brunner, Werner Conze, and Reinhardt Koselleck, edrs. *Geschichtliche Grundbegriffe: historisches Lexicon zur politisch-sozialen Sprache in Deutschland*, 543–91. Stuttgart: Klett-Cotta.
Jardine, Lisa (1996), *Worldly Goods: A New History of the Renaissance*. London: Macmillan.
Jardine, Lisa (2004), "Gloriana Rules the Waves: Or, the Advantage of Being Excommunicated (And a Woman)," *Transactions of the Royal Historical Society*, 14: 209–22.
Jinno, Takashi (2013), "The Development of Roman Catholic Church," Koichi Horikoshi and Takashi Jinno, eds., *Jugo no tema de manabu chusei yoroppashi (15 Topics of History of Medieval Europe)*, 38–60. Kyoto: Mineruva Shobo.
Johnson, James Turner (1984), "Two kinds of Pacifism: Opposition to the Political Use of Force in the Renaissance-Reformation Period," *The Journal of Religious Ethics*, 12 (1): 51–6.
Johnson, James Turner (1987), *The Quest for Peace: Three Moral Traditions in Western Cultural History*. Princeton NJ: Princeton University Press.
Kafadar, Cemal (1996), *Between Two Worlds: The Construction of the Ottoman State*. Berkeley and Los Angeles: University of California.
Kamen, Henry (1971), *The Iron Century: Social Change in Europe, 1550–1650*. London: Weidenfeld and Nicolson.
Kamen, Henry (2005) *Spain, 1469–1714: A Society of Conflict*, 3rd ed. Harlow: Pearson Longman.
Kaplan, Benjamin J. (2002), "Fictions of Privacy: House Chapels and the Spatial Accommodation of Religious Dissent in Early Modern Europe," *American Historical Review* 107: 1031–64.
Kaplan, Benjamin J. (2007), *Divided by Faith. Religious Conflict and the Practice of Toleration in Early Modern Europe*. Cambridge MA: Harvard University Press.
Karant-Nunn, Susan C. (1982), "Continuity and Change: Some Effects of the Reformation on the Women of Zwickau," *The Sixteenth Century Journal* 13: 17–42.
Katz, Dana (2008), *The Jew in the Art of the Italian Renaissance*. Philadelphia: University of Pennsylvania.

Keating, Jessica (2015), "Metamorphosis at the Mughal Court," *Art History*, 38: 733–47.
Keating, Jessica (2018), *Animating Empire: Automata, the Holy Roman Empire, and the Early Modern World*. University Park: Penn State University Press.
Keith, Robert G. and John H. Parry, eds. (1984), *New Iberian World: A Documentary History of the Discovery and Settlement of Latin America to the Early 17th Century*, vol. 1. New York: Hector & Rose.
Kempshall, Matthew S. (1999), *The Common Good in Late Medieval Political Thought*. Oxford: Oxford University Press.
Kettering, Alison McNeil (1998), *Gerard ter Borch and the Treaty of Münster*. The Hague: Mauritshuis.
King, Margaret (1986), *Venetian Humanism in an Age of Patrician Dominance*. Princeton: Princeton University Press.
Kingsbury, Benedict and Adam Roberts, (1992), "Introduction: Grotian Thought in International Relations" *Hugo Grotius and International Relations*, 1–64, eds. Hedley Bull, Benedict Kingsbury, and Adam Roberts. Oxford: Clarendon Press.
Kingsbury, Benedict and Benjamin Straumann, eds. (2010), *The Roman Foundations of the Law of Nations: Alberico Gentili and the Justice of Empire*. Oxford: Oxford University Press.
Kirshner, Julius, ed. (1994), *The Origin of the State in Italy; 1300–1600*. Chicago: University of Chicago Press.
Klaassen, Walter, ed. (1981), *Anabaptism in Outline: Selected Primary Sources*. Waterloo, Ont.: Herald Press.
Kline, A.S., *A.S. Kline's Free Poetry Archive* (http://www.poetryintranslation.com/PITBR/Latin/VirgilAeneidVI.htm#anchor_Toc2242942), accessed March 23, 2017.
Knecht, Robert J. (1994), *Renaissance Warrior and Patron: The Reign of Francis I*. Cambridge: Cambridge University Press.
Knecht, Robert. J. (2001), *The Rise and Fall of Renaissance France*. Oxford: Blackwell Publishers.
Knoppers, Laura Lunger and Joan B. Landes, eds. (2004), *Monstrous Bodies. Political Monstrosities in Early Modern Europe*. Ithaca, NY: Cornell University Press.
Kohl, J. (2018), "A Murder, a Mummy, and a Bust: The Newly Discovered Portrait of Simon of Trent at the Getty," *Getty Research Journal*, 10: 37–60.
Komaroff, Linda ed. (2011), *Gifts of the Sultan: The Arts of Giving at the Islamic Courts*. Los Angeles: Los Angeles County Museum of Art.
Konetzke, Richard (ed.) (1953), *Colección de documentos para la historia de la formación social de Hispanoamérica, 1493–1810*, vol. 1. Madrid: CSIC.
Koskenniemi, Martti (2010), "International Law and *raison d'état*. Rethinking the Prehistory of International Law," 298–339, in Benedict Kingsbury and Benjamin Straumann, eds., *The Roman Foundation*.
Kostial, Michaela, (2009), "Peace," in Manfred Landfester et al., eds., *Brill's New Pauly: Classical Tradition*, 329–34. Leiden-Boston: Brill.
Kunt, Metin and Christine Woodhead, eds. (1995), *Suleyman the Magnificent and His Age: The Ottoman Empire in the Early Modern World*. London and New York: Longman.
Langedijk, Karl (1976), "Baccio Bandinelli's Orpheus: A Political Message," *Mitteilungen des Kunsthistorichen Institutes in Florenz*, 20: 33–52.
Last Stone, Suzanne (2006), "Judaism and Civil Society," in Michael Walzer ed., *Law, Politics, and Morality in Judaism*, 12–33. Princeton: Princeton University Press.
Lausen-Higgins, Johanna (2012), "'All the Gold a Miser Desires': A New Reading for the Iconography of the Grotto of the Animals at Villa Castello," *Garden History*, 40: 253–67.

Lavenia, Vincenzo (2009), "Alberico Gentili: i processi, le fedi, la guerra," in Luigi Lacchè ed., *Ius gentium Ius communicationis Ius belli. Alberico Gentili e gli orizzonti della modernità*, 165–96. Milan: Giuffrè, 2009.

Lavenia, Vincenzo (2016), "Intorno ad Alberico Gentili. La formazione, i processi, l'esilio," in Lucia Felici ed., *Ripensare la Riforma protestante. Nuove prospettive degli studi italiani*, 255–68. Turin: Claudiana.

Lazzarini, Isabella (2015), *Communication and Conflict: Italian Diplomacy in the Early Renaissance, 1350–1520*. Oxford: Oxford University Press.

Le Moyne, Pierre (1647), *La Gallerie des femmes fortes*. Paris: Antoine de Sommaville.

Lecuppre-Desjardins, Élodie and Anne-Laure van Bruaene, eds. (2010), *De Bono Communi. The Discourse and Practice of the Common Good in the European City (13th–16th centuries)*. Turnhout: Brepols.

Lee, Alexander (2013), *The Ugly Renaissance: Sex, Greed, Violence, and Depravity in the Age of Beauty*. New York: Doubleday.

Lesaffer, Randall (2004), "Peace treaties from Lodi to Wesphalia", in Randall Lesaffer, ed., *Peace Treaties and International Law*, 9–44.

Lesaffer, Randall, ed. (2004), *Peace Treaties and International Law in European History. From the Late Middle Ages to World War One*, ed. by Randall Lesaffer. Cambridge: Cambridge University Press.

Levi, Peter (1998), *Virgil: His Life and Times*. London: Duckworth.

Lewis, Robert E. (1903), *The Educational Conquest of the Far East*. New York: F.H. Revell.

Lightbown, Ronald (1978), *Secular Goldsmiths Work in Medieval France*. London: Thames and Hudson.

Loh, Maria, ed. (2001), *Early Modern Horror*. Oxford: Oxford University.

Lopez, George A., ed. (1989), *Peace Studies: Past and Future*, special issue of *The Annals of the American Academy of Political and Social Sciences*, 504.

Losada, Ángel (1971), "The Controversy between Sepúlveda and Las Casas in the Junta of Valladolid," in Juan Friede and Benjamin Keen, eds., *Bartolomé de las Casas in History: Toward an Understanding of the Man and his Work*, 279–308. DeKalb: Northern Illinois University Press.

Louthan, Howard P. and Randall C. Zachman (2004), *Conciliation and Confession. The Struggle for Unity in the Age of Reform, 1415–1648*. Notre Dame: University of Notre Dame Press.

Lowe, Ben (2005). "Peace," in Maryanne Cline Horowitz, ed., *New Dictionary of the History of Ideas*. Farmington Hills MI: Thomson Gale.

Lowinsky, Edward E., ed. (1968), *The Medici Codex of 1518*. Chicago: University of Chicago.

Luria, Keith P. (2005), *Sacred Boundaries. Religious Coexistence and Conflict in Early Modern France*. Washington: Catholic University Press of America.

Luther, Martin (1962), *Temporal Authority: To What Extent It Should Be Obeyed*, 1523, in *Luther's Works*, vol. XLV, ed. William I. Brandt, trans. from the German by J.J. Schindel and rev. by Brandt, 75–129. Philadelphia: Muhlenberg Press.

Luther, Martin (1966), *Treatise on Good Works*, 1520, in *Luther's Works*, vol. XLIV, ed. James Atkinson, trans. from German by W.A. Lambert and rev. by Atkinson, 15–114. Philadelphia: Fortress Press.

Luther, Martin (1967), *Whether Soldiers, Too, Can Be Saved*, 1526, in *Luther's Works*, vol. XLVI, ed. Robert C. Schultz, trans. by C.M. Jacobs and rev. by Schultz., 46–87. Philadelphia: Fortress Press.

Lynn, John A. II. (2008), *Women, Armies, and Warfare in Early Modern Europe*. Cambridge: Cambridge University Press.

Machiavelli, Niccolò (1954), *La mandragola*. Bologna: Cappelli (*The Mandrake*, English version by F. May and E. Bentley in Eric Bentley, *The Classic Theatre*. New York, Doubleday, 1958, vol. 1, 1–57).

Machiavelli, Niccolò (1988), *The Prince*, ed. by Quentin Skinner and Russell Price. Cambridge-New York: Cambridge University Press.

Machiavelli, Niccolò (2001), *Discorsi sopra la prima deca di Tito Livio*, ed. by Francesco Bausi. Rome: Salerno; English edition Machiavelli, Niccolò (1998), *Discourses on Livy*, trans. by Harvey C. Mansfield and Nathan Tarcov. Chicago: University of Chicago Press.

Machiavelli, Niccolò (2006), *Il Principe*, ed. by Mario Martelli. Rome: Salerno; English edition Machiavelli, Niccolò (1998), *The Prince*, trans. by Harvey C. Mansfield. Chicago: University of Chicago Press.

Machiavelli, Niccolò (2010), *Opere storiche*, ed. by Alessandro Montevecchi and Carlo Varotti. Gen ed. Gian Mario Anselmi. Rome: Salerno.

Maclean, Ian (2009), *Learning and the Market Place. Essays in the History of the Early Modern Book*. Leiden: Brill.

MacPherson, Crawford Brough (1962), *The Political Theory of Possessive Individualism*. Oxford: Oxford University Press.

Major, J. Russell (1994), *From Renaissance Monarchy to Absolute Monarchy: French Kings, Nobles, and Estates*. Baltimore: Johns Hopkins University Press.

Malcolm, Noel (2010), "Alberico Gentili and the Ottomans," in Benedict Kingsbury and Benjamin Straumann, eds., *The Roman Foundations of the Law of Nations: Alberico Gentili and the Justice of Empire*. Oxford, Oxford University Press, 127–45.

Mallett, Michael E. (1974), *Mercenaries and their Masters: Warfare in Renaissance Italy*. Totowa, NJ: Rowman and Littlefield.

Mapel, David (1996), "Realism and the Ethics of War and Peace," in Terry Nardin, ed., *The Ethics of War*, 54–77.

Marcocci, Giuseppe (2014), "L'Italia nella prima età globale (1300–1700)," *Storica*, 20: 7–50.

Markus, Robert A. (1988), *Saeculum: History and Society in the Theology of St. Augustine*, 2nd ed. Cambridge: Cambridge University Press.

Marsilius of Padua (1928), *The Defensor Pacis*, ed. by Charles W. Previté-Orton. Cambridge: Cambridge University Press.

Martin, Gregory (2011), *Rubens in London: Art and Diplomacy*. London: Harvey Miller.

Matsumori, Natsuko (2005), *Civilización y barbarie: los asuntos de Indias y el pensamiento político moderno (1492–1560)*. Madrid: Biblioteca Nueva.

Matsumori, Natsuko (2009), *De la barbarie al orden: los asuntos de Indias y la Escuela de Salamanca*. Nagoya: The University of Nagoya Press (in Japanese).

Matsumori, Natsuko (2011), "The School of Salamanca in the Affair of the Indies: Toward an Alternative Theory of the Modern State," *International Relations–Comparative Cultural Studies* 10 (1): 27–48.

Matsumori, Natsuko (2012), "The Modern Political Order and the Affair of the Indies (1)–(2)," *Journal of International Relations and Comparative Culture*. University of Shizuoka, vols. 10 (2)–11 (1): 283–301, 85–108.

Matsumori, Natsuko (2014), "The School of Salamanca: 'The Barbarians' and Political Power," in Yoshie Kawade, ed., *Shuken to jiyu (Sovereignty and Liberty)*, 51–71. Tokyo: Iwanami Shoten.

Mattingly, Garrett (1955), *Renaissance Diplomacy*. Boston, MA: Houghton Mifflin.

May, Larry (1989), "Hobbes on the attitude of pacifism," in Martin Bertman and Michel Malherbe, eds., *Thomas Hobbes. De la métaphysique à la politique*, 129–40. Paris: Librairie philosophique J. Vrin.

Mayes, David (2015), "Divided by Toleration: Paradoxical Effects of the 1648 Peace of Westphalia and Multiconfessionalism," *Archiv für Reformationsgeschichte*, 106: 290–313.

McCall, Timothy and Sean Roberts. (2017), "Art and the Material Culture of Diplomacy," in Monica Azzolini and Isabella Lazzarini, eds., *Renaissance Diplomacy*, 214–33. Toronto: PIMS.

McNeal, Edgar Holmes and Oliver J. Thatcher, eds. (1905), *A Source Book for Mediæval History: Selected Documents Illustrating the History of Europe in the Middle Age*. New York: Scribner's.

Medici Codex, Florence: Biblioteca Medicea-Laurenziana, MS Acquisti e Doni 666.

Mendieta, Gerónimo de (1971a), *Códice Mendieta: documentos franciscanos, siglos XVI y XVII*, Vol. 2. Guadalajara: Edmund Aviña Levy.

Mendieta, Gerónimo de (1971b), *Historia eclesiástica indiana: obra escrita a fines del siglo XVI*, 2nd ed. México: Porrúa.

Menocal, María Rosa (2002), *The Ornament of the World: How Muslims, Jews, and Christians Created a Culture of Tolerance in Medieval Spain*. New York: Little Brown.

Meserve, Margaret (2008), *Empires of Islam in Renaissance Historical Thought*. Cambridge, MA: Harvard University.

Meurer, Peter (2008), "Europa Regina. 16th Century Maps of Europe in the Form of a Queen," *Belgeo*, 3–4: 355–70.

Meuwese, Mark (2011), "The Opportunities and Limits of Ethnic Soldiering: The Tupis and the Dutch-Portuguese Struggle for the Southern Atlantic, 1630–1657," in Wayne E. Lee, ed., *Empires and Indigenes: Alliance, Imperial Expansion, and Warfare in the Early Modern World*, 193–220. New York, NY: New York University Press.

Meyjes, Guillaume H.M. Posthumus (1997), "Tolerance et irénisme," in Cristiane Berkvens-Stevelinck, Jonathan Israel and Guillaume H.M. Posthumus Meyjes, eds., *The Emergence of Tolerance in the Dutch Republic*, 63–73. Leiden: Brill.

Miglietti, Sara (2010), "Amitié, harmonie et paix politique chez Aristote et Jean Bodin," *Asterion* Mis en ligne le 01 septembre 2010, consulté le 29 septembre 2016. URL: http://asterion.revue.org/1660.

Migne, Jacques-Paul, ed. (1986–8), *Innocentii III Romani pontificis Opera omnia (Patrologiæ cursus completus*, 214–17 vols.). Turnholti: Typographi Brepols.

Milazzo, Lorenzo (2012), *La teoria dei diritti di Francisco de Vitoria*. Pisa: ETS.

Mineo, Ennio I. (2009), "Liberté et communauté en Italie (milieu XIIIe-début XVe siècle)" in Claude Moatti and Michèle Riot-Sarcey, eds., *La République dans tous ses états. Pour une histoire intellectuelle de la république en Europe*, 215–50. Paris: Payot.

Minnucci, Giovanni (2016), *Silete theologi in munere alieno. Alberico Gentili tra diritto, teologia e religione*. Milan: Monduzzi.

Molina, Luis de (1614), *De iusticia et iure, opera omnia*, vol. 1. Venetiis: Apud Sessas.

Momigliano, Arnaldo (1996), *Pace e libertà nel mondo antico*. Florence: La Nuova Italia.

Montaigne, Michel de (1983), *Journal de voyage*, ed. by Fausta Garavini. Paris: Gallimard.

Monter, William (2012), *The Rise of Female Kings in Europe, 1300–1800*. New Haven, CT: Yale University Press.

More, Thomas (1965), *Utopia*, in *Works*, vol. IV. New Haven and London: Yale University Press.

Moreau, Pierre-François (1989), *Hobbes. Philosophie, science, religion*. Paris: Presses Universitaires de France.

Morínigo, Marcos A. (1946), "Sobre los cabildos indígenas de las Misiones," *Revista de la Academia de Entre Ríos*, 1: 29–37.

Mormando, Franco (1999), "'Just as Your Lips Approach the Lips of Your Brothers': Judas Iscariot and the Kiss of Betrayal," in Franco Mormando, ed., *Caravaggio and the Baroque Image*, 179–90.

Mormando, Franco, ed. (1999), *Caravaggio and the Baroque Image*. Boston: Museum of Fine Arts.

Muhanna, Elias I. (2010), "The Sultan's New Clothes: Ottoman-Mamluk Gift Exchange in the Fifteenth Century," *Muqarnas*, 27: 189–207.

Mumford, Jeremy Ravi (2012), *Vertical Empire: The General Resettlement of Indians in the Colonial Andes*. Durham: Duke University Press.

Musacchio, Jaqueline (2009), *Art, Marriage, and Family in the Florentine Renaissance Palace*. New Haven: Yale University.

Najemy, John (1993), *Between Friends: Discourses of Power and Desire in the Machiavelli-Vettori Letters of 1513–1515*. Princeton: Princeton University Press.

Naohiro, Asao (1991), "The sixteenth-century unification," trans. by Bernard Susser, ed. by John Whitney Hall, *The Cambridge History of Japan*. Vol. 4: *Early Modern Japan*, 40–95. Cambridge: Cambridge University Press.

Nardin, Terry, ed. (1996), *The Ethics of War and Peace: Religious and Secular Perspectives*. Princeton, Princeton University Press.

Nederman, Cary J. (1988), "Nature, Sin, and the Origins of Society: The Ciceronian Tradition in Medieval Political Thought," *Journal of the History of Ideas*, 49 (1): 3–26.

Negro, Emilio and Nicosetta Roio (1998), *Francesco Francia e la sua scuola*. Mantua: Artioli.

Netzloff, Mark (2011), "The Ambassador's Household: Sir Henry Wotton, Domesticity, and Diplomatic Writing," in Robyn Adams and Rosanna Cox, eds., *Diplomacy and Early Modern Culture*, 155–71. London: Palgrave Macmillan.

Neuschel, Kristen (1989), *Word of Honor. Interpreting Noble Culture in Sixteenth Century France*. Ithaca: Cornell University Press.

Niccoli, Ottavia (1990), *Prophecy and People in Renaissance Italy*, trans. by Lydia G. Cochrane. Princeton: Princeton University Press.

Niccoli, Ottavia (2007), *Perdonare. Idee, pratiche, rituali in Italia tra Cinque e Seicento*. Bari-Rome: Laterza.

Nirit Ben-Aryeh Debby (2001), "War and peace: the description of Ambrogio Lorenzetti's Frescoes in Saint Bernardino's 1425 Siena Sermons, *Renaissance Studies* 15 (3): 272–86.

O'Malley, John W. (2013), *The Council of Trent. Myths, Misunderstandings and Unintended Consequences*. Rome: Gregorian and Biblical Press.

Oakley, Francis (2003), *The Conciliarist Tradition. Constitutionalism in the Catholic Church*. Oxford: Oxford University Press.

Ortu, Gian Giacomo (2003), *Lo Stato Moderno. Profili storici*. Rome-Bari: Laterza.

Pagden, Anthony (1995), *Lords of All the World: Ideologies of Empire in Spain, Britain and France c. 1500–c. 1800*. New Haven: Yale University Press.

Palmer, Allison L. (2001), "The Walters' 'Madonna and Child' Plaquette and Private Devotional Art in Early Renaissance Italy," *The Journal of the Walters Art Museum*, 59: 73–84.

Panizza, Diego (1981), *Alberico Gentili giurista ideologo dell'Inghilterra elisabettiana*. Padua: La Garangola.

Panizza, Diego (2010), "Alberico Gentili's *De armis Romanis*: The Roman Model of the Just Empire," in Benedict Kingsbury and Benjamin Straumann, eds., *The Roman Foundations*, 53–84.

Paoletti, John T. and Gary M. Radke (2005), *Art, Power, and Patronage*. New York: Prentice Hall.

Parchami, Ali (2009), *Hegemonic Peace and Empire: The Pax Romana, Britannica and Americana.* London: Routledge.
Parker, Geoffrey (1987), *The Thirty Years War.* New York: Military Heritage Press.
Parker, Geoffrey (1988), *The Military Revolution. Military Innovation and the Rise of the West 1500–1800.* Cambridge: Cambridge University Press.
Parry, John H. (1963), *The Age of Reconnaissance.* New York: Mentor Books.
Patterson, William B. (1997), *King James and the Reunion of Christendom.* Cambridge: Cambridge University Press.
Pedullà, Gabriele (2004), "Paura e virtù," in Alessandro Fontana and Jean-Louis Fournel, eds., *Langues et ecritures de la Republique et de la guerre: études sur Machiavel,* 299–334. Genova: Name.
Pereña, Luciano (1984), "La escuela de Salamanca y la duda indiana," in Demetrio Ramos et al. eds., *La Ética en la conquista de América. Francisco de Vitoria y la Escuela de Salamanca,* 291–344. Madrid: CSIC.
Persson, Fabian (1999), "The Kingdom of Sweden: The Courts of the Vasas and Palatines, c. 1523–1751," in John Adamson, ed., *The Princely Courts of Europe: Ritual, Politics and Culture Under the Ancien Régime, 1500–1750,* 275–93. London: Weidenfeld and Nicolson.
Phelan, John Leddy (1970), *The Millennial Kingdom of the Franciscans in the New World,* 2nd ed. Berkeley: University of California Press.
Phillips, Andrew (2010), *War, Religion and Empire. The Transformation of International Orders.* Cambridge, Cambridge University Press.
Pierce, Leslie (1993), *The Imperial Harem: Women and Sovereignty in the Ottoman Empire.* Oxford: Oxford University Press.
Pilliod, Elizabeth (2001), *Pontormo, Bronzino, Allori: A Genealogy of Florentine Art.* New Haven: Yale University.
Pinker, Steven (2011), *The Better Angels of Our Nature: Why Violence Has Declined.* New York: Viking Penguin.
Pirenne, Henri (1963), *Early Democracies in the Low Countries. Urban Society and Political Conflict in the Middle Ages and the Renaissance.* ed. by John H. Mundy, New York: Norton.
Pirillo, Diego (2010), *Filosofia ed eresia nell'Inghilterra del tardo Cinquecento. Bruno, Sidney e i dissidenti religiosi italiani.* Rome: Edizioni di Storia e Letteratura.
Pizan, Christine de (2003), *The Book of Deeds of Arms and of Chivalry,* trans. Sumner Willard and Charity Cannon Willard. University Park, PA: Pennsylvania State University Press.
Plancher, Urbain (1781), *Histoire generale et particuliere de Bourgogne,* t. IV. Dijon: N. Frantin.
Plassmann, Thomas et. al. (1949), "Special Issue Dedicated to the Memory of Don Fray Juan de Zumárraga, First Bishop and Archbishop of Mexico," *The Americas,* 5 (3): 259–378.
Pocock, John G.A. (1975), *The Machiavellian Moment: Florentine Political Thought and the Atlantic Republican Tradition.* Princeton: Princeton University Press.
Polin, Raymond (1954), "Sur la signification de la paix d'après la philosophie de Hobbes," *Revue française de science politique,* 4: 252–77.
Power, Daniel (2013), "Who Went on the Albigensian Crusade?" *English Historical Review,* 128 (534): 1047–85.
Procacci, Giuliano (1995), *Machiavelli nella cultura europea dell'età moderna.* Roma-Bari: Laterza.
Prosperi, Adriano (1999), "Europa 'in forma virginis': aspetti della propaganda asburgica del '500?" in Id., *America e Apocalisse e altri saggi,* 127–5. Pisa-Roma: Istituti Editoriali e Poligrafici.

Prosperi, Adriano (2000), *L'eresia del Libro Grande. Storia di Giorgio Siculo e della sua setta.* Milan: Feltrinelli.

Prosperi, Adriano (2001), "Un papato spirituale: programmi e speranze nell'età del Concilio di Trento," in Gabriele de Rosa, ed., *Il Papato e l'Europa*, 239–54. Soveria Mannelli: Rubettino.

Prosperi, Adriano (2005), "'Guerra giusta' e cristianità divisa tra cinquecento e seicento," in Mimmo Franzinelli and Riccardo Bottoni, eds., *Chiesa e guerra: dalla benedizione delle armi alla* Pacem in terris, 29–90. Bologna: Il Mulino.

Prosperi, Adriano (2009), *Tribunali della coscienza: inquisitori, confessori, missionary.* Turin: Einaudi.

Prosperi, Adriano (2015), "Lo stato della religione tra l'Italia e il mondo: variazioni cinquecentesche sul tema," *Studi storici*, 1: 29–48.

Pucci, Francesco (1580 [1579]), *Informatione della religione christiana.* Florence [London]: n.p.

Pucci, Francesco (1955–9), *Lettere, documenti e testimonianze*, ed. by Luigi Firpo and Renato Piattioli. 2 vols. Florence: Olschki.

Quaglioni, Diego and Giovanni Minnucci (2014), "Il *De papatu Romano Antichristo* di Alberico Gentili (1580/1585–91): primi appunti per l'edizione critica," *Il pensiero politico* 2: 145–55.

Queller, Donald E. (1967), *The Office of Ambassador in the Middle Ages.* Princeton, NJ: Princeton University Press.

Randolph, Adrian (2014), *Touching Objects: Intimate Experiences of Italian Renaissance Art.* New Haven: Yale University.

Reed, Marcia, ed. (2015), *The Edible Monument: The Art of Food for Festivals.* Los Angeles: Getty.

Reeves, Marjorie (1969), *The Influence of Prophecy in the Later Middle Ages. A Study in Joachimism.* Notre Dame: University of Notre Dame Press.

Reichberg, Gregory, Henrik Syse, and Endre Begby, eds. (2006), *The Ethics of War: Classic and Contemporary Readings.* Malden, Oxford and Carlton: Blackwell Publishing.

Reid, Anthony (1988), *Southeast Asia in the Age of Commerce, 1450–1680.* Vol. I: *The Lands Below the Winds.* New Haven, CT: Yale University Press.

Renaudet, Augustin (1942), *Machiavel.* Paris: Gallimard.

Restall, Matthew, Lisa Sousa, and Kevin Terraciano, eds. (2005), *Mesoamerican Voices: Native-Language Writings from Colonial Mexico, Oaxaca, Yucatan, and Guatemala.* Cambridge: Cambridge University Press.

Ricard, Robert (1966), *The Spiritual Conquest of Mexico: An Essay on the Apostolate and the Evangelizing Methods of the Mendicant Orders in New Spain, 1523–1572.* Berkeley: University of California Press.

Rieber Robert, ed. (1991), *The Psychology of War and Peace: The Image of the Enemy*, Plenum Press; New York and London.

Rispoli, Tania (2015), "Imitation and Animality: On the Relationship between Nature and History in Chapter XVIII of The Prince," in Filippo Del Lucchese, Fabio Frosini, and Vittorio Morfino, eds., *The Radical Machiavelli: Politics, Philosophy, and Language*, 190–203. London: Brill.

Rivère de Carles, Nathalie, ed. (2016), *Early Modern Diplomacy, Theatre and Soft Power: The Making of Peace.* London: Palgrave Macmillan.

Roberts, Penny (2013), *Peace and Authority During the French Religious Wars c. 1560–1600.* Houndmills: Palgrave Macmillan.

Roberts, Sean (2014), "Inventing Engraving in Vasari's Florence," *Intellectual History Review*, 24: 367–88.

Roberts, Sean (2016), "The Lost Map of Matteo de' Pasti: Cartography, Diplomacy, and Espionage in the Renaissance Adriatic," *Journal of Early Modern History* 20: 19–38.
Rodin, David and Richard Sorabji, eds. (2006), *The Ethics of War. Shared Problems in Different Traditions*. Aldershot: Ashgate.
Roelker, Nancy L. (1968), *Queen of Navarre: Jeanne d'Albret, 1528–72*. Cambridge, MA: Harvard University Press.
Rosand, David (2001), *Myths of Venice: The Figuration of a State*. Chapel Hill, NC: University of North Carolina Press.
Rosas Lauro, Laura and Akira Saito, eds. (2017), *Reducciones: la concentración forzada de las poblaciones indígenas en el virreinato del Perú*. Lima: FEPUCP.
Rosenthal, Lisa (2006), *Gender, Politics, and Allegory in the Art of Rubens*. Cambridge: Cambridge University Press.
Roser, Max, *Our World in Data*. Available online: https://ourworldindata.org.
Rotondò, Antonio (1991), "Anticristo e Chiesa romana: diffusione e metamorfosi di un libello antiromano del Cinquecento," in Antonio Rotondò, ed., *Forme e destinazione del messaggio religioso: aspetti della propaganda religiosa nel Cinquecento*, 19–164. Florence: Olschki.
Roussel, Bernard and Michel Grandjean, eds. (1998), *Coexister dans l'intolérance. L'édit de Nantes (1598)*. Genève: Labor et fides.
Ruggiero, Guido (2002), "Introduction: Renaissance Dreaming: In Search of a Paradigm," in Guido Ruggiero, ed., *A Companion to the Worlds of the Renaissance*, 1–20. Oxford: Blackwell.
Ruggiero, Guido (2015), *The Renaissance in Italy: A Social and Cultural History*. Cambridge: Cambridge University Press.
Russell, Joycelyne G. (1986), *Peacemaking in the Renaissance*. London: Duckworth.
Safley, Thomas M. (1984), *Let No Man Put Asunder: The Control of Marriage in the German Southwest: a Comparative Study, 1550–1600*. Kirksville, MO: Sixteenth Century Journal Publisher.
Safley, Thomas M., ed. (2011), *A Companion to Multi-confessionalism in the Early Modern World*. Leiden: Brill Publishers.
Salmon, John H.M. (1979), *Society in Crisis: France in the Sixteenth Century*. London: Routledge.
Salmon, John H.M. (2004), "Sovereignty, Theory of," in *Europe 1450–1789. Encyclopedia of the Early Modern World*, 447–50. New York: Thompson Gale.
Sánchez, Magdalena S. (2009), "Sword and Wimple," in Anne J. Cruze and Mihoko Suzuki, eds., *The Rule of Women in Early Modern Europe*, 64–79. Urbana, IL: University of Illinois Press.
Sandberg, Brian (2004), "'Generous Amazons Came to the Breach': Besieged Women in the French Wars of Religion." *Gender and History* 16: 654–88.
Sandberg, Brian (2010), *Warrior Pursuits: Noble Culture and Civil Conflict in Early Modern France*. Baltimore, MD: Johns Hopkins University Press.
Sandys, Edwin (1605), *A Relation of the State of Religion*. London: Simon Waterson.
Sandys, Edwin (1673), *Europae Speculum or A View or Survey of the State of Religion in the Western Parts of the World*. London: Thomas Basset.
Sarpi, Paolo (1620), *The Historie of the Council of Trent*, trans. by Nathanael Brent. London: Robert Baker and John Bill.
Sarreal, Julia J.S. (2014), *The Guaraní and their Mission: A Socioeconomic History*. Stanford: Stanford University Press.
Sassen, Saskia (2006), *Territory, Authority, Rights. From Medieval to Global Assemblages*. Princeton: Princeton University Press.

Sasso, Gennaro, (1993), *Niccolò Machiavelli*. Bologna: Il Mulino.
Saupin, Guy (1998), *Naissance de la tolérance en Europe aux Temps modernes*. Rennes: Presses Universitaire de Rennes.
Sauzet, Robert (1979), *Contre-Réforme et Réforme catholique en Bas-Languedoc au XVIIe siècle: le diocèse de Nîmes de 1598 à 1694*. Bruxelles-Louvain: Nauwelaerts.
Schalk, Ellery (1986), *From Valor to Pedigree: Ideas of Nobility in France in the Sixteenth and Seventeenth Centuries*. Princeton: Princeton University Press.
Schilling, Heinz (1992), *Religion, Political Culture and the Emergence of Early Modern Society: Essays in German and Dutch History*. Leiden: Brill.
Schmitt, Carl (2006), *The Nomos of the Earth: In the International Law of the* Jus Publicum Europaeum, trans. by G.L. Ulmen. New York: Telos Press.
Schrader, Stephanie, ed. (2013), *Looking East: Rubens's Encounter with Asia*. Los Angeles: Getty.
Schulte, Regina (2006), "Introduction: Conceptual Approaches to the Queen's Body," in Regina Schulte, ed., *The Body of the Queen: Gender and Rule in the Courtly World, 1500–2000*, 1–15. New York, NY: Berghahn Books.
Scott Dixon, C. (2007), "Urban Order and Religious Coexistence in the German Imperial City: Augsburg and Donauwörth, 1548–1608," *Central European History*, 50: 1–33.
Scott Dixon, C. (2009), "Introduction: Living with Religious Diversity in Early-Modern Europe," in Scott, Freist and Greengrass, *Living with Religious Diversity in Early-Modern Europe*, 1–20.
Scott Dixon, C., Dagmar Freist, and Mark Greengrass, eds. (2009), *Living with Religious Diversity in Early-Modern Europe*. Farnham: Ashgate.
Scribner, Bob and Ole Peter Grell, eds. (1996), *Tolerance and Intolerance in the European Reformation*. Cambridge: Cambridge University Press.
Seidel Menchi, Silvana, ed. (2016), *Marriage in Europe. 1400–1800*. Toronto, Buffalo, London: University of Toronto Press.
Selwyn, Jennifer D. (2004), *A Paradise Inhabited by Devils: the Jesuits' Civilizing Mission in Early Modern Naples*. Ashgate: IHSI.
Sepúlveda, Juan Ginés de (1997), *Demócrates segundo* (*Obras Completas* III), trans. A. Coroleu Lletget. Pozoblanco: Ayuntamiento de Pozoblanco.
Setton, Kenneth (1978), *The Papacy and the Levant, 1204–1571*, vol. II, *The Fifteenth Century*. Philadelphia: The American Philosophical Society.
Shay, Jonathan (1994), *Achilles in Vietnam: Combat Trauma and the Undoing of Character*. New York: Touchstone.
Shephard, Tim (2010), "Constructing Identities in a Music Manuscript: The Medici Codex as a Gift," *Renaissance Quarterly*, 63: 84–127.
Shogimen, Takashi (2013), *The Birth of European Political Thought*. Nagoya: The University of Nagoya Press (in Japanese).
Simon, Erika (1988), *Eirene und Pax: Friedensgöttinnen in der Antike*. Stuttgart: Franz Steiner.
Simon, Robert B. (1985), "Bronzino's 'Cosimo I de'Medici as Orpheus'," *Philadelphia Museum of Art Bulletin*, 81: 16–27.
Simpson, Lesley Byrd (1966), *The Encomienda in New Spain: The Beginning of Spanish Mexico*. Berkeley: University of California Press.
Skard, Torild (2014), *Women of Power: Half a Century of Female Presidents and Prime Ministers Worldwide*. Bristol: Policy Press.
Skinner, Quentin (1978), *The Foundations of Modern Political Thought*, vol. 1, *The Renaissance*. Cambridge: Cambridge University Press.

Skinner, Quentin (1987), "Ambrogio Lorenzetti: The Artist as a Political Philosopher." *Proceedings of the British Academy*, 72: 1–56.
Skinner, Quentin (2002), *Visions of Politics*, vol. II, *Renaissance Virtues*. Cambridge: Cambridge University Press.
Sluga, Glenda and Carolyn James (2016), "Introduction: The Long International History of Women and Diplomacy," in Glenda Sluga and Carolyn James, eds., *Women, Diplomacy and International Politics since 1500*, 1–12.
Sluga, Glenda and Carolyn James, eds. (2016), *Women, Diplomacy and International Politics since 1500*. London: Routledge.
Smith, Pamela H. (2007), "Making and Knowing in a Sixteenth-Century Goldsmith's Workshop," in Lissa Roberts, Simon Schafer, and Peter Dear, eds., *The Mindful Hand: Inquiry and Invention between the Late Renaissance and Early Industrialization*, 20–37. Amsterdam: KNAW.
Soll, Jacob (1995), *Publishing the Prince. History, Reading, and the Birth of Political Criticism*. Ann Arbor, MI: University of Michigan Press.
Solomon, Norman (2006), "The Ethics of War: Judaism," in David Rodin and Richard Sorabji, eds., *The Ethics of War*, 108–37.
Sonnino, Paul (2008), *Mazarin's Quest: The Congress of Westphalia and the Coming of the Fronde*. Cambridge, MA: Harvard University Press.
Soucek, Priscilla (1997), "Byzantium and the Islamic East," in Helen C. Evans and William D. Wixom, eds., *The Glory of Byzantium*, 402–11. New York: Metropolitan Museum of Art.
Spangler, Jonathan (2009), *The Society of Princes: The Lorraine-Guise and the Conservation of Power and Wealth in Seventeenth-Century France*. Farnham: Ashgate.
Spencer, Rafael Aguayo, ed. (1970), *Don Vasco de Quiroga: taumaturgo de la organización social*. México: Ediciones Oasis.
Spicer, Andrew, ed. (2012), *Lutheran Churches in Early Modern Europe*. Farnham: Ashgate.
Stollberg-Rilinger, Barbara (2009), "The Impact of Communication Theory on the Analysis of the Early Modern Statebuilding Processes," in Wim Blockmans, André Holenstein and Jon Mathieu, eds. *Empowering Interactions: Political Cultures and the Emergence of the State in Europe, 1300–1900*, 313–8. Farnham: Ashgate.
Stollberg-Rilinger, Barbara (2015), *The Emperor's Old Clothes: Constitutional History and the Symbolic Language*, trans. Thomas Dunlap. New York, NY: Berghahn, 2015.
Strehlke, Carl Brandon, ed. (2004), *Pontormo, Bronzino, and the Medici: The Transformation of the Renaissance Portrait in Florence*. Philadelphia: Philadelphia Museum of Art.
Strong, Roy (1977), *The Cult of Elizabeth: Elizabethan Portraiture and Pageantry*. Berkeley, CA: University of California Press.
Strong, Roy (1984), *Art and Power: Renaissance Festivals 1450–1650*. Los Angeles and Berkeley: University of California.
Stuard, Susan M. (2006), *Gilding the Market: Luxury and Fashion in Fourteenth-Century Italy*. Philadelphia, University of Pennsylvania.
Suárez, Francisco (1944), "A Work on the Three Theological Virtues: Faith, Hope and Charity, divided into Three Treatises to Correspond with the Number of the Virtues Themselves," in Gwladys L. Williams, et al., eds., *Selections from Three Works of Francisco Suárez, S.J.*, vol. 2. Oxford: Clarendon Press.
Subrahmanyman, Sanjay (2007), "Par-delà de l'incommensurabilité: pour une histoire connectée des empires aux temps modernes," *Revue d'histoire moderne et contemporaine*, 54: 34–53.
Subrahmanyam, Sanjay (2011), *Explorations in Connected History: From the Tagus to the Ganges*. New Delhi: OUP.

Te Brake, Wayne (2009), "Emblems of Coexistence in a Confessional World," in C. Scott Dixon, Dagmar Freist and Mark Greengrass, eds., *Living with Religious Diversity*, 53–79.
Tenenti, Alberto (1973), "The Sense of Space and Time in the Venetian World," in John R. Hale, ed., *Renaissance Venice*, 17–46. Totowa, NJ: Rowman and Littlefield.
Terry-Fritsch, Allie and Erin F. Labbie, eds. (2012), *Beholding Violence in Medieval and Early Modern Europe*. Burlington, VT: Ashgate.
The Origins of Modern State in Europe, 13th to 18th Centuries (1994–9), 6 vols. Oxford: Clarendon.
Thornton, John K. (1991), "Legitimacy and Political Power: Queen Njinga, 1624–1663," *Journal of African History* 32: 25–40.
Thornton, John K. (2006), "Elite Women in the Kingdom of Kongo: Historical Perspectives on Women's Political Power," *Journal of African History* 47: 437–60.
Tibi, Bassam (1996), "War and Peace in Islam," in Terry Nardin, ed., *The Ethics of War*, 128–45.
Tilly, Charles (1975), *The Formation of National States in Western Europe*. Princeton: Princeton University Press.
Todorov, Tzvetan (1982), *La conquête de l'Amérique. La question de l'autre*. Paris: Éd. du Seuil.
Torre Villar, Ernesto de la (1974), "Fray Pedro de Gante: maestro y civilizador de América," *Estudios de historia novohispana*, 5: 1–81.
Tranchedini, Nicodemo (2001), *Vocabolario italiano-latino. Edizione del primo lessico dal volgare. Secolo XV*, ed. by Federico Pelle. Florence: Olschki.
Tuck, Richard (1999), *The Rights of War and Peace. Political Thought and the International Order from Grotius to Kant*. Oxford: Oxford University Press.
Valdivia Giménez, Ramón (2010), *Llamado a la misión pacífica: la dimensión religiosa de la libertad en Bartolomé de las Casas*. Madrid: CSIC.
Valleriani, Matteo (2011), "The War in Ariosto's *Orlando furioso*: A Snapshot of the Passage from Medieval to Early Modern Technology," in Marco Formisano and Hartmut Böhme, eds., *War in Words: Transformations of War from Antiquity to Clausewitz*, 375–90. Berlin/New York: Walter de Gruyer GmbH & Co. KG.
van Gelder, Maartje and Tijana Krstic, (2015), "Introduction: Cross-Confessional Diplomacy and Diplomatic Intermediaries in the Early Modern Mediterranean," *Journal of Early Modern History* 19: 93–105.
van Veen, Henk Th. (2006), *Cosimo I de' Medici and his Self-Representation in Florentine Art and Culture*. Cambridge: Cambridge University.
Vander Auwera, Joost and Irène Schaudies, eds. (2013), *Jordaens and the Antique*. Brussels and New Haven: Marcatorfonds and Yale University.
Verástique, Bernardino (2000), *Michoacán and Eden: Vasco de Quiroga and the Evangelization of Western Mexico*. Austin: University of Texas Press.
Viroli, Maurizio (1992), *From Politics to Reason of State: The acquisition and transformation of the language of politics 1250–1600*. Cambridge: Cambridge University Press.
Visceglia, Maria Antonietta, ed. (2013), *Papato e politica internazionale nella prima età moderna*. Rome: Viella, 2013.
Viti, Paolo, ed. (1994), *Firenze e il concilio del 143*. Florence: Olschki.
Vitoria, Francisco de (1967), *Relectio de Indis, o libertad de los indios*, Luciano Pereña and Josè Manuel Pérez-Prendes y Muñoz de Arracó, eds. Madrid: CSIC.
Vitoria, Francisco de (1991), *Political Writings*, trans. by Jeremy Lawrance, ed. by Jeremy Lawrance and Anthony Pagden. Cambridge: Cambridge University Press.

Vives, Juan Luis (1529), *De concordia et discordia*, In *Opera omnia*. Basel: ed. Nic. Junios Episcopius.
Walker, Leslie J., ed. (1950), *The Discourses of Niccolo Machiavelli*, 2 vols. London: Routledge & Kegan Paul.
Walker, Stephanie (1991), "A Pax by Guglielmo della Porta," *Metropolitan Museum Journal*, 26: 167–76.
Wallace, Ronald S. (1988), *Calvin, Geneva and the Reformation: A Study of Calvin as Social Reformer, Churchman, Pastor and Theologian*. Edinburgh: Scottish Academic Press.
Wallerstein, Immanuel M. (1974), *The Modern World-System*, vol. I: *Capitalist Agriculture and the Origins of the European World-Economy in the Sixteenth Century*. New York and London: Academic Press.
Wallerstein, Immanuel M. (1980), *The Modern World-System*, vol. II: *Mercantilism and the Consolidation of the European World-Economy, 1600–1750*. New York and London: Academic Press.
Walsham, Alexandra (2006), *Charitable Hatred. Tolerance and Intolerance in England, 1500–1700*. Manchester and New York: Manchester University Press.
Walzer, Michael (1996), "War and Peace in the Jewish Tradition," in Terry Nardin, ed., *The Ethics of War*, 95–114.
Warren, Fintan B. (1963), *Vasco de Quiroga and His Pueblo-Hospitals of Santa Fe*. Washington: AAFH.
Watkins, John (2008), "Toward a New Diplomatic History of Medieval and Early Modern Europe," *Journal of Medieval and Early Modern Studies* 38: 1–14.
Watts, John (2009), *The Making of Polities. 1300–1500*. Cambridge: Cambridge University Press.
Webel, Charles (2014), *The Politics of Rationality: Reason Through Occidental History*. New York and London: Routledge.
Weber, Benjamin (2014), *Lutter contre les Turcs. Les formes nouvelles de la croisade pontificale au XVe siècle*. Rome: École française de Rome.
Wellman, Kathleen (2013), *Queens and Mistresses of Renaissance France*. New Haven, CT: Yale University Press.
Westbury-Jones, John (1971), *Roman and Christian Imperialism*. Port Washington: Kennikat Press.
Wiesner-Hanks, Merry E. (2002), "Women's Authority in the State and Household in Early Modern Europe," in Annette Dixon, ed., *Women Who Ruled*, 27–39.
Wiesner, Merry E. (1987), "Beyond Women and the Family: Towards a Gender Analysis of the Reformation," *Sixteenth Century Journal* 18: 311–21.
Williams, George Huntston (1962), *The Radical Reformation*. London: Weidenfeld and Nicholson.
Williams, Robert A. (1992), *The American Indian in Western Legal Thought: The Discourses of Conquest*. New York: Oxford University Press.
Williamson, George C. (1901), *Francesco Raibolini called Francia*. London: George Bell & Sons.
Wilson, Peter (2009), *The Thirty Years War: Europe's Tragedy*. Cambridge, MA: Belknap Press.
Wolfthal, Diane (2004), *Images of Rape: The 'Heroic' Tradition and its Alternatives*. Cambridge: Cambridge University.
Wood, Christopher (1993), *Albrecht Altdorfer and the Origins of Landscape*. London: Reaktion.
Woodacre, Elena (2016), "Familial Ties, Political Ambition and Epistolary Diplomacy in Renaissance Europe," in Glenda Sluga and Carolyn James, eds., *Women, Diplomacy and International Politics since 1500*, 30–45.

Woolett, Anne T. and Ariane van Suchtelen, eds. (2006), *Rubens and Brueghel: A Working Friendship*. Los Angeles: Getty.
Wright, Alison (2005), *The Pollaiuolo Brothers*. New Haven: Yale University.
Yates, Frances A. (1975), *Astraea. The Imperial Theme in the Sixteenth Century*. London and Boston: Routledge & Kegan Paul.
Yates, Frances A. (1988), *The French Academies of the Sixteenth Century*. London: Routledge.
Young, Nigel J. (2010), "Editor's Introduction," in Nigel J. Young, ed., *The Oxford International Encyclopedia of Peace*, I: xxiii–xxxvi.
Young, Nigel J., ed. (2010), *The Oxford International Encyclopedia of Peace*. Oxford: Oxford University Press.
Zemon Davis, Natalie (1973), "The Rites of Violence: Religious Riot in Sixteenth-Century France," *Past and Present*, 59: 51–91.
Ziegler, Karl-Heinz (2004), "The Peace Treaties of the Ottoman Empire with European Christian Powers" in Randall Lesaffer, *Peace Treaties and International Law*, 338–64.

CONTRIBUTORS

Andrea Guidi is the author of *Un Segretario militante* (Bologna 2009), a monograph which investigates Niccolò Machiavelli's work in the Florentine chancery. He also co-edited two volumes of the series *Legazioni. Commissarie. Scritti di governo*, which present autograph documentation of Machiavelli's activities in the chancery, as well as two books and a special issue of *European History Quarterly* on the history of the archives in the early modern age. Guidi is currently *Stipendiat* of the Herzog August Bibliothek, Wolfenbüttel. He was *Gast* of the Sonderforschungsbereich 948 "Helden–Heroisierungen–Heroismen," Albert-Ludwigs-Universität Freiburg, Felix Gilbert Member of the Institute for Advanced Study at Princeton (2017), Research Fellow at Birkbeck–University of London, in the project "AR.C.H.I.ves" funded by the European Research Council (2012–16), and a Fellow of *Villa I Tatti*, the Harvard University Center for Italian Renaissance Studies in Florence (2011–12).

Isabella Lazzarini studied at the Scuola Normale Superiore, Pisa, and qualified as Professor of Medieval History in 2013; she teaches at the University of Molise. Her research interests focus on the political, social, and cultural history of late medieval Italy, with an emphasis on Renaissance diplomacy and the growth of different political languages in documentary sources. She has been a Leverhulme Trust visiting professor and a Marie Curie COFUND senior research fellow at the University of Durham; a visiting fellow at All Souls College, Oxford, and a professeur invité at the Ecole Nationale des Chartes, Paris. Among her main publications, *L'Italia degli stati territoriali (secoli XIII–XV)*, Bari-Rome, Laterza, 2003; *Amicizia e potere. Reti politiche e sociali nell'Italia medievale*, Milan, Mondadori 2010; *The Italian Renaissance State*, A. Gamberini, I. Lazzarini eds., Cambridge, CUP, 2012; *Communication and Conflict. Italian Diplomacy in the Early Renaissance (1350–1520)*, Oxford, OUP 2015; *Social Mobility in Medieval Italy (1100–1500)*, Rome 2018, ed. with Sandro Carocci.

Filippo Del Lucchese is Senior Lecturer in History of Political Thought at Brunel University, London, Senior Research Associate, University of Johannesburg, and chair at the Collège International de Philosophie in Paris. His research interests are in the early modern period (from the Renaissance to the Enlightenment), history of philosophy and Marxism. He has been a Marie Curie fellow, and holds degrees from the universities of Pisa and Paris IV (Sorbonne). He is the author of *Conflict, Power and Multitude in Machiavelli and Spinoza* (Continuum Press, 2009, published in French by Éditions Amsterdam) and *The Political Philosophy of Niccolò Machiavelli* (Edinburgh University Press 2015). He has also published articles on the history of early modern philosophy and political theory in journals such as *History of Political Thought*, *European Journal of Political Theory*, *Dialogue*, *International Studies in Philosophy*, *Differences*. He has taught in Italy, France, Lebanon and the United States and is currently working on a project on "Monstrosity in Ancient Thought."

Alastair Mordaunt is a PhD student at Brunel University studying under the supervision of Filippo Del Lucchese. Alastair completed his BA in politics at York University and MA in political science at San Francisco. His research centers on agonistic theories of democracy and the influence of the early modern period.

Brian Sandberg is a Professor of History at Northern Illinois University who works on religion, violence, and political culture during the European Wars of Religion. He authored a monograph entitled, *Warrior Pursuits: Noble Culture and Civil Conflict in Early Modern France* (Baltimore: Johns Hopkins University Press 2010). Sandberg has held fellowships from the Institut d'Études Avancées de Paris, the Fulbright Scholar Program, the Institute for Research in the Humanities (University of Wisconsin-Madison), the National Endowment for the Humanities (at the Medici Archive Project), and the European University Institute. He recently published an interpretive essay, *War and Conflict in the Early Modern World, 1500–1700* (Cambridge: Polity Press 2016) and a collective volume, *The Grand Ducal Medici and their Archive (1537–1743)*, edited by Alessio Assonitis and Brian Sandberg (Turnhout: Brepols, 2016). He is currently working on several research projects, including a monograph on *A Virile Courage: Gender and Violence in the French Wars of Religion 1562–1629*.

Elena Bonora is Full Professor of Early Modern History at the University of Parma. Her main areas of research are the religious crisis of the sixteenth century and the origins of the Counter-Reformation, with a special focus on their impact on Italian and European history. She has looked into the transition from the Renaissance to the Counter-Reformation in the perspective of religious and political history, taking into account also the cultural dimension and the issue of censorship. Recent monographies: *Giudicare i vescovi. La definizione dei poteri nella Chiesa postridentina*, Roma-Bari, Laterza, 2007; *Roma 1564. La congiura contro il papa*, Roma-Bari, Laterza, 2011; *Aspettando l'imperatore. Principi italiani tra il papa e Carlo V*, Torino, Einaudi, 2014.

Sean Roberts is Associate Professor of Art History at Virginia Commonwealth University's School of the Arts in Qatar and President of the Italian Art Society (2017–19). His research is concerned with the interactions between Italy and the Islamic lands, the cultural history of maps, and the place of prints in the histories of art and technology. He is the author of *Printing a Mediterranean World: Florence, Constantinople and the Renaissance of Geography* (2013) and co-editor of *Visual Cultures of Secrecy in Early Modern Europe* (2013). Recent essays have appeared in the *Journal of Early History, Source,* and *I Tatti Studies*. He is currently writing an examination of skulduggery and malfeasance among early engravers titled *Sabotage! Rivalry, Technology, and the Making of Renaissance Prints*.

Diego Pirillo (Ph.D., Scuola Normale Superiore) is Associate Professor of Italian Studies at the University of California, Berkeley. Along with several articles and book chapters, he is the author of *The Refugee-Diplomat: Venice, England and the Reformation* (Cornell: Cornell University Press, 2018), *Filosofia ed eresia nell'Inghilterra del tardo Cinquecento: Bruno, Sidney e i dissidenti religiosi italiani* (Rome: Edizioni di Storia e Letteratura, 2010) and (with O. Catanorchi) *Favole, metafore, storie. Seminario su Giordano Bruno* (Pisa: Edizioni della Normale, 2007).

Rebecca Ard Boone is Professor of History at Lamar University, USA. Her publications include *War, Domination, and the Monarchy of France* (2007), *Mercurino di Gattinara and the Creation of the Spanish Empire* (2014), and *Real Lives in the Sixteenth Century* (2018).

Kazuhisa Takeda is Senior Assistant Professor of Spanish Language and Latin American History at Meiji University, Tokyo, Japan. Takeda's research concerns the historical evolution of Native American christianization in South America under Spanish rule, during the sixteenth to eighteenth centuries. He focuses particularly on Jesuit mission history, seeking to clarify the development of globalization since the "discovery" of America in 1492, from the viewpoint of Christian expansion and its socio-cultural impact upon the indigenous South American peoples. Takeda has published "The Jesuit-Guaraní Confraternity in the Spanish Missions of South America (1609–1767)" in *Confraternitas* (2017); "Las milicias guaraníes en las misiones jesuíticas del río de la plata" in *Revista de Historia Social y de las Mentalidades* (2016); "Los padrones de indios guaraníes de las misiones jesuíticas (1656-1801)" in *Surandino Monográfico* (2016); and "Cambio y continuidad del liderazgo indígena en el cacicazgo y en la milicia de las misiones jesuíticas" in *Tellus* (2012).

INDEX

Page numbers in **bold** refer to figures.

Accolti, Giulio, 83
accommodation, 7
Africa, **57**, 58
agency, individual, 11
aggression, 31, 35–6
Albigensian crusade, 137
Aliciati, Andrea, 85
allegory, 74, 85, 97–100
alliances, 41
Altdorfer, Albrecht, *Battle of Isus*, 86
Amalia Elisabeth, Landgravine of
    Hesse-Cassel, 64
amazons, 58–60, **59**
ambassadors, 61–2
Amboise, royal edict of, 74, 75–6
Ambrogius, 16
Amerindian societies, 58, 137–47, **144**, **145**,
    146
Amsterdam, 81
Anabaptists, 20, 21–2, 42
Andreae, Johann Valentin, 24
angelic pope, myth of the, 107
Angelico, Fra, *Last Judgement*, 89–90, **89**
Anne d'Autriche, 54, 64
Anne de Bretagne, duchesse de Bretagne, 53
antiquity, re-evaluation of teachings, 36–7
Antitrinitarians, 22
Aragon, 55
Ariosto, Ludovico, 37–8, 38, 69
Aristophanes, 25
Aristotle, 16, 26, 28, 50, 134–5, 139
art historians, 85
artillery, 37
atrocities, 120
Augsburg, peace of, 15, 62–3, 74, 75, 76
Augsburg Confession, 20
Augustine of Hippo, 16, 19, 33, 33–4, 36, 37,
    38, 44, 72, 139
Augustus, Emperor, 25
Auslauf, 81
autonomy, political, 10

balance of power, 15, 30
Barbaro, Ermolao, 126
Baron, Hans, 3, 127
Baudin, Louis, 148
Bégat, Jean, 74
beliefs, shared, 31–2
Beneficio di Cristo, 105
benefits, 1
benevolence, 43
Benin, 57
Berlin, Isaiah, 40
Bodin, Jean, 27–8, 45, 129
Boleyn, Anne, 52
Boniface VIII, Pope, 135
Bonora, Elena, 11
Borch, Gerard ter, *The Ratification of the
    Treaty of Münster*, 86, **87**, 100
Borgia, Lucrezia, 93–4
Bosch, Hieronymus
    Christ Carrying the Cross, 35, **36**
    The Mocking of Christ, 35, **35**
Bosse, Abraham, 50, **51**
Bronzino, Agnolo, *Portrait of Cosimo I as
    Orpheus*, 99–100, **99**
brotherhood, 43
Brueghel, Jan, the elder, *The Return from War*
    (with Rubens), 97–8, **98**
Bullinger, Heinrich, 20
Bünting, Heinrich, **69**
Burckhardt, Jakob, 3

Caferro, William, 3
calendar reform, 79
Callot, Jacques, 23
Calvin, John, 20, 104
Calvinism, 70, 73, 78, **78**
Campanella, Tommaso, 24
canon law, 6, 31, 38
Caravaggio, *Arrest of Christ*, 90
Cardiel, José, 147
Carneades, 19

Carnesecchi, Pietro, 103, 106
Castelvetro, Giacomo, 114
Castiglione, Baldassare, 51–2
Catalina, Queen of Portugal, 55
Catherine of Aragon, 52
Cellini, Benvenuto, 92
change, pace of, 49
charitable hatred, 72–3
Charlemagne, 136
Charles V, Holy Roman Emperor, 15, 69, 70, 105, 116, 117–18, 122, **123**, 129, 142
Charles VIII, King of France, 53
Charles IX, King of France, 54, 63
Charroux, synod of, 136
China, 57–8, 147
chivalry, 38
Christendom, 31–2
   dissolution of, 38
Christian humanism, 18–20
Christian Republic, 137–47, **144**, **145**, **146**
Christian world, rupture of, 5–7
Christin, Olivier, 74, 75
Christina, Queen of Sweden, 55, 64
Christine de Lorraine, 52
chronology, 3
Church, the
   claim for political power, 25
   decline of, 15
   moral authority, 6
   public function, 73–4
   relations with the state, 111–12, **113**, 114–15, 116
Cicero, 16, 25, 26
civic humanism, 127
civilians, 38
Clement VIII, Pope, 107–8
Coates, Anthony, 33
coexistence, 77–80, **78**
   daily, 10–11
collective identity, 32
colonial expansion, 93, 137–47, **144**, **145**, **146**
Columbus, Christopher, 15, 122, 138, 149n2
Comenius, Jan Amos, 24
commerce, and peace, 30
common good, the, 25
communication, codes of, 5
confessional relations, 7
Confucian thought, 32
Constance, council of, 21
Constantine, donation of, 112
Constantine, Emperor, 20

Controversy over the sword, Poland, 22
Cortright, David, 2
Counter-Reformation, the, 15, 103–4, 107–11
cross-confessional marriage, 79–80
Crouzet, Denis, 78
Crucé, Emeric, 29
cruelty, 39
crusades, 136–7, **137**
cultural background, 16
cultural history, 2–3, 5
cultural identification, 31–2
Cusanus, Cardinal, 18
Czechowic, Martin, 22

Dadler, Sebastian, *Medal of Emperor Ferdinand III with the Allegory of the Peace of Westphalia*, **9**
d'Admont, Engelbert, 25
d'Albret, Jeanne, 54
Dante Alighieri, 25, 108, 132, 132–5
definition, 1–2, 3–4, 6–7, 15–30
   Christian humanism, 18–20
   cultural background, 16
   political dimensions, 16, 23–30
   the Reformation, 20–3
   religious dimensions, 16, 16–23
   sovereignty, 24–8
   supra-national dimension, 28–30
   utopian, 23–4
d'Este, Anna, duchesse de Guise, 54
diplomacy
   birth of, 9
   development of, 125–8
   gendered, 60–1
   marriage, 61
diplomatic gifts, 94–5
diplomatic language, 63–4
Discovery, Age of, 7–8
divine inspiration, 38–9
Dixon Annette, 50
Dordrecht, synod of, 29
Dutch East India Company, 29, 94–5, 131
Dutch Reformed Church, 81
Dutch Republic, 130–1, **130**

economic changes, 15
economic competition, 30
edenic state, 1
educational conquest, 143, **144**
El Greco, *The Adoration of the Name of Jesus (Allegory of the Holy League)*, **6**
Eleonora de Toledo, 52

Elizabeth I, Queen of England, 52, **53**, 95, 130
Elshtain, Jean Bethke, 58
embassies, 61–2
embodiment, 97–100, **98, 99**
encomienda, 138–9
Encounters, Age of, 7–8
enemy, the, 31, 33–4
English revolution, 28
Enlightenment, the, 81
Erasmus, 12
Erasmus, Desiderius, 12, 18–19, 34–6, 38, 39, 43, 44, 72
Erastianism, 104, 111–12, **113**, 114–15, 116
Erastus, Thomas, 104, 111, 114
ethics, 33
Euhemerus, 23
Europe, virgin metaphor, 67–72, **68, 69, 71**
extra-European cultures, 3 *see also* Islamic world, Japan; New World

Fairland, Thomas, *George Fox*, **22**
female rulers, 50, 52–8, **53, 56, 57**
feminine power, 50–2, **51, 53**, 65
Fernández-Santamaria, José, 43
Ferrara–Florence, council of, 10
feudalism, 117
Finden, Paula, 3
Florence, 126–7, 130
Ford, Ford Madox, *The Trial of Wycliffe*, **21**
Foucault, Michel, 137–8
four causes, doctrine of the, 114
Fox, George, **22**, 23
framework, 3–5
France, 50, 53–4, 117, 118–20, 132
Francesca, formerly Piero della, *Ideal City*, **2**
Franciscans, 11, 143–5
Franck, Sebastian, 22
François I, King of France, 53–4, 61, 62
French Wars of Religion, 44, 54, 63, 74, 119–20, 129
    peace of Amboise, 75–6
friendship, 27–8
friendship pacts, 11, 76–7
Fronde Civil War, 54

Gattinara, Mercurino di, 128
gendered diplomacy, 60–1
Gentili, Alberico, 41, 104, 111–12, **113**, 114–15, 116
George of Kunštát, 25–6
gifts of peace, 93–7, **96**

Gittings, John, 2
globalization, 5, 125, 129–32
God, estrangement from, 92
God's peace, representations, 89–93, **89, 91**
Gonzaga, Giulia, 106, 107
Graf, Urs, 23
grand narrative, 3, 5, 9–10
Grandjean, Michel, 83
Gratian, 20
Great Britain, Navigation Acts, 30
Grebel, Conrad, 21
Greece, Ancient, 24, 25
Gregory VII, Pope, 137
Gregory XIII, Pope, 79
Grosseteste, Robert, 21
Grotius, Hugo, 12, 29–30, 47, 131
Guicciardini, Francesco, 1, 7, 28, 36, 37, 38, 39, 42, 115, 127
Gurevich, A.J., 139–40

Habermas, Jurgen, 31
Habsburg, Maria Maddalena von, 52
Habsburg–Valois Wars, 62
Hale, John, 37, 38, 39, 43
Hampton, Timothy, 62, 63
Harrington, James, 28
Hellenistic period, 24
Helvetic Confession, 20
Henri IV, King of France, 54
Henry IV, king of France, 110, 112, **119**, 120
Henry VIII, King of England, 52, 114
heretics, 137
Hideyoshi, Toyotomi, 120, **121**
Historic Peace Churches, 23
historiographical background, 5
historiographical traditions, 5
Hobbes, Thomas, 28, 45
Holy Roman Empire, 34, 50, 54–5, 125
holy war, 94–5
honor, 38
Horodowich, Elizabeth, 7
human nature, 31–47
    aggressive, 31, 35–6
    Anabaptists and, 42
    anthropological explanations, 43–4
    collective identity, 32
    and divine inspiration, 38–9
    Erasmus's doctrine, 34–6, 44
    Guicciardini on, 39, 42
    Hobbes' conception of, 45
    humanist views of, 36–7
    irrationality, 35

Islam and, 32–3
Jewish thought, 32
Latin Christendom and, 33–4
Machiavelli on, 39, 39–41, 42
negative view, 35, **35**, **36**
psychological explanations, 39
respectful, 31
shared beliefs, 31–2
and technological innovation, 37–8
tension within, 31
virtus, 37
humanism, 18–20, 36–7
Hürrem Sultan, 55
Hus, Jan, 21, 25

Iambulus, 23
iconoclasm, 78
imperial ideology, 117–18, 122–5, **123**, **124**
Incas, 147–8
individual agency, 11
infantry, rise of, 118–19
Innocent III, Pope, 137
Inquisition, the, 105, 107
integration, 12, 132, 138–9, 147–8
intellectual climate, 8
international law, 30, 47
international society, 30
intolerance, 72–3
iron century, the, 70, 74
irrationality, 35
Isabel Clara Eugenia, Infanta, 54–5
Islamic world, 5, 32–3, 55–6, 95–6, 122–3, **124**
Italian heretics, 103–4, 107–11, **108**, **109**, 114, 116
Italian Renaissance, 3
Italian Wars, 34, 37–8, 118

James I, King of England, 101, **103**
James, William, 61
Japan, 58, 117, 118, 120, **121**, 132
Jesuits, 11, 43, 67, 97, 142, 145, **146**, 147
Jews, 32
John XXIII, antipope, 21
Johnson, James Turner, 34, 42–3
juridical interpretation, 41
just war, 19, 20, 32, 33, 36, 44, 123
classic doctrine, 34
denial of, 21
the enemy, 33–4
humanist abandonment of, 37
juridical interpretation, 41

moral duty, 34
theory of, 8–9, 16

Kamen, Henry, 70
Kaplan, Benjamin J., 11, 76
Kappel, peace of, 74
Keating, Jessica, 96
Kettering, Alison, 100
kinship structures, 61
Knox, John, 50

language, 1, 75, 128
las Casas, Bartolomé de, 139
Latin Christendom, human nature and, 33–4
Latin nouns, 1
Latini, Brunetto, 28
Lazzarini, Isabella, 52, 126
League of Nations, 24
Lee, Alexander, 85
Leonardo da Vinci, 85
Livius, 26
Lodi, peace of, 9, 10, 12, 85, 86, 130
Lollardism, 21
Lorenzetti, Ambrogio, 25, 33, **34**
Louis XII, King of France, 53
Louise de Savoie, 53, 62
Lucretius, 26
Luther, Martin, **18**, 19–20, 20, 70, 104, 114
Lutheranism, 70, 75
Lynn, John A., 60

Machiavelli, Niccolò, 12, 26–7, **27**, 28, 36, 39, 39–41, 42, 92, 109, 127
Mahayana Buddhism, 57
Mantegna, Andrea, *Mars and Venus*, 97
Mantua, diet of, 10
Margaret of Austria, 54, 62
Margaret of Parma, 54, 63
Marguerite de Navarre, 53–4
Marguerite de Valois, 54
marital peace, 93–4
marriage alliances, 61
Mars, 97–8, **98**
Marsilius Ficinus, 18–19, 19, 25
martyrdom, theology of, 21
Mary of Burgundy, 54
Mary of Hungary, 54
Mary Stuart, 50, 52
Mary Tudor, 50, 52
materialism, 26
materially, paxes, 90–2, **91**, 94
Matsumori, Natsuko, 139

Mattingly, Garrett, 49, 126
Medici family, 52
Medici, Catherine de', 54, 61, 63, 119
Medici, Cosimo I de', 52, 99–100, **99**, 107
Medici, Ferdinando I de', 52
Medici, Marie de', 54, 61
Medici Codex, 93
Melanchthon, Philip, 104
Mennonites, 23
mercantilism, 30
mercenaries, 42
Mexico, 143–5, **144**, 147
Meyjes, Guillaume H.M. Posthumus, 111
Michelangelo, 86
Middle Ages, the, 2, 12, 20–1, 25, 136, 140
Milan, Edict of, 20
militarism, 117
Mirandola, Giovanni Pico della, 18–19
missionaries, 67, 138, 142, 143, 147
Montaigne, Michel de, 77, 79
moral duty, 34
moral skepticism, 39
morality, 40
More, Thomas, 23–4, 144
Morone, Giovanni, 105, 107
Mouton, Jean, 93
Moyne, Pierre Le, 50, **51**
Mughal Empire, 56–7, **56**
Muhammad, the Prophet, 33
multi-confessionalism, 7
Münster, Sebastian, **68**
Münster, Treaty of, 9, 85
music, 93, 95, 149n2
Muslim raiders, 41–2

Nantes, edict of, 74, **78**
natural justice, 43–4
natural law, 43–4, 47
natural state, 28
nature, laws of, 28
Navarre, 55
Netherlands, the, 63
new diplomacy, 49, 61–4
new diplomatic history, 49
New Model Army, 23
New World, 125
    cabildos, 147
    colonial expansion, 137–47, **144**, **145**, **146**
    discovery of, 5, 15, 138
    educational conquest, 143, **144**
    encomienda, 138–9
    reducciones, 11, 145, **145**, **146**, 148

noblewomen, role, 51–2
Nur Jahan, Empress, **56**, 57

Ochino, Bernardino, 112
original sin, 139
Orpheus, 99–100, **99**
Osnabrück, Treaty of, 9
Ottoman Empire, 5, 15, 16, 17, 18, 55, 92, 122–3, **124**, 129–30
Oxford International Encyclopedia of Peace, 2

pacifism, 12, 18, 20–1, 23, 25, 30
    radical, 22
Pagan world, 140
Palacios Rubios, Juan López de, 140
Palaeologus, Jacob, 22
papacy, 10, 34, 112
Paraguay, 145, **145**, **146**, 147, 148
patronage, 52, 130
Paul III, Pope, 140
Paul IV, Pope, 106, 107
pax, 24–5
pax Christi, 132–5
pax et treuga Dei, 135–7
pax Hispanica, 137–47, **144**, **145**, **146**
pax Romana, 25, 132–5
Paz, Matias de, 140
peace movements, 12, 101–16
    Erastianism, 104, 111–12, **113**, 114–15, 116
    Italian heretics, 103–4, 107–11, **108**, **109**, 114, 116
    the *spirituali*, 103, 104–7, 107, 115–16
peace studies, 2–3, 85
Peace Testimony, 23
peace treaties, 9, 41
peacemaking, 11, 61–4
    women, 60–1
Peasants' War, the, 21, 149n4
Penn, William, 23
Perrot, François, 112
Petrarca, Francesco, 108
Petrarch, 37
Philip II, King of Spain, 63
Pius II, Pope, 95
Pius IV, Pope, 107
Pius V, Pope, 17
Pizan, Christine de, 59
Podiebrad, king of Bohemia, 25–6
Poland, Controversy over the sword, 22
Pole, Reginald, 105–6
political autonomy, 10
political culture, 49

political dimensions, 16, 23–30
  sovereignty, 23, 24–8, 29
  supra-national, 28–30
  utopian, 23, 23–4
political keywords, 3–5
political language, 128
political organization, paradigm shift in, 15
political patronage, 52
political realism, 36
Polybius, 26
Portugal, 55
positive concept, 90
processions, conflict over, 77–8
Protestantism, 6, 20–3
Pucci, Francesco, 104, 107–11, **108, 109**, 111, 112, 116
pugnare mihi non licet, 20
Putsch, Johannes, 67, 71, 82

Quakers, 23
Quiroga, Vasco de, 144–5
Qur'an, 33

realism, 26
reducciones, 11, 145, **145, 146**, 148
Reformation, the, 2, 5, 10, 15, 16–17, 20–3, 62, 70, 73, 101, 109, 129
religion, 12
  demarcation lines, 70
religious choice, 10
religious councils, 9
religious dimensions, 16, 16–23
  Christian humanism, 18–20
  the Reformation, 20–3
religious diversity, 82–3
religious identity, consolidation of, 70
religious migrations, 62
religious peace, 10–11, 67–83, 132–7
  application, 76
  characteristics, 74–5
  coexistence, 77–80, **78**
  definition, 75
  implementation, 75–7
  language, 75
  need for, 82–3
  obstacles to, 72–4
  preservation, 83
  promotors, 75
  resistance to, 76
  spatial compromises, 80–2, **80, 82**
  virgin metaphor, 67–72, **68, 69, 71**
religious tolerance, 22

Renaissance, definition, 3, 11–12, 49
Renaissance worlds, 49
representations, 85–100
  diplomacy, 95–6, **96**
  gifts of peace, 93–7, **96**
  God's peace, 89–93, **89, 91**
  Islamic world, 95–6
  paxes, 90–2, **91**, 94
  peace embodied, 97–100, **98, 99**
  see also individual artists
respect, 31
Respublica christiana, 69–70
Roberts, Sean, 3
Roman law, 122–3
Rubens, Peter Paul, 47, 97, 98, 100
  Consequences of War, 45, **46**, 47, 71–2, **71**
  Minerva Protects Pax from Mars ("Peace and War"), **46**, 47
  The Return from War (with Jan Brueghel the elder), 97–8, **98**
rulers, female, 50, 52–8, **53, 56, 57**

Safavid Empire, 55–6
St. Bartholomew's Day massacre, 27, 63, 108
Saint-Pierre, Abbé de, 24
Salamanca, School of, 11, 44, 45, 123, 139–41, 145
Salic Law, 50, 53
Sandberg, Brian, 11
Sandys, Edwin, *Relation of the State of Religion*, 101–2, **102**, 115
Sanzio, Raffaello, *The School of Athens*, **4**
Sarpi, Paolo, 10, 104
Sassen, Saskia, 2, 83
Savonarola, 38
Savonarola, Girolamo, 108, 109
Sayf ad-Din Inal, 95–6
Schleitheim Confession, 21
Schmalkaldic Wars, 62–3
Schmitt, Carl, 139
scholasticism, 8
Schuilkerk (hidden church), 81
Schulte, Regina, 60–1
Scotland, 52
secularization, 44
Seyssel, Claude de, 128
Sfondrati, Paolo Camillo, 110
Sforza, Giovanni, 93–4
shared churches, 80–1, **80, 82**
Shogimen, Takashi, 135
Siam, 60
Sidney, Algernon, 28

Siena, 25, 33, **34**
Skinner, Quentin, 37
slavery, 139
Sluga, Glenda, 61
social justice, 29
soft power, 60
sovereign, the, 45
sovereignty, 15, 23, 24–8, 29, 44, 45, 47, 126, 131
    development of, 128–9
    and feminine power, 50–2
Spain, 115, 123
    Reconquista, 92, 122, 125, 138
Spanish Armada, 63
Spanish Empire, 11, 122, 123, 137–47, **144, 145, 146**
spirituali, the, 103, 104–7, 107, 115–16
Spranger, Bartholomeus, 90
state, the
    birth of, 5
    Bodin on, 27–8
    emergence of, 15
    relations with Church, 111–12, **113**, 114–15, 116
    rise of, 38–9
Stollberg-Rilinger, Barbara, 62–3, 63–4
Striggio, Alessandro, 100
Suleiman the Magnificent, 117–18, 122–3, **124**
supra-national dimension, 28–30
Sweden, 55
Swiss Reformed Churches, 20
sympathy, 31

technological innovation, 37–8
themes, 8–11
theologians, 72
Theopompus, 23
Thirty Years War, 15–16, 44, 54, 55, 64, 86, 131
Thomas Aquinas, 16, **17**, 19, 36, 37, 44, 123, 139
Thucydides, 26
Tintoretto, Jacopo, 60
Tokugawa, Ieysu, 120
tolerance, 4, 7, 22, 75, 80–1, 102, 105
trade, 118, 125, 129–32, **130**
Tranchedini, Nicodemo, 1
Trent, council of, 10, 103, 104–7, **105**, 107, 112, 115
Tridentine reforms, 92
trust, 39

Tuck, Richard, 131
turning points, 5–8

United Nations, 24, 132
unity, 69
universalism, 29–30
Urban II, Pope, 136
utopia, 23, 23–4
utopianism, 43

Valdés, Juan de, 104, 106
Vattel, Emer de, 30
Velazquez, Diego, *The Surrender of Breda*, **8**
Venice, 28, 94–5, 126–7, 129, 130
Venus, 97–8, **98**
Vermigli, Peter Martyr, 115
Veronese, *Allegory of the Battle of Lepanto*, 86
Verrocchio, Andrea del, candelabrum, 87–9, **88**
violence
    abhorrence toward, 31
    anthropological explanations, 43–4
    control of, 42
    justification of, 40–1
    psychological explanations, 39
virgin metaphor, 67–72, **68, 69, 71**
virtus, 37
Vitoria, Francisco de, 29, 44, 45, 123, 139, 140–1
Vives, Juan Louis, 19

Waldensian movement, 20–1
Waldo, Peter, 20–1
war
    causes of, 114
    changing nature of, 128, 131–2
    dangers of, 118
    Erasmus on, 43
    Hobbes' conception of, 45
    limitation of, 30
    Machiavelli on, 26, 40–1, 42
    preparation for, 24
    proliferation of, 117–18
    as the status quo, 117
    and trade, 118, 125
    as weakness, 28
War of the Public Good, 118
warrior women, 58–60, **59**
Warsaw Confederation, 74
Washington, George, 30
wedding gifts, 93–4

Weenix, Jan Baptist, *The Dutch Ambassador on his Way to Isfahan*, 96–7, **96**, 100
Wellman, Kathleen, 53–4
Werner, Anthon von, *Luther at the Diet of Worms*, **18**
Westphalia, Peace of, **9**, 10, 12, 16, 74–5, 86, 131
Whitehall Palace, London, 98
Wolff, Christian, 30
women
    campaign community, 60
    diplomatic activities, 60–1
    epistolary networks, 52
    Islamic world, 55–6
    letter-writing activities, 52
    peacemaking, 60–1
    power, 50–2, **51**, 65
    role, 51–2
    rulers, 50, 52–8, **53**, **56**, **57**
    soft power, 60
    warrior, 58–60, **59**
Women, Diplomacy and International Politics since 1500, 65
Woodacre, Elena, 52
Wycliffe, John, 21, **21**

Young, Nigel, 2

Zemon Davis, Natalie, 78
Zumárraga, Juan de, 143